WHITEWASHING THE SOUTH

Perspectives on a
Multiracial America Series
Joe R. Feagin, Texas A&M University,
Series Editor

WHITEWASHING THE SOUTH

White Memories of Segregation and Civil Rights

Kristen M. Lavelle

ROWMAN & LITTLEFIELD
Lanham • Boulder • New York • London

Published by Rowman & Littlefield
A wholly owned subsidiary of
The Rowman & Littlefield Publishing Group, Inc.
4501 Forbes Boulevard, Suite 200, Lanham, Maryland 20706
www.rowman.com

Unit A, Whitacre Mews, 26-34 Stannery Street, London SE11 4AB,
United Kingdom

British Library Cataloguing in Publication Information Available

Library of Congress Cataloging-in-Publication Data Available

ISBN 978-1-4422-3279-2 (cloth : alk. paper)
ISBN 978-1-4422-3925-8 (pbk. : alk. paper)
ISBN 978-1-4422-3280-8 (electronic)

∞ ™ The paper used in this publication meets the minimum requirements of
American National Standard for Information Sciences Permanence of Paper
for Printed Library Materials, ANSI/NISO Z39.48-1992.

Printed in the United States of America

CONTENTS

ACKNOWLEDGMENTS

First of all, with deep humility, I am grateful to each person who agreed to be interviewed for this project.

This research first found its footing through guidance from Joe Feagin, Jane Sell, Wendy Moore, Joseph Jewell, and Albert Broussard, and the Department of Sociology at Texas A&M University where I received my doctoral training. I received funding from the College of Liberal Arts, the Race and Ethnic Studies Institute, and the Department of Sociology, all at Texas A&M University. While conducting interviews, I lived and worked full-time in North Carolina; the folks at Salem College (Terry Smith in particular) always supported my project. With interviewing, transcribing, and historical research, I had invaluable help from research assistants, including Nego Crosson, Jodi Staley, Kris Monroe Dearmin, Kimber Heinz, Lesley Lamb, and Stephanie Parker. Most of this book was written while I lived and worked full-time in Montana, and I am grateful for the collegial environment in the Department of Sociology and Anthropology at Montana State University and my multidisciplinary writing group.

Many colleagues have joined me on my journey through this work and helped me become a better scholar and writer, especially Jennifer Mueller, Krista McQueeney, Rosalind Chou, Michelle Christian, Kim Nguyen, Chris Chambers, Glenn Bracey, Ruth Thompson-Miller, Tami Eitle, and Leah Schmalzbauer. Sarah Stanton and the editorial team at Rowman & Littlefield have the honors of helping me publish my first book and answering all my beginner's questions. I am especially grateful to the four anonymous reviewers of the manuscript. Finally, I thank Nick Bentley, whose daily influence enhances both my scientific lenses and my passion for social change.

I

"OUR GENERATION HAD NOTHING TO DO WITH DISCRIMINATION"

For segregation has worked brilliantly in the South, and, in fact, in the nation, to this extent: it has allowed white people, with scarcely any pangs of conscience whatever, to create, in every generation, only the Negro they wished to see. As the walls come down they will be forced to take another, harder look at the shiftless and the menial and will be forced into a wonder concerning them which cannot fail to be agonizing. It is not an easy thing to be forced to re-examine a way of life and to speculate, in a personal way, on the general injustice.

—James Baldwin, 1961, "A Fly in the Buttermilk"

In January 2009 I was seeking participants for my research on white southerners' memories of segregation and civil rights in Greensboro, North Carolina, and I phoned the home of a man recommended to me for an interview. After a few rings, an elder woman answered ("June"), and I began my pitch in the typical way: "Hello, my name is Kristen, and I'm a student doing a research study with people who've lived their whole lives here in Greensboro." This phone solicitation happened in the latter stage of my research—I had already interviewed more than thirty people—and yet the conversation unfolded in an unforeseeable way. "What's this all about?" she wanted to know. "Well, my project is on race relations and how people remember the racial past, and someone I already interviewed gave me your husband's name and phone number." Before I provided any further details, June responded with anger, reprimanding me for pursuing what she considered a negative research project, on "how terrible it was for the blacks." She told me I should be looking at the positive things about the past and insisted, "Listen, I've had black people I've *loved*, second only to my mama. Our generation had *nothing to do with discrimination!*"

June tried to convince me that what I must be assuming about the segregation era was inaccurate, and she demanded to know what I was trying to prove. Taken aback by her assumptions and vehemence, I tried to calmly explain that I wanted to learn how ordinary white people remember experiencing segregation and civil rights and that there was no agenda driving the research study. I said I was listening to how people described living through the past and experiencing race. But she was adamant that I must be trying to wrest confessions from innocent white southerners. And then—perhaps my repeated claims that I had no vendetta against white southerners finally became convincing—a shift occurred. June morphed into a compassionate elder, gushing about how she loved young people like me and wanted to help me out in any way she could. She suggested that perhaps both she and her husband would be good candidates for my interview study after all, and she said she very much looked forward to meeting me.

Like her initial vitriolic response, I was taken aback by this shift. Up to that point, June had been making her emphatic arguments and asking me pointed questions, and I had listened quietly and answered her respectfully but honestly. For example, she had asked, "Now don't you agree that black people have all the same opportunities as whites today?" And I said, "Actually, no, that's not my understanding from everything I've learned in school." Through our dialogue June and I had certainly reached no agreement about the racial realities of the past or present or how I should be conducting my study. And yet, there she was graciously offering herself and her husband up for an interview at my convenience. As the rather lengthy phone call ended, I said I would try to phone her home again to schedule an interview.

I was perplexed and exhausted by the exchange and prematurely ended my phone solicitations for the day, needing to process what had occurred. I first typed up fieldnotes. I had rarely encountered a delivery of so much venom and honey in any circumstance: mental health seemed a potential explanation. But, as I read over my notes and got some mental distance from the incident, I reached the insight that I had encountered all of the themes in June's perspective in previous interviews. I had heard numerous nostalgic portrayals of the past, inclusive of the racial arrangement. Like her, many people had acknowledged the reality of past racial oppression in indirect ways, through arguing that dwelling on *those* things was counterproductive. I had listened while people expressed frustration toward commemorations and activist efforts that highlighted the oppression of black Americans and would seem to indict the white South. I had also been repeatedly struck by people's willingness to sit for an interview with me, even when they knew nothing about me and claimed to have little personal interest in discussing the research topic. The phone conversation with June was able to clarify, with heightened emotional poignancy, that elder white southerners are not unconnected to or unaffected by race and the racial past. Rather, white southerners across differences of politics, religion, socioeconomics, and gender discussed the racial past in ways that affirmed white southern goodness.

The encounter with June helped to crystallize the perspective this book takes on elder white southerners—they are as complex as any other population, they can simultaneously hate and love their past, they can both acknowledge and deny structural realities, and they are managing both their past and present. It is my aim in this book to critically analyze these complexities using sociological lenses. I view the interview participants as ordinary people who constructed knowledge around race, region, history, and identity through interaction with racial structures and ideologies. A key point I make throughout the book is that elder white southerners reveal their investment in seeing themselves—individually and collectively—as good people through the ways they use memory and storytelling. In the contemporary post–civil rights "color-blind" era, being a "good" person means being nonracist, and a "good" society is a nonracist one. Elder white southerners' current identity maintenance is linked inextricably to their perceptions and portrayals of the racial past.

On the other hand, there is good reason to view elder white southerners as a unique population. Unlike younger generations, they are tasked with constructing themselves as good people in the face of a damning racial history. While white southerners have not been harshly chastised for their participation in segregation, that era is now considered to have been a time of overt racism. Elder white southerners spent their formative years socialized in a Jim Crow society that consistently articulated and institutionalized white superiority and black inferiority. At the same time, white southern families proudly taught values of fairness and equality, and many had black people in their lives that they claim to have loved and been loved by in return. We can imagine how difficult it would be, without a developed racial consciousness, to make sense of these contradictions—rendering understandable why so few elder white southerners have produced and disseminated their own critical accounts of life as a privileged caste under Jim Crow.[1]

In having experienced the legal segregation era of institutionalized white supremacy, the civil rights era that challenged and dismantled it, and the contemporary racial era, elder white southerners are an invaluable population for study. Yet there are surprisingly few social science analyses of this group. I interviewed forty-four elder white southerners about how they experienced living through the racial past. They were people who had lived their whole lives in the South—specifically in Greensboro, North Carolina, a city well known for its pivotal role in the civil rights movement (dubbed the birthplace of the 1960 sit-in movement). The analysis herein of these lifelong white southerners' memories explores the complexities, seeming contradictions, consequences of, and potential alternatives to their racial narratives. It also makes a case for the contemporary relevance of these narratives.

RESEARCHING WHITE SOUTHERNERS

How elder white Americans make sense of the racial past is not well understood. Collective memory scholars have produced numerous analyses of historical and cultural artifacts, such as museum exhibits and commemoration ceremonies, but have done few investigations of how ordinary people interpret history.[2] Much research incorporating a historical perspective documents how people of color have borne the brunt of a white-dominant society—how they cope, strategize, mobilize, and manage to thrive within a society that marginalizes them. Researchers less often have investigated the culture's dominant members—their interpretations of unequal structures and their identities and emotions.[3] The majority of such studies have focused on younger Americans, and there is surprisingly limited research on ordinary white southerners, particularly those who lived through Jim Crow segregation.[4] Establishing dominant group members' participation and investment in the racial status quo is crucial in understanding how racial ideologies and structures are maintained.[5] As numerous race scholars argue, racial stratification in the United States is not upheld by the callous irrational acts of rabid racists but by rational actions that support the society's racial hierarchy and racial inequalities.[6] This book works toward addressing these gaps by analyzing the memories and racial perspectives of the oldest living generation of white Americans. By taking this approach, this book speaks to how whites construct the racial past and present, and how they reconcile their identities with multiple racial eras.

During the legal segregation era of the late-1800s through the 1960s, white southerners had a largely unquestioned understanding of Jim Crow.[7] Along with the legal mandates, such as whites-only businesses and segregated public spaces, by adulthood people had internalized Jim Crow knowledge "almost instinctively" and understood "just what is expected of them in all situations."[8] People were socialized to follow not only segregation laws and policies but also an elaborate set of social norms. For example, there was a taboo of black women drinking alcohol with white women; but black men could drink with a white man as long as he did not put his lips to the white man's bottle, while a white man was free to drink straight from a black man's bottle if he chose.[9] As shown by this example, the rules were intricate—and situational variations likely countless—but ultimately Jim Crow laws and social conventions were designed to reinforce white supremacy.

The people interviewed for this book were "ordinary" white southerners who grew up immersed in the logic and practice of white supremacy and then witnessed the activism of the civil rights movement that forced the demise of Jim Crow. I use the term "ordinary" to emphasize that the interview participants were like the vast majority of the white South—those who were not key actors in the institutional enforcement of Jim Crow policies (such as government officials), or actively involved in white supremacist organizations, or antiracist activists. Neither were they uninvolved bystanders; ordinary does not imply passivity. The interview participants represent white southerners who were socialized by their families and communities to follow a white supremacist culture, who then went on to socialize others, and who accepted or resisted to varying degrees the civil rights movement and the changes it ushered in.[10]

Greensboro, North Carolina, was the site for this study, first, because of its notoriety as a place of civil rights activism where white residents could be expected to have formed interpretations and memories of the racial past. Second, Greensboro has historically been reputed as a progressive southern city in a progressive southern state.[11] The tension between racial oppression and seeming racial progressivism mirrors and interacts with tensions I will explore throughout this book in the interview narratives. Between 2007 and 2009 I lived in Greensboro and conducted in-depth interviews with forty-four white southerners who were born between the early 1910s and early 1950s (old enough to remember segregation) and were lifelong residents of the area (so they could comment on local events). To locate individuals who fit my parameters, I primarily used snowball sampling through word of mouth, referrals, and community organizations. At the time of the interview, participants ranged in age from late 50s to early 90s (median age of 74). All were children of Jim Crow, but they spanned nearly two generations: while some were young adults in the 1960s, others were parents of young adults. Primarily due to the age requirement, I had to make special efforts to interview men, but in the end thirty-three of the participants were women. Most interviews were conducted one-on-one in participants' homes, and a few involved married couples.

In the audio-recorded interviews that lasted an hour and a half on average, I asked each person to talk about growing up and living in the segregated South, memories of key civil rights–era events, and their perspectives on social change and the contemporary racial landscape. In addition, I asked them to comment on the importance of remembering the racial past. I learned that few deemed the study of high importance—arguing it was better to move on or focus on more positive things—though most said they were happy to help me complete it. Nevertheless, I came to conclude that the people I interviewed *were* invested in the racial past and portrayed it in ways that enhanced their identities and rationalized their racial views. In other words, even when people argued that the racial past was bygone history, my analysis highlights the ways in which they utilized that past to construct self and society.

I want to be clear that this book does not see the interview participants as representing a monolithic "white southerner." The interviews were conducted in one southern city, and there were important variations among the participants. For example, they were diverse by socioeconomic status, educational attainment, political leanings, and religious affiliations—factors that can impact both racialized experiences and views of racial issues. Throughout the analysis, I highlight notable variations among participants' views and backgrounds and share interview excerpts that diverged from the dominant themes.

On the other hand, this book also takes the perspective that the participants had a collective experience as whites born and raised and coming of age in the segregated South. While things like socioeconomic status are always at play (for example, poor whites had much in common with poor blacks, while wealthier white families employed black workers), race was *the* key boundary that structured the Jim Crow South, and it was maintained by the actions of both white elites and less powerful whites and justified by a white supremacist ideology. Furthermore, the participants live now in a "different" racial era, but one in which being white is still a privileged social location, continuing to confer systematic advantages.[12] The dominant way to think and talk about race today—referred to by such terms as "color-blind racism" and "laissez-faire racism"—explains away racial inequalities and argues against (whites) taking steps to address them.[13] As sociologist Matthew Hughey points out, even though whites are diverse, they have much in common:

> Differently-oriented whites . . . do not make their choices, interact, or build a sense of their racial selves within entirely different social worlds but within a larger space of interaction and common meanings. . . . They are together influenced by the ideas, unequal resources, and patterns of interaction that historically benefit and privilege whiteness.[14]

In fact, in a recent study, Hughey identified striking similarities in racial discourse and identity among white nationalists and white antiracists.[15] Indeed, the key themes that emerged from my analysis spanned many differences among participants.

The interviews are concerned primarily with memory and identity and are best viewed as negotiations with ideas about the racial past.

Trying to use these interviews to establish "white southern *experiences*" during Jim Crow and the civil rights movement would miss the mark. Memory scholars have made clear that remembering is fundamentally a contemporary interpretive process rather than a straightforward portrayal of a past reality; it is intimately connected to culture, politics, and self-image.[16] As communication scholar Barbie Zelizer explains: "Collective memories allow for the fabrication, rearrangement, elaboration, and omission of details about the past, often pushing aside accuracy and authenticity so as to accommodate broader issues of identity formation, power and authority, and political affiliation."[17] The interview participants were people in or nearing their twilight years who were being asked to reflect back on a long lifetime. Thus, what they did in the interviews was to create a narrative through storytelling about their lives. Narratives are "constructed, creatively authored, rhetorical, replete with assumptions, and interpretive."[18] At the same time, narratives are "true to life," for they hold meaning and truth for the speaker.[19] I viewed the participants' narratives as constructed yet authentic stories about their perceptions of the racial past.

Because of the research topic, who I was, and who the participants were, there were often layers of tensions in the interviews. How do you respond when being told by an elder that the Jim Crow era had nothing to do with racial oppression? I often felt conflicted trying to negotiate my self-presentation and multiple standpoints (young, white, female, southern, race scholar, antiracist). At the time of the interviews, I was in my mid-20s and pursuing my PhD in sociology with a focus on race and ethnicity. I am sure I looked to the participants rather like a youngster, and I did not fight that perception—I was reserved, respectful, and genuinely grateful. Although by that time in my life I had developed an antiracist and feminist perspective and a knowledge base of contemporary and historical dynamics of race and racism in the United States, I needed to build rapport with participants to make the research study work. However, my politeness and active listening practices meant that I struggled with what to do with my own knowledge and convictions—conflicts captured frequently in the fieldnotes I wrote after each interview and throughout the data collection process.[20]

Ultimately, although I sometimes found people's statements ill-informed or condescending, I saw my primary role as a facilitator of narrative construction; I viewed them as the experts of their own experience. The key function of this approach was to encourage an analysis that would maintain them as ordinary people—not as aberrations or people whom I ought to convince to hold different views. Although I highlight inaccuracies and denials and propose alterative narratives that could be productive with regard to reconciling with the racial past and black southerners, my approach as an interviewer and critical analyst was to determine what ordinary white southerners recalled about the racial past and how they constructed themselves (individually and collectively) in relation to it.

FRAMING, IDEOLOGY, AND IDENTITY

I never did secure an interview with "June," but she strongly advised me to consider her perspective as I continued with the research project. In the notes I wrote after the call, I summarized her recommendations:

> In some ways blacks were better off when they were all "working together" (slavery, sharecropping, segregation). Even way back when, she is certain that blacks were well taken care of and were quite satisfied with their lives, no complaints. "Discrimination" happened, but *not* at the hands of her "generation." Hey, women have been oppressed too, but look how far we've come, and let's focus on that. She has *loved* black people, and that's what really matters. Past racial inequalities have been *way* overemphasized—what about the wonderful things? In a nutshell, we should stop talking about the negative things, if anything must be said about the past let's have it be positive, and most of all let's celebrate how far we've come, how wonderful things are today, and let's share our dreams for the future.

Several conflicting ideas are embedded in this list of recommendations. First, June believed that African Americans were not oppressed under segregation: they were generally better off, satisfied, and well taken care of by whites. On the other hand, she subtly acknowledged that black southerners had in fact been oppressed ("women have been oppressed *too*"). Second, her assertions undercut African American perspectives and deflate the rationale for the civil rights movement (inequalities have been overemphasized, while "the wonderful things" have been ignored). On the other hand, June seemed to acknowledge the societal benefits brought by desegregation ("let's celebrate how far we've come"). Third, June presented her perspective as objective and vital to understanding the past (having assessed common portrayals of the southern past and found them dangerously biased). On the other hand, she expressed a variety of strong emotions, including defensiveness, mistrust, anger, optimism, and pride. These complexities are echoed in the accounts throughout this book.

For the analysis, I looked critically at *what* participants said, *how* they said it, and viewed those patterns alongside historical evidence. When it came to describing race during Jim Crow, the participants demonstrated a mix of acknowledgment, denial, and factual confusion, and often deemphasized the racialized power dynamics inherent to the era. There were frequent mentions of both structural inequalities and perceived "good" relations between white and black southerners. When remembering the civil rights era, many people focused on the chaos and threat of the time period, devalued the actions of civil rights activists, and claimed also to have been ready for desegregation. Commentaries on the contemporary racial milieu included much frustration toward black activists, racial commemoration efforts, and an African American community that they saw as squandering the opportunities won in the 1960s. Participants also presented today's interracial friendships as points of hopefulness and proof that past racial problems had become irrelevant.

In the chapters to come, I arrange these themes chronologically and frame them by three key complexities: (1) acknowledging and downplaying the racial oppressions of the Jim Crow South (in chapters 2 and 3); (2) expressing appreciation for desegregation while criticizing the civil rights movement and its activists (in chapters 4 and 5); and (3) assessing favorably the racial changes witnessed over a lifetime and resenting reminders of unpleasant aspects of the racial past (in chapter 6). While these complexities could be viewed simply as contradictions, I argue that they work together rather than against each other. They are produced through use of an ideological worldview that upholds racial inequalities through furthering notions of whites/white society as good, African Americans/black culture as deficient, and social institutions as generally race-neutral. In the interest of establishing their own nonracism/racial innocence and the nonracism of the mainstream society, elder white southerners acknowledge historical realities to a certain extent while asserting the society's structures as race-neutral.

My analysis draws from research on contemporary racial discourse and the *white racial frame* concept. Sociologist Joe Feagin argues that Americans (especially but not exclusively whites) view the racial landscape through this interpretive frame that enables justifications for white-dominant structures and practices.[21] Entrenched through white elites' control of cultural, economic, and political processes (for example, scientific theories, mainstream media narratives and images, race-based laws and policies), the white racial frame continues to shape interpretations through its foundational notions of white goodness and black (and other nonwhite) deficiency. These notions were expressed as whites' biological superiority during the slavery and segregation eras and as whites' cultural superiority now in the post–civil rights era. While research on post–civil rights racial discourse emphasizes what is "new" about how we think and talk about race, the white racial frame accounts for both the stability and flexibility of the racial hierarchy across time to maintain its purpose—to justify structures of white domination. The white racial frame also posits emotions as intricately involved in how we process information about the racial world.

The racial narratives of elder white southerners are not purely ideological, working to make sense of and legitimate the racial status quo, but are involved also in identity maintenance. And these are not purely separate functions. Whites' identity work is central to reproducing the racial order.[22] I propose that participants' racial narratives reveal their construction of a *white moral identity*. Sociologists have theorized moral identity making as the process of constructing oneself as morally superior—an interpretive effort that involves marking others as deviant/immoral and failing to acknowledge aspects of oneself that contradict the moral identity.[23] I apply this concept to make sense of how participants constructed a positive sense of self in light of the purview of the research topic—reflecting on living through a history of white domination now maligned in the post–civil rights era. I argue that the elder white southern participants construct a white moral identity of virtuousness and racial innocence through acknowledging blatant inequities while also highlighting the goodness of the segregation era and, when referencing the civil rights and post–civil rights eras, criticizing African

Americans, emphasizing white victimization and loss, and asserting
equal opportunity.

OVERVIEW OF THE BOOK

In chapter 2, I share how interviewees discussed growing up during
legal segregation, focusing on the private realm of white homes and
families, where white supremacist codes of interracial etiquette often
operated alongside cross-racial intimacy. Their accounts of black domestic workers and employees have themes of mutual affection and
good treatment. *White protectionism* is a term I introduce to describe
how people worked to establish their parents and other family members
as nonracist, good people. I provide some context by quoting available
accounts from black domestic workers, who typically did not share a
view of the white home as a safe haven from racial oppression. Although
interviewees usually claimed that Jim Crow had no ill effects on them, I
discuss the impact of Jim Crow on white children, including the need to
reconcile teachings of equality and teachings of white superiority.
Contrary to participants' claims, I argue that white southerners were
inevitably deeply affected by Jim Crow.

Chapter 3 focuses on accounts of segregation in the public realm,
including restaurants, city streets, and regional travel. Although many
people emphasized the safety and security of their childhood and its
easygoing racial interactions, they acknowledged also the blatant racial
inequality embedded in segregated public facilities. However, in many
explanations, Jim Crow was an inevitable period in southern history,
stemming from mysterious origins and maintained by unknown forces.
In analyzing their limited reflection on the white supremacy of segregation, I develop the concept of white protectionism further, arguing that
it operates on a level more collective and more structural than was
evident in the previous chapter.

The next two chapters analyze the civil rights era. Chapter 4 looks at
narratives of local civil rights activism, especially Greensboro's notorious sit-in protests that began in 1960 at segregated businesses. Sharing
participants' accounts of witnessing civil rights activism firsthand, I
present the major theme of chaos, uncertainty, and danger. I analyze
also how participants demonstrated a collective symbolic distance from

the civil rights movement through lacking awareness, inaccurate recall, and criticizing protestors and activist leaders, despite claiming to have supported the movement and desegregation on principle. I assert that their civil rights narratives work to lighten the weight of Jim Crow oppression, present white southerners as racially enlightened and even vulnerable targets, and downplay the importance of the movement.

Chapter 5 analyzes narratives of Greensboro's school integration process (1963–1971). At that time, most interviewees were parents of schoolchildren, so the issue was one that directly and intimately affected them. For many, the memories were vivid and their emotions still raw; claims of *white victimhood* were abundant. Respondents justified white resistance to school desegregation as a nonracist stance and presented integrating schools and busing programs as disruptive and traumatic for vulnerable white children. In both chapters 4 and 5, the contrast between participants' stated agreement with desegregation and their criticism of the process is a key theme. I argue that these two phenomena work in concert to support notions of white virtuousness, both individual and collective.

Chapter 6 analyzes participants' perceptions of racial issues in the post–civil rights era. First I discuss participants' portrayals of racial changes over their lifetimes, ranging from admissions of personal enlightenment and positive regard for current interracial relations to sadness and criticism toward the current state of racial affairs and what they believe has been lost in recent decades. Next I share people's accounts of the 1979 "Greensboro massacre" (an incident in which white supremacists ambushed a protest march of multiracial labor organizers and five organizers were murdered, but no one was found guilty at trial) and their commentary on the early 2000s truth and reconciliation effort that sought to address lingering wounds in the community. Many interviewees expressed bitter resentment toward both the original event and the recent reconciliation process.

In chapter 7 the book ends by further discussing the connections between white southerners' memories and identities and makes a case for the relevance of this analysis beyond the world of elder white southerners. Recent sociological research has found that whites who deem the civil rights movement an important historical event have a more accurate understanding of the contemporary racial landscape—namely, that systemic racial bias continues to benefit whites and hinder the advancement of people of color.[24] Remembering accurately, then, is not simply valuable in and of itself; since it is linked to our comprehension of current inequalities, memory impacts our ability to recognize the changes needed to move U.S. society toward its ideal of liberty and justice for all. How we view the past is linked with how we view the present; these perceptions help to determine whether and how we will engage in the work required to build a more just society.

2

"ONLY LOVE UNDER OUR ROOF"

Jim Crow at Home

While the system of legal segregation enforced the separation of whites from blacks in many public areas, the white supremacist ideology that undergirded legal segregation permeated the public and private realms alike.[1] Most historical research on Jim Crow life has focused on the public aspects, such as segregation of businesses and accommodations, even though the home was a primary site of whites' socialization to Jim Crow.[2] Thus, U.S. society has a limited view of this time period and lacks a comprehensive understanding of the intricate dynamics of Jim Crow, which manifested not only in separate accommodations, but also in the private realm of homes, neighborhoods, and churches, where people spent the majority of their time and learned most of their lessons about race.

Even at the time, Jim Crow whites had a limited understanding of the role that the home, family, and white community played in socializing them to segregation. Black southerners felt the contrast between their supportive all-black neighborhoods and the white-dominant outside world. To the extent that it could be, the black community was a safe haven from racial oppression.[3] Through frequent teachings, black children learned how to recognize, manage, avoid, and cope with white racism.[4] Black communities fostered a critical race consciousness to maintain a sense of dignity and pride and to survive on a day-to-day basis. Jim Crow whites, on the other hand, did not experience a sharp contrast between the safety and ideology of their communities and mainstream society, and they did not require training in survival strategies and coping mechanisms to maintain a positive identity under legal segregation. Rather, the white community tended to teach the same lessons as the mainstream culture, preparing their children to become enforcers of Jim Crow.[5]

It is in this more private realm of white communities where our analysis begins. When the interview participants for this research were asked about their racialized experiences as childhood members of white families and communities, they recalled primarily interracial harmony, tolerance, and the indoctrination of equality, not white supremacist ideology or practice. Many had grown up in homes with black domestic workers employed and portrayed these relationships as having been respectful and often family-like—genuine impressions on the part of participants, but which downplay the power dynamics inherent between employers and employees. There were frequent memories of how parents and churches had taught love and brotherhood, and assertions that *these* were the formative values that had shaped their racial perspectives. Some rationalized even the overtly racist views displayed memorably by family members, part of a dynamic I refer to as *white protectionism*. Overall, the Jim Crow white home was constructed as a site immune from, and even opposed to, racism.

THE SANCTITY OF THE WHITE HOME

In her 1949 memoir, Lillian Smith described the contradictions of the segregated South and their devastating effects on her childhood understandings of the world. Jim Crow culture taught her white supremacy; family and church taught her principles of human equality. Smith explained that the messages were deeply contradictory and yet coexisted largely without question.[6] In *Growing Up Jim Crow: How White and Black Southern Children Learned Race*, historian Jennifer Ritterhouse corroborated Smith's insight that white southerners simultaneously taught their children both "decency" and racism. In Ritterhouse's research of historical documents, however, few whites expressed that they had learned racism from their families. She explained that, through adolescence, the rules of segregation became stricter and white youth stopped asking questions about Jim Crow and began participating in socializing the next generation. Whites' segregation sensibilities were well entrenched by young adulthood, and their childhood curiosity had been forgotten or rationalized away.

Similarly, the participants portrayed the white home as a site mostly untouched by racial prejudice and rarely if ever the source of contradictory messages regarding race and equality. When people told stories about their family's racial views during their childhood, the majority described their loved ones' colorblindness, racial progressiveness, and goodwill to black southerners. They recalled loving, respectful relationships, free from racial animosities, with African American nannies, maids, cooks, "yard men," and farm workers. Parents were especially revered; when racism or anti-black prejudice was personified, it was usually in neighbors, acquaintances, or older relatives. Those who did share memories of close family members' racial prejudice often went on to employ strategies of *white protectionism* to lighten the racist association or rationalize their loved one's perspectives.

Teachings of Equality and Love

All of the participants were born and raised in the segregated South and experienced Jim Crow as children, teenagers, and young adults. The oldest participants lived at least four decades under Jim Crow and thus attended college, served in the military, married, established households, held down careers, and parented their own children before legal segregation was dismantled. Most people portrayed the Jim Crow era as one of greater morality, obedience to elders, and warm neighborly relations. Most also recalled their parents and families with fondness and said that they were taught explicit lessons about human equality and entitlement to respectful treatment rather than anti-black beliefs, constructing racism as something hateful that was not promoted by their families. In a typical portrayal, one of the older participants, Arnold, a man in his 80s,[7] said his parents were respectful toward black people and were not like white supremacists:

> If my parents had been a member of the Ku Klux Klan or some other hate group or something, why, that'd be different. But they were *neither* like that. And they *never* talked about (pause) black people,

or did not use the n-word, or did not talk in a derogatory way. They treated black people with respect.[8]

Harmony, also in her 80s, raised her own children during segregation. She said that, when it came to race, she taught her children

> that we are *all* equal and we do not discriminate. There are things that we have to abide by, that the law has set down for us—you know, that we have no choice on some things, but our own personal ideas of things are what we make them. And we're supposed to always hope for better things and do the best we can and treat every-body alike.

Harmony said she instructed her children to believe in equality and progress, but also to follow the rule of law and accept the way things were.

Lillian Smith observed that religious teachings in the white South during Jim Crow were contradictory, both reflecting and enhancing the contradictions white children learned about race:

> We were taught . . . to love God, to love our white skin, and to believe in the sanctity of both. We learned at the same time to fear God and to think of Him as having complete power over our lives. As we were beginning to feel this power and to see it reflected in our parents, we were learning also to fear a power that was in our body and to fear dark people who were everywhere around us, though the ones who came into our homes we were taught to love.[9]

A perceptive white critic of Jim Crow segregation, Smith argued that teachings of equality in churches and homes did not elevate the white South above racism. Rather, religion coexisted with and reinforced the anti-black racism pervasive throughout the society. However, most of the people interviewed for this book viewed things differently from her. They asserted that church teachings complemented family teachings, but they did not identify racism in those teachings. In their recollections, home lessons of goodwill and equality were reinforced by religious doctrine.

Certainly, religious teachings of human equality and justice *could* provide tools for developing a critical race consciousness. One of the eldest participants, Gracie, spoke at length in her interview about having long had fairly progressive racial views, and she claimed that her religious upbringing helped her solidify those views, even as she stood out from many of her contemporaries:

> Many people have asked me how did I grow up with the feeling about black people that I had, and I said, "Well, I went to a small church, and we were taught that we were all God's children, and there was no east and there was no west," and I said that I was so thoroughly indoctrinated by the time I realized it was a difference that it stuck with me. (chuckles)[10]

Gracie indicated that she had been recognized throughout her life by "many people" as a white person who broke from the overtly racist norm. In her view, religious messages of equality were the first and most influential messages she received in her life, and she believed that she was able to draw upon that ethical system when it came to interpreting race. In subsequent chapters we will return to Gracie and see how she described having had a more positive view of integration than the majority of whites around her.

Many participants recalled having been taught about equality through church and home influence. Several people also recounted incidents that they had not personally witnessed, but which were recounted as part of their family's racial story. Usually these were accounts that demonstrated the presence of racial kindness or progressiveness in the family line, and those from middle and upper middle class families in particular often had a paternalistic tone. For example, Mack, 80s, offered a generations'-old family story about freeing enslaved laborers prior to the Civil War. He implied that, in the antebellum South, there were, in contrast to his own family, "unscrupulous" white people who worked to maintain racial oppression:

> Mack: I know that my *great-great*-grandfather, had, I think it was sixteen or eighteen slaves, and he took them individually *north* . . . in groups of four and five in a wagon, and released them up there and gave them their emancipation papers, *long* before the Civil War. And the reason he did it, according to family tradition, he *knew* that if he released 'em *here* unscrupulous white people would capture them again, tear up their papers, and put 'em back in slavery. So he took 'em north . . . where that wouldn't happen. Okay?
> Interviewer: Mm-hm.

> Mack: So even though my family served in the War between the States, I remember sitting on my *great*-granddaddy's lap and his tellin' me stories. . . . I never heard him justify slavery. I never heard him justify segregation, or try to.

Originally his great-grandfather's story, this had become Mack's own that he invoked to represent his ancestry. He presented his ancestors as decent men for choosing to free enslaved workers and for not attempting to "justify" slavery or segregation. By saying to me pointedly, "Okay?," Mack let me know that he expected me to grasp the significance of his story: his family put forth significant effort to treat black people well, even if they fought in the Civil War for southern slave states. He asserted throughout the interview that his family was able to be critical of systemic racial inequalities. Carrying on the family tradition, Mack told several similar family stories of more recent incidents of racial goodwill. He maintained that his family had always done everything they could to counteract the hurtfulness of anti-black racism, unlike many of their contemporaries.

Similarly, Arnold, 80s, proudly told a story of his father's kindness to an illiterate black man. But, unlike Mack, he portrayed the act of racial goodwill as perhaps typical of the era:

> This black man who was a customer of my [dad] . . . he couldn't write his name. . . . My dad said, "No, John"—or whatever his name was—"you ought to be able to write your name." And he said, "I'm gonna write it for you." And my dad wrote it *several* times on a piece of paper, in pretty good-sized letters. And then he gave the guy a pencil and some paper and he said, "Now you go home and you copy that. And you just write." Next time he came . . . he wrote his name. . . . He was very proud that he was able to write his name. Well, he probably never learned to write anything else—he was an elderly man. But I thought, Well now that's what people oughta do. We all oughta do stuff like that. . . . Nowadays, people wouldn't have time to be bothered, but that was a much slower time, and my dad took the pains to spend time with him. [11]

Arnold indicated that, during Jim Crow, the pace of life and social relations were more easygoing, such that kindnesses of this type were perhaps more possible. As will become clear in the following chapter, many participants conflated the legal segregation era with a more congenial, neighborly time in American history.

White Protectionism: Rescuing the Family from Judgment

Many people portrayed their families and parental lessons as immune from racial prejudice and rooted in good morals. However, several people did speak voluntarily of particular family members who harbored anti-black prejudice or who opposed civil rights efforts. But, when asked to elaborate on these family members, there was a frequent phenomenon of backtracking or downplaying their original portrayals, rationalizing the prejudice or claiming it was not actually racist in essence. In these ways, they modified their initial statements and actively reconstructed themselves and their family members as nonracist, or at least not *that* racist. I term these rescue maneuvers *white protectionism*.

In the following exchange, Bernice, 80s, brought up her grandfather's anti-black views. I tried to get her to elaborate and also to think through the implications of having equality-minded parents and a racist grandpa:

> Bernice: But my grandfather, he wadn't much for the blacks.
> Interviewer: Why do you say that?
> Bernice: I don't know, I don't know. He—he—he never did voice his opinion much or anything. But he lived with us for a number of years.
> Interviewer: Mm-hm. So how did you know that about him?
> Bernice: Well, he—he'd, uh, like I said, never talked about it much but just (pause) little things sometime I would hear or something, you know . . .
> Interviewer: So, if your parents teach you to respect people no matter what their race is or what their color is, and you have an idea maybe that your grandfather who lives in the home with you doesn't like black people—
> Bernice: (takes a deep breath) Well it wadn't, uh, [that] he didn't like 'em . . . Now, he would never mistreat anybody, but uh, I—I just had that feeling that he just was not too gung ho with a lot of things that went on.

Bernice first volunteered that her grandfather "wadn't much for the blacks," but then struggled to articulate how she knew that. When I reworded her statement, saying that he "doesn't like black people," she rejected that characterization and asserted that "he would never mistreat anybody," that he opposed "a lot of the things that went on" rather than black people themselves. Thus, what began as an admission of a family member's anti-black prejudice turned into denying that image and asserting the person's goodness instead.

Similarly, Gertie, 70s, had described her mother as racially liberal in contrast to her father, so I asked her to explain how she had come to realize the difference between her liberal mother and her less liberal father. In her response she shared a specific account:

> He never voiced it, and he was a very kind, sweet person, but I can remember one time, when Martin Luther King was becoming very popular, that my father said very sternly that he thought he was a rabble-rouser. And I argued it with him, you know, vehemently, but I realized at that time that that's what he really felt. And other than that I don't know that I had any other indication, because he was very sweet and kind.

Just before relaying the memorable argument over King, Gertie claimed that her father "never voiced it." Just after, she said that the King comments had been her only clue to his racial views. Both before and after relaying the account of her father's angry response to Martin Luther King Jr., Gertie emphasized that he was a good person. There are two ways to interpret this: Gertie was attempting to ensure that her father was not condemned as a racist, or she was demonstrating that she had not reconciled in her own mind how her father could have been both a nice person and racially prejudiced.

In Darla's, 70s, case, white protectionism maneuvers were more clear-cut. She used overly moderate terms to describe her mother's racial views, such as "concern" and "awareness":

> My mother was a dear, dear person, but mother was a little more aware and concerned with black people. I mean, you know, wasn't her fault, but she was raised in an entirely different *era* from us, and she probably had seen 'em in a different light. I'm sure they had black people workin' for them when she was growin' up. She was

never not nice to black people, but in the way she talked sometimes I felt like maybe she didn't think they were as good as we were. . . . My daddy was entirely different. He was very, very friendly and nice and had great compassion. I never heard him say anything derogatory about blacks. And mother didn't really either, but she was just aware, you know, that there was a difference.

Like Gertie, Darla explained that her parents were kind, compassionate people. Darla drew a distinct contrast between her mother and father, describing them as "entirely different." However, she minimized that contrast in subsequent statements—for example, in the way she described how neither her mother nor her father had said "anything derogatory about blacks." A few minutes later in the interview, Darla claimed that her mother did in fact say negative things about African Americans, but she offered only benign examples not tinged with racial animosity: "The only thing *my mother* ever said that was derogatory was that she'd say somethin' about, 'Well, she's a black person,' or, 'They have to go into that bathroom,' or something. I mean, she was just aware of what was goin' on, and she would make a comment." Darla did not give a consistent portrayal of her mother. What she did say indicated that she had a clear sense of her mother's anti-black views and saw them as markedly different from her father's, but the pieces of evidence she shared did not support that assessment. Darla hinted at her mother's overtly racist views, but in her explanations she buffered her mother from criticism.

In the above excerpt, Darla rationalized her mother's views using a generational explanation: "she was raised in an entirely different era." As other participants spoke of their family members, this kind of rationale was common. This is naturalistic reasoning that asserts people as products of their environment/generation and believes that anti-black racism naturally wanes over time. For example, Chuck, 70s, explained that his family's anti-black prejudice had gradually lost its potency in each generation:

Interviewer: It's hard for *me* to understand having close personal relationships with some black people and then at the same time having separate places to sit in public. How do you make sense of that?

Chuck: It bothered me as a kid. I just couldn't see why it was. . . .
Well, I think the answer to your question is it's a generational thing.
My grandmother had one very, very strong attitude about race relations. My dad came along, and you could see the influence of her
attitude about that on him, but to a *much* less degree. And then
when I came along, I really don't think I had any. I mean, I have to
confess that there were jokes sometimes that would make you believe that my generation had the discriminatory attitudes, but we
really didn't. It was pretty much gone. And then when our kids came
along, it was pretty well gone.

Chuck argued that, with the exception of some racist joking, the "discriminatory attitudes" were "pretty much gone" by the time of his own
Jim Crow generation. He rationalized racism as something that
stemmed from a person's attitudes (rather than, for example, social
structures), that was largely dictated by their generation, and that had
steadily improved with the passage of time.

Bernice's grandfather "just was not too gung ho with a lot of things
that went on," Gertie's father "never voiced it" and "was very sweet and
kind," Darla's mom was "a little more aware and concerned with black
people," and Chuck's family showed that bias against blacks was merely
"a generational thing." In each of these examples, the participants first
called out their family members' racial prejudice, however mildly, and
then rationalized that racism as a product of their time or of experiences, or they backtracked and contradicted their initial claim. We can
view these moves as strategies, not necessarily intentional, of both explaining and *explaining away* the alignment of one's own family with
overtly racist ideology.

Mack, 80s, astutely pointed out the contradiction whereby white
southerners were able to respect individual African Americans while
still remaining racist toward blacks as a whole:

I grew up knowing a *lot* of black people individually. And as I *look* at
it, in those days white people had individual blacks that they were
very close to, but they didn't like black people. Okay? In other words,
they didn't like *black* people, but they liked the individual black
people. Like, I liked [our housekeeper], I liked [the men who
worked for the family].

Mack seemed to be explaining, from his own experience, how white southerners could feel great warmth toward select African Americans and still be strongly aligned with white supremacy. But a few minutes later in the interview, when asked to say more about this dynamic about "liking" individuals but then "not liking" the group, he indicated that it did not apply to his own family:

> Interviewer: So did your parents or grandparents talk about black people as a whole in a way that would make you think they didn't like them?
> Mack: I was—I was—*No*, don't think so. I was never, *ever* allowed to use the n-word. Never. I've *never* heard my father use it, I never heard my grandfather use it.
> Wife: It didn't occur to you, I'm sure.
> Mack: It didn't *occur* to me to use it. It was just not *done*.
> Wife: They were known to you by way of names?
> Mack: Yeah.
> Wife: Instead of anything else, not as a race.

Here, Mack's wife lent support to his response that indicated his family did not serve as an example of his previous claim that white southerners were prejudiced even if they "liked" individual black people. She helped him build his argument that his own family's positive, personal relationships with individual black people superseded any inclination to view African Americans negatively.

This final excerpt illustrates white protectionism done collectively: a married couple worked together to squelch the suggestion that Mack's family was racially prejudiced toward African Americans. White protectionism came into clearest focus through interaction—often between interviewer and participant. Most of these cases began with a simple admission of the family member's prejudiced views, which were sometimes watered down or vague. This is what we might consider a first phase of white protectionism. Second, my seeking clarification or elaboration often prompted rescuing maneuvers, as people regained control over the portrayal of their loved one(s). White protectionism maneuvers are defensive—minimizing negative implications, deflecting criticism, and rationalizing whites' participation in systemic racial inequality and racist ideology. Through white protectionism maneuvers, a person is able to acknowledge systemic racism and still assert the family's immu-

nity, or to reveal and then explain away a white loved one's racial prejudice.

DOMESTIC WORKERS: "HELP" ACROSS THE COLOR LINE

Interracial closeness and intimacy were in some ways more common in
the Jim Crow South than today, especially in the white household.
Today, white Americans are highly segregated from people of color and
especially black Americans in housing and schools (indeed, whites are
the most segregated race-ethnic group in the United States).[12] During
legal segregation the white home was a regular site of interracial interactions.[13] African American domestic workers were employed in a majority of middle- to upper-income white homes and in many working-
class white homes, as well as in well-to-do black homes.[14] Female domestic workers were often integrally involved in many matters of the
household, from maintaining the home and grounds and completing
daily chores to caring for children and acting as confidantes, and their
presence itself provided a symbolic status marker for the white family.[15]
Historian Grace Hale points out that Jim Crow white identity was given
shape by the employment of African Americans in the home: "Racial
identity within the culture of segregation depended in more ways than
one upon the symbolic power of the mammy—being white meant having black help."[16]

Despite the close physical proximity of worker and family member
in the white home, the set of behaviors expected of black employees
was stringent. Historian Leon Litwack explains that "they would sit at
their own table, eat from separate plates, drink out of separate buckets
and dippers, use their own toilets, and enter the house only by the back
door. They would abide by the same rules of etiquette in how they
addressed members of the family, and of course they would not expect
such courtesies to be reciprocated."[17] Black women and men were usually either called by their first names or generic names for their status,
like "Mammy" or "Mamie" and "Uncle." African Americans were, in
turn, expected to call white adults by titles and last names, such as
"Mister and Missus Johnson." White children often got the privilege of
a title as well, like "Mister Tommy" or "Miss Ann."[18] These titles were
one of the many reminders of blacks' status of inferiority within the

white home. Additionally, the domestic work itself could be dehumanizing and exhausting. As a mother who had worked in domestic service for thirty years reported in 1912, "I am the slave, body and soul, of this family," and "I am not permitted to rest. It's 'Mammy, do this,' or 'Mammy, do that,' or 'Mammy, do the other,' from my mistress all the time. . . . I live a treadmill life."[19]

While the emotional attachments between workers and family members could be deep and mutually felt, white employers, unlike black employees, generally perceived the closeness as genuine and unadulterated by racism.[20] White employers most often were not aware of this difference in perception, however. In her novel *The Color Purple*, Alice Walker offered a scene illustrative of this common lack of awareness. The characters in the scene are a white woman, Eleanor Jane, and her black domestic laborer, Sofia, who has been forced to work without pay or vacation for many years as penance for punching Eleanor Jane's father, the town mayor. In the scene, Eleanor Jane is at Sofia's house and is trying to get Sofia to agree that her (Eleanor Jane's) baby son, Reynolds Stanley, is "sweet." Sofia silently ignores the repeated requests, but finally explains, "I don't feel nothing about him at all. I don't love him, I don't hate him." Eleanor Jane is taken aback by the seemingly callous remark and responds, "I just don't understand. All the other colored women I know love children. The way you feel is something unnatural." Sofia replies, "I love children. But all the colored women that say they love yours is lying. They don't love Reynolds Stanley any more than I do. But if you so badly raise as to ast 'em, what you expect them to say?"

Eleanor Jane, a white southern daughter of privilege, had developed an inaccurate generalization of the regard that black women had for white children under their care. Only in the home of a black woman, who was forthright with her, was she confronted with the erroneousness of her impression. In the 1980s, anthropologist Susan Tucker interviewed white and black women who had participated in the Jim Crow domestic employer-employee relationship. Her interviews revealed that black women former employees were acutely aware of their status as employees, although they often did feel fondness toward their employers and the children under their care. On the other hand, white women former employers rarely acknowledged the inherent power dynamics in the relationship; rather, most of them emphasized closeness and intimacy.[21] This perception that ignores or downplays the power differential was frequent in my participants' narratives as well.

The Language of "Help"

The majority of the people interviewed had grown up in households where African Americans were employed. This was the case especially, but not exclusively, among those who had been raised in middle and upper middle class families. Due to how low the wages could be and the fact that employing domestic laborers was a marker of status, even some who said they had been "poor" had experienced having domestic workers. Essentially, all but the poorest of white families had enough excess money to enable them to hire black "help," at least on occasion.[22] And the wealthiest families often employed domestic workers on a daily basis and saw them as quite permanent fixtures of the home.[23]

One would imagine that household members must have had a wide variety of relationships with black employees, for a spectrum of personalities had to be negotiated within the home. However, of the forty-four people interviewed for this book, only one recalled having had a strained relationship with a domestic laborer. A woman in her 70s said, "I didn't like Lenora, and it didn't have anything to do with her color, she just was sort of a grumpy lady and she didn't talk to me much and I just didn't enjoy her company especially."[24] The other participants spoke kindly, warmly, or even glowingly, about the black people who had come into their homes to work. White families were portrayed as strictly upholding a standard of respect toward black laborers. For example, Bernice, 80s, mirthfully recalled an incident where her brother got punished for being mean to the housekeeper:

> Ol' Corina, this big fat nigra woman over on the hill, she had about over a half-dozen children, and she would come and stay with mother and help her and do ironing and stuff like that that mother wadn't able to do at the time. . . . She was a very loving person, and my oldest brother (chuckles) one time . . . Corina, this big ol' fat black nigra woman she said, "Miss Jenny, I can't work for you anymore," and Mama said "Corina, why? Why can't you work?" . . . and she says, "I can't tell you." [Mama] said, "Well you gotta tell me, and got to have some reason." And she said, "Bobby . . . called me a big black nigger." And my mother just about (laughing) fell out in the floor!

And boy you can bet he never said that again! (laughing) 'Cause my parents believed . . . in spanking. They didn't believe in (chuckles) half killing anybody but *you* got it.

Bernice heartily laughed while telling this story and clearly held this moment as a happy childhood memory where her brother learned through strict discipline to obey the family's standards. As Bernice's own language makes clear, there was an understanding in her family that a black domestic worker should never be called the hostile term "nigger," but could acceptably be called the slightly less potent term "nigra."

Nearly all participants who had lived in a home that employed black domestic workers portrayed the interracial relationships as friendly and warm. Numerous people went further and described their childhood domestic workers as family-like. For example, Florence, 80s, described the attachment felt mutually between her family and their employees:

I lived out in the country, but we still had black servants, and they almost felt like they were a member of [our] family, and we felt that way too. And we would invite them to sit at the table with us if they wanted to—that was their choice, to either decide to or not to eat with us. I remember [soon] before my mother died, she wanted to go see Marla, who was the black lady who had worked with us, and they had the *nicest visit*—it was like sisters talking, you know, they both knew that this was their last time together. But we loved Marla, and the color of her skin did not make any difference to us whatsoever. And then later when our children were little, we had a maid, and she even carried a picture of our son in her wallet. She said he was her baby.

Florence presented her parents' domestic employee Marla as a woman who was treated as an equal, being invited to sit with them at family meals and serving as a longtime confidante—"almost" family. And then Florence shifted into describing a similar relationship she felt she had had as an adult with her own maid, where the woman cared so deeply about her childcare duties that she kept a photograph of Florence's son in her wallet at all times.

Like Florence, other people said that their familial connection to black domestic workers transcended the term of employment and lasted for many years. For Sally, 70s, the family's loving relationship with her mother's employee stood the test of time:

> We had a woman who helped my mother. . . . To my children, she's just like another grandmother or another aunt. She has been to all of their college graduations. . . . So, she's just been a member of our family for all those years. . . . Paulette [and my mother] were *very* close. We would go [inside], and mother and Paulette would be at the table discussing life.

Sally presented her mother's relationship with her employee Paulette as "*very* close," like peers or sisters. In fact, from her word choice, it is not entirely clear that Paulette was an employee at all ("a woman who helped my mother"). Similarly, John, 70s, said that his parents' treatment of live-in black domestics in the 1940s and 1950s was as if they were members of the family: "Quite often Mother and Dad would hire a young black male. We had a room that they lived in . . . rent-free. And they would help some with maybe yard work or serve meals. . . . And they were not treated any different than Mother and Dad treated me. They were welcomed, they had the run of the house, they could do whatever they wanted." In John's portrayal, the workers were "welcomed," treated just like their own son, and they "would help some." Like Sally, John's language implies that this was not so much an employer–employee relationship, but rather one where both parties helped each other out when they needed it.

In the Jim Crow era, domestic workers were regularly referred to as "the help."[25] Although this term was common in the segregated South, in the participants' narratives, its usage extended beyond using it simply in place of "employee." As is evident in Bernice's, Sally's, and John's excerpts above, black domestic workers were described as people who "helped" the family. In Florence's terms, their domestic employee worked "with" the family. These descriptions leave the impression that the labor was minimal or easy and often collaboratively accomplished with members of the household. Furthermore, the construction of employee-as-helper implies that the labor was done voluntarily and with generosity.

Several people also gave accounts illustrating how *they* had helped and assisted their black employees, by providing a good job in a good home, treating them well, and doing special favors.[26] As Bernice, 80s, explained, her family's excess clothing and food became gifts to employees: "My mother *gave* them a whole lot of things—you know things that *we* would outgrow and so forth. 'Course time they passed down through our family there wasn't much left of 'em. (laughing) But . . . somebody working in our home . . . she'd always send 'em food home 'cause we did have plenty food. We had big gardens and chickens and things." Arnold, 80s, said that his father helped a black employee to purchase a home, something the man would not have been able to do otherwise: "[My dad] encouraged this black man to buy a house back when [African Americans] didn't know how to do any of those things. He told him save his money so he'd have some money to pay down, and he walked him through doing all that." In these stories, people are constructing their family's standpoint on race under Jim Crow, defining how their family treated African Americans, how their family was treated in return, and illustrating how much goodwill was demonstrated across the color line within the confines of the white home.

Goodwill or Power?

The language of "help," very common in the narratives of black domestic workers, clouds the core reality that the basis of the relationship between white families and black employees was an exchange of labor for low wages, set within a larger racist social and economic environment in which non-white southerners had extremely limited opportunities to earn wages anywhere near the "white" rate, even when they had education and valuable skills. But participants' portrayals of domestic workers rarely indicated that there was a power dynamic undergirding the relationship between employer and employee. For example, Mack, 80s, told a story about how black employees voluntarily protected his family's property after a storm:

> Mack: [A] tornado . . . tore the roof off my granddaddy's house. . . .
> When we went *over* there . . . there was Jonny Brand on the front
> porch with a shotgun and a police dog. And his *son* was on the *back*
> porch with a shotgun and a police dog. And they assured us that my
> [family was] going to be *very* safe, and there was not gonna be any-
> thing *stolen* from that house, and [we] weren't gonna be both-
> ered. . . .
> Interviewer: Why did they do that?

> Mack: Protection. . . . They were black people who worked for my granddaddy . . . and they were close, they were just—they were *family*, but they were black.

According to Mack, these were people who worked for the family, but more important, "were family," and therefore invested in protecting the family's assets from harm and ensuring their sense of security in the world. We must note that in several of these cases, there is a clear class element operating within the participants' experiences with black Americans. Because of their stature in the community, social networks, and economic means, well-to-do white families could come to expect to feel looked out for by black employees and acquaintances, who, in turn, could expect favors from time to time. However, interview participants tended to present the good deeds done for them as favors done by good (black) people for good (white) people, not acknowledging the social class and racial power differentials that incentivized sometimes ingratiating behaviors on the part of black southerners.[27]

Additionally, Patti, 80s, began her interview by explaining that her family felt both a "closeness and responsibility" that drove them to assist black people connected to the family through a history of labor:

> It was our family, but it wasn't our family in any way, you know, except this feeling of closeness and *responsibility*. When my father died his estate had a little money that was left to pay for taxes on a piece of property . . . where some of the descendants of my great-grandfather's slaves still lived. And our family paid the taxes every year so they didn't have to do it. And my father was a big family man . . . he would always go and see all the people every time. . . .
> But I was just raised with this thought that you helped those who are good to you—you return it.

Through using the term "responsibility," Patti pointed out her family's elevated status relative to the descendants of people they had once owned. On the other hand, in the end, she argued that she had learned a universal lesson about giving and receiving through how kindly her father treated them through both money and social visits. In recalling a well-liked black male employee of the family, Arnold, 80s, also pointed out the employer–employee relationship, and in more forthright terms than Patti:

I became very fond of a black man that worked for my dad. . . . I thought [it] was a really high day that I'd get to spend the day with him, and I'd ride around in the truck with him as he made his deliveries and pickups. . . . He was wonderful to me. He treated [me] with—'course I was his employer's son, I know that, but I mean, he was nice and, you know, he was a good man.

As Arnold explained how his fondness for a black employee was reciprocated, he quickly acknowledged his status as the boss's son. In this way, Arnold went further than most other participants by acknowledging that domestic employees' kindnesses may have been driven, at least in part, by obligation due to the nature of the relationship.

In an essay entitled "The Servant in the House," early black sociologist W. E. B. Du Bois described the demeaning nature of African Americans' segregation-era domestic labor: "700,000 washerwomen and household drudges,—ignorant, unskilled offal of a millionaire industrial system. Their pay was the lowest and their hours the longest of all workers. The personal degradation of their work is so great that any white man of decency would rather cut his daughter's throat than let her grow up to such a destiny."[28] Du Bois argued that the position of black domestic worker was so exploitative that Jim Crow white southerners would have dreaded the thought of their own children doing that labor. However, the participants did not portray the white home as a site of socioeconomic, physical, or psychological exploitation. Sally, 70s, attempted to make clear how her family's domestic employee was never made to do "demeaning work":

> We did grow up to be very respectful. Paulette . . . I never did see her like on her knees scrubbing the floor. Do you know what I'm trying to say? It was not demeaning work. Although my mother would do it, and I scrubbed the floors. (laughs) But I'm saying there was nothing that Paulette did that we didn't do. Do you know what I'm trying to say, within the house?

Sally explained that because her family respected their employee, they shared with her the most taxing duties, such as cleaning floors. Here, Sally stressed that her family did their best *not* to be exploitative. Similarly, Gertie, 70s, told of how her mother, though quite poor, had opted to pay the maid double the standard rate: "I asked [my mother] one time later, I said, 'We didn't have any money, how did you afford a maid?' She came once a week. And she said, 'Well, that's true, but she had even less than we did.' And she said, 'Most people paid twenty-five cents a day, and I paid her fifty cents a day.'" In account after account, the participants portrayed their families as benign, beneficent employers of African Americans.

Gertie's was one account that hinted at the larger racialized economic environment, indicating that the wages paid to black domestic workers were so low that even a low-income white family could afford to pay double. But it was uncommon for participants to acknowledge the overarching realities of the economic system of the segregated South. For example, in contrast to Gertie's portrayal was a married couple's rationale for their long-term employment of a college-educated black woman. They claimed that this woman had her pick of good jobs, but that she lacked that kind of ambition and preferred the conveniences of domestic labor:

> Wife: Wanda went to college. Oh, her mother was a domestic servant, [but] Wanda could have done anything.
> Husband: Yeah, she could have gotten a job in any office downtown.
> Interviewer: Why didn't she?
> Husband: I've asked her that question many times—I said, "Wanda, you know you could get a job anywhere you want to." And she said, "I'd rather not." And she was very, very close to our kids.
> Wife: And I think she kinda liked the hours—she could be home by two o'clock . . . and then she had a lot of time for church. So I think that's really what it was. And again, she was of that generation where (pause) she did not take advantage—she just didn't assert herself.

This couple implied that there were plentiful job opportunities for educated African Americans and reasoned that, despite having attended college, the woman was stuck in a nonassertive "generational" black mind-set and perhaps preferred the domestic's work schedule. They left the impression that black southerners relinquished other opportunities and willingly chose to make a lifelong career of working in white homes.

Working class white families often employed poor or working class black women in the home, although less extensively than families with higher means, and so the interpersonal and economic dynamics were undoubtedly different.[29] In my interviews with people from a working class background, there were several accounts in which their families had at times relied on their employees to bail *them* out of economic difficulties. For example, Verna, 80s, accepted free labor when the woman who had been her childhood housekeeper came to work for her once a week when she was a young mother on a low income: "She was with Mother before I was born. And then when my mother was very ill . . . [she] would come and visit her . . . she promised Mother that she would take care of me. . . . She would come with me when I had my children. And I could not afford to pay her 'cause we didn't have any money." These accounts were not presented as exploitative either, but rather as evidence of mutual care and respect. Delilah, 70s, spoke of not always paying for services provided: "When they came other times during the week . . . they didn't charge, they just came. We couldn't afford *that*. (pause) And if they saw we were out of [a grocery item] or something, they'd get somebody to stop by the store and get it and bring it the next day. So you could see how family-oriented it was." Delilah's family received free labor and groceries from their domestic workers, and she presented this as proof of how the relationships had been family-like.

Arlene, 70s, was one of the few participants to refer to the injustice of the low pay received by African Americans when working for white families: "We also had household help who were African American, and they too were there for years and were treated well. And, I mean, I think the pay was *awful*, but it was . . . what was done at that time." Arlene demonstrated some critical perspective on the standard practice of paying exploitative wages, and also asserted that her family's employees were "treated well." Overall, when it came to portraying the employment of black southerners by whites, if they shared a critical consciousness, it was not extended to their own families. There was little connection made between systemic racial discrimination and the actions taken by their families. Rather, families were constructed as having paid fair wages and treating their employees with respect.

CONSTRUCTING BLACK PERSPECTIVES

Largely lacking also in the interviewees' portrayals of black domestic laborers was a consideration that their employees' views may have been quite different from their own. From the perspectives of Jim Crow–era black domestic laborers, it was abundantly clear that white supremacy shaped the terms of their employment and their treatment on the job.[30] African Americans' accounts of laboring in white homes are markedly less rosy than the accounts of white employers.[31]

Several interview participants shared what they believed were blacks' perspectives on working for whites. For example, Sharon, 60s, claimed that African Americans were grateful for the opportunity to work for her grandparents as agricultural day laborers: "My grandparents were still making a living on the farm. . . . Many times they'd have blacks to come and work, and (pause) you know my family was very good to the blacks. And they were thankful for the work, and they paid them and everything." Here, Sharon's assertion that "they were thankful for the work" arguably came from her own family's judgment, rather than an accurate read on how those individuals felt.

Arnold, 80s, however, did indicate that black employees' perspectives varied from white employers', but then the example he gave made the case that whites like his own family wanted *more* equality in their interracial interactions than blacks did:

> You have to think about it from the black standpoint. We had a black woman who worked for us. . . . She helped raise our children, and she had never married, and she thought they were her children. I mean, she considered them as her children. (chuckles) . . . But she would *not* sit down at our table and eat with us. (pause) So, I don't know why. We begged her, and our children just never understood why she wouldn't, but they began to realize that was, like I said, the way things are. She would sit on a stool at the kitchen counter; she would not sit at our table. (pause) She would not ride up front when we would take her home. . . . That's just the way she was raised, I reckon.

Here, Arnold equalized the perspectives of Jim Crow whites and blacks; they both were uncomfortable breaking with segregation traditions. He portrayed African Americans' acquiescence to Jim Crow conventions as a matter of them being "raised" that way by their own families, as opposed to, for example, employing survival strategies in dealing with whites. The way Arnold presented it, blacks held to Jim Crow etiquette even more strictly than whites like his family who desired to have more peer-like interracial interactions, such as eating meals together.

According to historian Leon Litwack, in the postslavery South, the ever-present tension between white employers and African Americans was most apparent in domestic labor, because "those tensions reached deep into the family circle and involved the closest contact between blacks and whites."[32] However, few of the participants spoke of any significant tension in their relationships with domestic workers, and only a few recalled having witnessed a white family member being less than cordial to a black worker in the home. Arlene, 70s, was one of those who alluded to strain between the white family and black workers. She stuttered markedly while describing how her family treated two domestic employees: "Barbra worked as a housemaid, and granted, uhh, she was, um (pause) um, I ca-cannot in good conscience say treated well, but I mean, she certainly was-was not, uh, treated badly. But she was treated like a servant. And, uh, as was Vernon." Arlene had great difficulty articulating her observation of the family's treatment of domestic workers. This contrasts with the vast majority of other participants, quoted throughout this section, whose narratives of mostly positive relationships flowed readily.

For Jim Crow African Americans there was a "powerful stream of popular knowledge used to teach young people to be constantly on guard lest they fall prey to the capricious actions of white folks."[33] Black Americans most often entered the employ of white homes with advice from other African Americans; for example, the importance of retaining one's independence by never borrowing money from the family, admonitions to remember that, to whites, blacks are interchangeable and replaceable despite a family's expressions of affection, and, for young women, preparation for white men's attempts at sexual exploitation.[34] These cautions were survival skills to endure an emotionally, psychologically, and physically difficult situation of not merely working for, but also being subjected to the private whims of the white southern employer.[35] Sociologist Ruth Thompson-Miller recently interviewed Jim Crow–era African American southerners, and her analysis demonstrated that many elder black Americans today carry the burden of segrega-tion-era traumas through a "segregation stress syndrome."[36]

It is important not to oversimplify the employer–employee relation-ship and racial exploitation under Jim Crow. Many of the black female domestic workers interviewed by anthropologist Susan Tucker and by the research team that produced *The Maid Narratives: Black Domestics and White Families in the Jim Crow South* claimed to have enjoyed their work and to have genuinely cared for the family, especially the young children they helped to nurse and raise.[37] These positive per-spectives were mirrored in my interviews with white southerners. But narratives of black Americans frequently include added layers of insight on the oppressiveness of Jim Crow domestic labor.[38] For example, one black woman, Willie Mae Fitzgerald, "saw the whites for whom she worked as stingy people who did not see their own material wealth, particularly relative to her own poverty. They saw her every day, but they never compared her life with theirs."[39] In Fitzgerald's words:

> The last place I worked at twenty-odd years—and they didn't raise my salary. Oh yeah, I thought they was crazy about me. I did. They loved my cooking. They were crazy about my dinners. . . . The sala-ries had went up then. Most people was getting eight, ten, twelve dollars and all. So one day I say to her . . . "I been working here for a long time." I say, "I'd like a raise." . . . She said, "I've got to talk it over with my husband." And they ain't talked it over now! . . . I stayed with her until I was sixty-seven. She never did raise me! . . . I say them white folks worked the hell out of me, and that's why I'm all sick and crippled up now. . . . My children was small then, and I knew I had to take care of them. I thought of my little children. . . . I stayed. I was quiet. That's how I worked.[40]

Here, Fitzgerald's long-lasting bitterness over her low salary, physical degradation, and financial inability to quit the job is palpable. Key also are her beginning statements reflecting how her employers' expressions of enthusiastic fondness for her ("I thought they was crazy about me") did not translate into truly good treatment or fair wages.

From my interviews it is impossible to know how the participants' employees felt about their jobs and how much bitterness or nostalgia tinges their memories of laboring in those white homes. But it is clear via other collections of narratives that black men and women retained criticism of the white employer-family and their economic exploitation, but they learned to hide their true feelings from whites.[41] The white southerners' narratives herein demonstrate, then, not necessarily a failure to listen to their employees' points of view, for it was unlikely that those employees felt free to voice their perspectives to them with full honesty. Rather, participants were focused on how *they* remembered and felt about these employees and rarely considered the overarching economic and psychological exploitations of the Jim Crow South that necessarily shaped these relations. Nevertheless, not seeing domestic work as rife with sacrifice and hardship—for example, never grappling with what it meant for black mothers to spend more time caring for whites' children than their own—is one part of a more generalized, and perhaps a willing, ignorance to the white supremacist structure of Jim Crow.

RECONCILING WHITE SUPREMACY AND "GOOD" PEOPLE

According to sociologist Joe Feagin, the historical reality of race in the Jim Crow South was such that "whites who enforced this devastating and comprehensive segregation were usually 'good' or 'warm' people, especially to their kin and friends. Racial oppression was, and still is, executed and imposed by otherwise normal human beings."[42] The normality of racism is an insight needed to understand how good people were also agents of racial oppression. Racism has long been embedded in the structures, laws, and practices of the society and ingrained in the minds of the American people through white supremacist ideology, imagery, and narratives.[43] Lillian Smith used spiritual terms to describe how her family and church socialized her to uphold Jim Crow racism and still maintain a sense of herself as a moral, just, and loving person:

> The mother who taught me what I know of tenderness and love and compassion taught me also the bleak rituals of keeping Negroes in their "place." The father who rebuked me for an air of superiority towards schoolmates . . . and rounded out his rebuke by gravely reminding me that "all men are brothers," trained me in the steel-rigid decorums I must demand of every colored male. They who so gravely taught me to split my body from my mind and both from my

"soul," taught me also to split my conscience from my acts and Christianity from southern tradition.[44]

Smith argued that white southern children were subjected to jarring contradictions between Jim Crow and Christianity. Their families (and they themselves) condoned and helped to enforce the "southern tradition" of exploiting African Americans, and yet they were taught to be good, moral people. Smith was able to identify how her family's teachings about race supported a white supremacist society. Unlike Smith, the people interviewed for this book largely did not see themselves or their families as having played a significant participatory role in Jim Crow racism and did not sense that they had been burdened by their socialization to segregation's norms.

However, Sharon, 60s, was one of the participants who spoke frankly and with nuance about how racism was reinforced within her family. She demonstrated an understanding that white southerners could embody simultaneously genuine cross-racial affection and white supremacy:

> I'm gonna be very, very honest. (pause) My parents and grandparents, they thought blacks had a place, (pause) and they just didn't think you crossed that line. They thought that the blacks had a purpose—to work—and that was their place. And you know, like I said, they were *good* to them (pause) but it stopped at a particular point. But I do want to share one thing from my mother, and she told me this just a few years ago. . . . For a while they had a black man that lived on their farm. . . . If my grandparents had to go away . . . they left Lester in charge of taking care of my mother and her sister. And my mother was telling me that they would get home on the school bus and that Lester would meet them. And she started *crying*—and of course Lester was black. . . . [My mother] was a very strong, dominating, woman—I mean was not weak *at all*. But she started crying [at] just the thought of Lester, she had such fond memories. And she said, "He was *so good to us*" and . . . "for a black man, he would've never harmed us," and she just *loved* him.

First, Sharon explained that, although her family treated African Americans well, they also closely aligned with the white supremacist ideology of the day. Then she shared a poignant story of how deeply her mother felt for her black childhood caretaker, while also indicating that her mother harbored clear prejudice toward black males ("she said . . . 'for a black man, he would've never harmed us'").

Most participants employed less forthrightness when speaking of their family's connection to white supremacist ideology and practice. For example, when asked to think about how her parents would have explained segregated public facilities to her as a child, Sally, 70s, responded by telling stories of her family's generosity toward, and good relationships with, black southerners:

> Interviewer: How do you think your parents would have explained segregation? So those sort of little rules, those regulations? If you had asked about it . . . back of the bus stuff, and those sort of separations?
> Sally: Uh (sighs) that's a hard question for me to answer, because they were southerners, but they did have a lot of compassion. So it would be hard to put words into that, because I think that is the difference between the North and the South too is that black and white people live together in a way that is hard to understand. [My husband's] family . . . had a black man that lived in their house. He was the son of a slave, and he was mentally challenged. . . . He *lived* with them, had a room and lived with them. And a lot of people in the North don't understand those kinds of relationships, but it happened. . . . [My grandfather] would make stew in a big black kettle over a fire in the backyard, and there was a man that he knew really well who would come—a black man—and I can *still* see them out in the backyard, you know, smokin' pipes in the chair. . . . And they cooked it all night long. . . . And granddaddy gave *money* for a black group to build a church not too really far from where they lived. . . . I mean, it was an *intimate* relationship. It's hard to explain to somebody that didn't grow up in that kind of, you know. . . . There was a *community* sense then. And of course, I was too young to be involved with the negative senses, and I'm sure there were . . . negative situations, but that happened between white and white. (laughs) I will tell you the worst thing you could be in North Carolina was white trash. That was the *worst* thing.

Sally began her explanation by pointing out that her parents were both compassionate people *and* southerners, hinting at that Jim Crow dichotomy of morality/goodness and racism. As her narrative took shape, though, it led to a series of examples of goodwill demonstrated by whites like her family and the friendly and intimate relations across racial lines. And then, last, bringing up the stigmatization of "white trash," Sally asserted that the more significant tension in the Jim Crow South was based on class rather than race. Using a similar argument, Arlene, 70s, said that the "real bigotry" was toward religious minorities rather than toward nonwhites:

> I think that there definitely were prejudices then. (pause) I think consideration wasn't really *given* so much to *blacks* in that regard. I think that was a given. I think the real bigotry and prejudice was more probably towards other white people—towards Jewish people, towards Catholics. I remember that much more vividly than I ever do any *negative* opinions about blacks.

Arlene indicated that anti-black prejudice "was a given"—understood and *accepted* and not necessarily blatantly voiced. In her perception, overt manifestations of prejudice did not take the form of white-on-black, but rather intraracially targeted Jewish and Catholic whites. She did not conceive of Jim Crow segregation as being replete with "negative opinions about blacks."

Numerous participants shared racial goodwill stories to attempt to explain the intricacies of Jim Crow life and how the segregation era was not in essence designed to maintain complete physical separation. Indeed, this is an important point for understanding how Jim Crow was lived. Our contemporary national narrative of segregation relies too heavily on the public markers of Jim Crow (for example, racially separate or exclusive facilities) and neglects the realities of the private realm.[45] Thus, younger Americans and non-southerners tend to believe that the segregation era was typified by whites' overt hatred or disgust with all blacks. Critiquing this inaccurate understanding may have, in part, motivated my interview participants to share so many accounts of close relationships across the color line.

However, so many of their narratives paint a picture of their own family's near-immunity from white supremacist ideology and their propensity for racial goodwill. Taken together, these stories of easygoing interracial relations underplay the pervasiveness of systemic racism and work also to establish the speakers as coming from good, nonracist families. Indeed, in her excerpt above, Sally ended her listing of family racial goodwill stories by shifting topics away from black–white relations, asserting that white classism was more potent than white racism ("I will tell you the worst thing you could be in North Carolina was white trash. That was the *worst* thing."), a stance that trivializes the racial oppression experienced by African Americans under Jim Crow, in both white homes and the public sphere. I have made the case that these narratives of home and family construct the white family as uninvolved in the racial oppression of African Americans under segregation. Interview participants acknowledged in various ways the unequal arrangements under Jim Crow, while most of their detailed storytelling highlighted the phenomenon of racial harmony.

A question I asked early in the interviews was to recall what is was like being a white kid in the South. Nearly all participants had great difficulty with this question. They could talk for hours about their youth, but they seemed to have no readily accessible notions about how being white had shaped their experiences. A typical response came from Arlene, 70s:

> I probably at that point in my life didn't realize that there was any other kind of life out there. Our lives were fairly insular, that we did what we did in our families and in our church and that was *life* and there wadn't a *whole* lot of consideration given to what other kind of lives might have existed at the time. It just wasn't a factor. . . . I don't have a precise *memory* of anything relating to being white, because that was the only life I knew. Didn't have any other concept to relate to.

Many people claimed, like Arlene, that, because of segregation, their lives were extremely "white" and therefore they had no awareness of *being* white. Even those who had long-term relationships with African Americans (usually domestic workers) had little sense that they had learned anything in particular about whiteness through those interactions.

When I asked people to talk about the experience of growing up *white* in the South, most had difficulty with this question. While many spoke readily, and proudly, about what being southern meant to them, few could begin to articulate what being white and southern meant. Given the hegemonic nature of Jim Crow white supremacy, it is understandable that they would claim to have had little to no sense of themselves as white children and teenagers. On the other hand, that so many elder white southerners today do not conceive of their childhoods as having been shaped by whiteness and segregation's racial logic is noteworthy. Furthermore, they encountered the civil rights movement, which explicitly challenged white domination, and more than four decades had since passed. They have had ample time to reflect on what it means that they were born and raised under Jim Crow. Indeed, as chapter 6 makes clear, many participants had taken the mental space to formulate quite opinionated commentaries on race and whiteness in more recent eras.

As was clear earlier in this chapter, participants could talk at length about African Americans they had known and infer as to how those relationships had affected their views of race and humanity. However, they appeared to not see the role of their own whiteness in contributing to their identity. Whites have long depended on people of color to give their racial identity meaning: whiteness takes on meaning through its contrast with non-whiteness.[46] Even though they grew up white in the segregated South, the participants were unable to, and likely unpracticed in, articulating the meaning that being white had lent to their lives. This is despite the reality of the segregated South, again, that Jim Crow whites had innumerable interactions across the color line. As historian Grace Hale points out, "the white home became a central site for the production and reproduction of racial identity precisely because it remained a space of integration within an increasingly segregated world."[47]

However, we can garner some insight about the experience of growing up white in the segregated South, and its meaning, from what participants said elsewhere in the interviews. From Lillian Smith's psychospiritual perspective, white southern children were deeply impressionable beings whose capacity for empathy and the fullness of humanity was constrained by white supremacist ideology and practice. Numerous participants spoke of remembering having been confused about the expectations and contradictions of segregation. Hope, 70s, recalled noticing the contradiction between the equality role modeled by her parents and the messages of segregated public facilities:

> Hope: That's why I never been prejudiced, you know, Mom and Daddy would bring— they'd come right in and eat at our table . . . That's the way my mom and dad was.

> Interviewer: So when you would go downtown, was there more of a separation?
> Hope: Yeah, uh-huh.
> Interviewer: What was that like?
> Hope: Well it felt eerie, sort of eerie. Why would people want to be like that? And I just don't understand a lot of it, but maybe one of these days we all will you know. (chuckles) I hope so.
> Interviewer: So it was unclear why it was like that?
> Hope: . . . Well my mom and daddy said you just stay clean, keep your nose clean and you'll be alright. They said don't mess around with people that hates other people . . . no matter what color their skin.

Hope recalled childhood confusion, an "eerie" feeling, when confronted with the reality of Jim Crow inequality. She indicated that, despite her parents' teachings (e.g., "keep your nose clean"), this tension was not yet reconciled either in her own mind or in the broader society ("Why would people want to be like that? I just don't understand a lot of it, but maybe one of these days we all will").

Similarly, a few people mentioned that they felt helpless or unable to comprehend or challenge the things they saw happening around them. Sharon, 60s, recalled a shocking moment in her childhood when she learned of the reality of racial inequality upon realizing that an African American domestic worker was illiterate:

> I remember being at [a neighbor's] house and [the] daughter told me that the maid . . . couldn't read. . . . I said, "No! That can't be!" I could *not* believe that an adult could not read—it didn't matter to me what color they were. . . . So we got this little plot—we got a book . . . and we were gonna ask her a word. . . . We went in the kitchen—I think she was washing dishes or something—and so I asked her what was the word, acting like we were reading a book and didn't know the word. And I could tell she was very embarrassed and I could just tell that . . . she did not know how to read. And it bothered me tremendously. I just couldn't believe that an adult couldn't read. It was (pause) sort of a wake up to the fact that things weren't equal and I didn't know it. I didn't know it could possibly *be*, but it was.

This was a moment of shock and clarity. Sharon vividly remembered being confronted with the fact that, contrary to her assumption, education was not a right extended equally to all people. Sharon also remembered having had more progressive racial views than her parents, but explained that she did not feel free to challenge them:

> The way I was raised you just didn't (pause) choose conflict with your parents. It was just better to keep your mouth shut and do your thing more or less. But you know, if I had been very vocal, they would have listened. But it wouldn't have changed anything. (pause) We just sort of went along with the way they thought. But then, when my sister and I got out on our own, we could think the way we wanted to.

Sharon recalled that she and her sister felt differently from her parents, but they chose the strategy of deference and did not confront their parents' entrenched views. Her statements indicate that there was little space available for sensitive, curious white children to challenge white elders or raise serious concerns about the racial status quo; the Jim Crow white world was not invested in building a critical race consciousness.

While we would never equate white southerners' experience with that of African Americans, it is evident white children were also victims of Jim Crow—of the racial system set up by their forebears and condoned by their parents and grandparents.[48] In the poetic language of Lillian Smith: "We learned the dance that cripples the human spirit, step by step by step, we who were white and we who were colored, day by day, hour by hour, year by year until the movements were reflexes and made for the rest of our life without thinking. Alas, for many white children, they were movements made for the rest of their lives without feeling."[49] In the interviews, few people openly displayed empathy for black southerners' ordeals under Jim Crow, even though many claimed to have loved and respected individual African Americans deeply and for many years. In fact, it was very rare for a participant to indicate that they had gained enlightenment on racial oppression *through* their interactions with black loved ones (for example, Sharon's account, above). This narrative absence helps demonstrate the social distance and power dynamics inherent in those relationships. African American employees could not and did not bare all to white family members, especially when it came to their experiences with white racism.[50]

It was difficult for whites to develop genuine empathy across the color line. Undoubtedly white children had moments of empathetic curiosity about the plight of African Americans, but they were rarely encouraged by adults to ruminate on those thoughts and feelings. Bernice, 80s, said she wondered about the different lives lived by whites and blacks, but she only went so far as to feel sympathy for poor black children:

> Interviewer: I know you said you thought about, maybe "I have a nice dress, why doesn't this little black girl have a nice dress?" Did you ever think about what if you were that black girl—like what it would have been like growing up black?
> Bernice: (sigh) I don't think I ever did. I used to feel *sorry* for 'em a lot of times, you know. But no, I never put myself in their place *really*.

Also, Mack, 80s, said he understood the inherent inequality of Jim Crow by adolescence, but acknowledged that his empathy for African Americans was lacking, a phenomenon he guessed might have been rooted in his being male:

> [Segregation] made no sense to me when I was 12, 13, 14, 15 years old. I didn't cry out about it. I didn't join any marches or whatever. But I had never been one to join a union or a pressure group or whatever. I was an independent thinker, an independent person in my entire philosophy and thinking. (pause) And I don't know that I ever empathized with people to the point that I should've. That was probably part of my male genes, I don't know. (chuckles)

Because, during segregation, few whites were expected or encouraged to empathize with black southerners' experiences, empathy work would have to be done on reflection, connecting with what memories they had, and seeking out black Americans' accounts. Carla, 60s, pointed this out, revealing that she had only recently begun to "humanize" the treatment black southerners endured daily under segregation:

> [A black coworker told me] she could remember when they had to sit in the balcony at the movies. And when they couldn't even go through the drive-thru at McDonald's, that they would get out of the car and her [very light-skinned] brother could drive through the drive-thru at McDonald's and get their food. And then that's when you begin to humanize it. Because I was not really exposed to it from

lookin' at it as discrimination. You know what I mean? It was not on my radar. . . . It's like for so long it didn't really affect me. I didn't think about, I didn't really have much of an opinion about it.

The legacy of white children's empathy deficit is hinted at within select stories of lingering sadness, confusion, and even racial apathy.

Alexithymia is a term used by psychiatrists to describe an individual who cannot understand the emotions of others and thus cannot empathize. Sociologists Joe Feagin and Hernán Vera propose the term *social alexithymia* to conceptualize the emotional damage done to dominant group members who are socialized to live in a society that systematically privileges them and mistreats others. Social alexithymia is "a significantly reduced ability, or an inability, to understand or relate to the emotions, such as recurring pain, of those targeted by oppression."[51] A white dominant society, then, depends upon whites socializing each other *not* to empathize fully with people of color. This emotional disconnect helps legitimize, and prevent a critique of, the racial status quo.

Segregation's white children were trained in social alexithymia from a young age. Subjected to Jim Crow racial logic and socialization, they were discouraged from extending full empathy to their neighbors of color, even to loved ones. Of course, as favored citizens in a white supremacist society, however, they did not bear the social assault to self-esteem and identity that black children experienced. Instead, they constantly received messages, mostly subtle, of their goodness and racial superiority. However, unlike black children, white children had few opportunities to sort through their confusions or critical questions about anti-black oppression, racial inequality, and white privilege. White children typically repressed or forgot their curiosity and lost the sense that things could have been different had white southerners made different choices.[52]

FORGOTTEN ALTERNATIVES

Participants' memories of the private spaces during segregation, recounted a half century later, offered little critique of the contradiction between teachings of equality and socialization to Jim Crow. When speaking of home, Jim Crow racial oppression and white supremacy were virtually absent from childhood memories and silent in family histories. Segregation laws may have been unjust, they acknowledged, but only love and respect crossed the threshold into white homes, and the African Americans employed by their families received fair wages and good treatment. They remembered Jim Crow etiquette rules, such as eating meals separately or the use of formal addresses exclusively for whites, as comfortable for both parties and mutually enforced.

Historian C. Vann Woodward first used the term *forgotten alternatives* to point out that race in the South was contested for decades after the Civil War and that segregation laws had not in actuality been inevitable.[53] Proposed just after the *Brown v. Board* (1954) Supreme Court decision on the unconstitutionality of segregated schools, his assertion that the South could have been different, and thus could be changed, invigorated antisegregation activists.[54] Ritterhouse states that "adult white southerners tried, consciously and unconsciously, to teach both black and white children to 'forget' any possible alternatives to white supremacy at the same time they energetically *repressed alternatives* that actually arose in both the public and private spheres."[55] These efforts could not have been successful with black children, for the black community was heavily invested in resisting white supremacist ideology. The opposite is true for white children, who could accept the logic of white supremacy more readily—embracing the notion of their own racial superiority—and "forget" any alternatives to Jim Crow.

The next chapter analyzes memories of segregation in public spaces, as people recall separate water fountains, separate movie theater seating areas, whites-only restaurants, and the like. We will see further evidence of forgotten alternatives, as people struggle to pinpoint why or by whom the Jim Crow system was created. Many people will describe segregation matter-of-factly, as "just the way it was," and we will analyze the functionality of that explanation. Additionally, we will see more forgotten alternatives in chapters 4 and 5, as people construct themselves as victims of the civil rights era as opposed to, for example, having been enlightened by the movement and its activists to the injustices of Jim Crow.

3

"JUST THE WAY IT WAS"

Jim Crow in Public

Whether in public or private spaces, the distance between white and black southerners during the period of legal segregation from the late 1800s through the 1960s was physical only to a certain extent. Black and white southerners intermingled so much, and often in rather intimate ways, that it was actually social and emotional distance that characterized the Jim Crow experience.[1] These frequent interracial interactions were structured by an elaborate set of racialized norms, whereby whites and people of color were expected to engage in different behaviors. Undergirding these racialized interaction rules as well as segregation laws was an ideology of white supremacy.[2] White superiority was the guiding principle of de jure (legal) segregation and de facto (informal) segregation. The rules about behavior and how to "stay in one's place" were concerned with the subordination of African Americans and the elevation of whites/whiteness.

Few of the participants interviewed for this book expressed outright an understanding of this reality. Although every participant lived large portions of their lives under segregation, most portrayed Jim Crow–era white racism as episodic and individualized more so than as an all-encompassing structural arrangement. In their view, this era included some racial inequalities, but more importantly was typified by safety, generosity, a sense of community, and even easygoing race relations. Furthermore, when reflecting on the origins of segregation, white people were rarely identified as the creators and enforcers. The explanation that segregation was "just the way it was" was invoked innumerable times throughout the interviews, and so in this chapter we explore what that means. In describing those who followed segregation expectations, like themselves and their families, being a law-abiding citizen was presented as a good thing and as the only option. While many participants shared memories of segregated spaces and recalled childhood confusion, there was a theme of nostalgia that ran through the narratives.

A 1956 quarterly report of the Southern Regional Council outlined some of the contradictory beliefs common in the pre–civil rights period. White southerners

> possessed a conviction that segregation was "best for both races" and that blacks desired it; respected "law and order"; believed in blacks' rights to "an equal chance"; supported public education; took pride in the South and hoped that "outsiders" would not think it "benighted"; and feared that, if integration came, blacks would "take advantage" of whites.[3]

This chapter analyzes interview participants' narratives of the legal segregation era in the public realm. They shared their stories and perspectives of what it was like growing up in their neighborhood and city and how they encountered and made/make sense of the public markers of Jim Crow.

In this chapter especially, it will be clear that the people interviewed for this book have reflected on their experiences during segregation and hold a complex set of beliefs around Jim Crow. As historian Jason Sokol has argued, "few southerners achieved, much less desired, a clean break from the past."[4] On the whole, participants freely assessed segregation laws as unfair or unjust. Many also rationalized and minimized those stark racial inequalities, indicating that the period of legal segregation included some hardship for black southerners, but that racial injustice was not what typified the era. Recall, from the opening of this book, the woman's adamant assertion that her "generation had nothing to do with discrimination."

THE SYSTEM OF LEGAL SEGREGATION

Legal segregation was not a set of laws and practices dictating that whites and African Americans be kept completely separate. Racial separation was enforced only in certain public facilities, businesses, and social spaces, and segregation statutes varied by state, region, and locality.[5] Even in formally segregated spaces, interracial interactions were common. For example, at Greensboro's downtown cinema, the Carolina Theatre, black patrons had to use a side entrance, buy from a separate concession stand, and sit in the balcony, but they viewed the same movie showings as the white patrons who were seated below them. Woolworth's five and dime store employed both black and white lower-level staff and sold products and take-out food to any paying customer, but only white patrons were allowed to sit down and eat in the dining area. Segregation was typified as much by racial interaction as by racial separation in the public sphere. What rounded out the Jim Crow structure was its racial ideology (white superiority) and its set of expected behaviors, often called the racial "etiquette," but which I will refer to as "norms" in this chapter.[6] The markers of segregation gave whites access to more services and superior accommodations, and Jim Crow norms dictated deference from blacks toward whites. The styles of separation and racial norms reinforced the structure and ideology of white supremacy.

First published in 1959, Stetson Kennedy's *Jim Crow Guide* explained the racial norms that one ought to understand if visiting the South, such as how to make an introduction between a white person and a black person, how a person of color could challenge whites and get away with it, and when to remove one's hat. His detailed explanations laid bare the complicated system of Jim Crow.[7] Here is just one example, teaching a non-southern African American the unspoken rules of partaking of tobacco or alcohol in the presence of whites:

> If you are a male, you are free under the etiquette to drink intoxicating liquors with males of the other race. . . . However, if a white man should offer you a drink, he will hardly expect you to drink from the bottle after the manner of his white fellow workers, but rather to find a receptacle of some kind. On the other hand, should you offer a white man a drink from your bottle, he may drink from it if there is no receptacle at hand. . . . As for smoking, if you are male you may

also feel free to indulge with males of the other race. But if you are a female, you are not thus privileged . . . white women would still regard it as highly presumptuous if a nonwhite woman were to drink or smoke in their presence. However, it is permissible to partake of snuff in the presence of white women.[8]

Although the rules may seem illogical, Kennedy pointed out that this set of expected behaviors was "a compulsory ritual denoting first- and second-class citizenship."[9] It was necessary to follow these "rules," and the intent was to reinforce the idea that African Americans were inferior to whites. Within this system, interracial interactions could be experienced as friendly and easygoing, but this reality does not diminish the racist ideology that deemed blacks to be lazy, ignorant, dangerous, and threatening, and thus in need of white institutional subordination in order to protect white society from negative influence.[10] For black southerners, the norms were an assault on their humanity and a matter of survival. It was crucial for people of color to follow Jim Crow norms at all times; if they challenged Jim Crow convention and were deemed threatening by whites, their physical safety, economic livelihood, or civil liberties could be jeopardized. For whites, on the other hand, following Jim Crow norms saved face and helped them maintain self-esteem and a positive racial identity.

It is clear from writings and oral histories that African Americans had to manage the structure of segregation on a daily basis. Black children were taught Jim Crow expectations, which were clearly rooted in notions of white supremacy, as a "game" they must learn to play so that they could retain self-respect and develop skills for navigating white spaces and interacting with white people.[11] It was a game with rules white children had little incentive to deconstruct, as they were systematically being bestowed advantages by Jim Crow.[12] White children learned the "rules" of legal segregation occasionally by explicit instruction but mostly via observation and subtle forms of socialization.[13] Lillian Smith explained:

We learned the intricate system of taboos, of renunciations and compensations, of manners, voice modulations, words, feelings, along with our prayers, our toilet habits, and our games. I do not remember how or when, but by the time I had learned that God is love, that Jesus is His Son and came to give us more abundant life, that all men are brothers with a common Father, I also knew that I was better than a Negro, that all black folks have their place and must be kept in it . . . that a terrifying disaster would befall the South if I ever treated a Negro as my social equal.[14]

During the segregation era, southern whites had a largely unquestioned understanding of Jim Crow, which they deeply socialized into their children.[15] "Southerners, whites and Negroes alike, having been steeped for generations in the atmosphere engendered by the interracial etiquette, usually know precisely—almost instinctively—just what is expected of them in all situations."[16] "Instinct" is a key term here: Jim Crow norms came naturally to people because they were so thoroughly indoctrinated to segregation expectations by everyone and everything around them. And while black children learned how to develop a critique of Jim Crow, white children were rarely if ever encouraged to even question segregation.[17]

A TIME OF SAFETY AND EASYGOING RACE RELATIONS

lack of fear, feeling of comfort

A prominent theme in participants' narratives of childhood in the public realm was recalling the safety and security of day-to-day life. Parents allowed children to roam the neighborhood streets without fear as they went to and from school or play. Youth could ride the trolley or walk to downtown and browse shops or watch a movie. If we consider the pervasiveness of segregation practices in these spaces, it is clear that this level of childhood safety was part of a white experience and would not have been available to youth of color to the same extent. However, many participants discussed this bubble of childhood safety as if it had been a universal rather than racialized experience, talking about how much safer and simpler life used to be in general, when people learned they could count on mutual respect, trust, caring, and neighborliness from most everyone they might encounter, whether white or black.

For example, when I asked Patti, 80s, to talk about segregation, she explained the era in general terms, with no hint at a racial component: "It was a quieter, gentler time. You never locked the door of your house. You never took the keys out of the car, even when you went shopping downtown. That was a *different time*. People didn't *steal*. . . . Even hungry people didn't steal." Patti offered a contrast between the safe, trusting reality of her youth and later eras. Similarly, as with many other participants, Gertie, 70s, thought it unfortunate that children were able to be more carefree in her youth than they can be today: "I had the most wonderful childhood. I mean, I *really* think that it's a shame that people nowadays don't have the freedom that I did. I could go around the corner when I was four years old on my tricycle to see my friend and no one was going to bother me. It was a much more free time; I could be much more independent." From many people's memories and perspectives, what shaped day-to-day life during the segregation era was the security of knowing you could trust people and would not be victimized.

Numerous participants remembered the segregation era generally as one of happiness and safety. Certainly we would expect to hear of nostalgia for one's childhood. However, there were claims also that, racially, some things were significantly better then. In particular, people noted the easygoing nature of interactions between white and black southerners. For example, Harmony, 80s, said that racial issues seemed to be more of a problem currently than in her youth: "Racial things were not a big item back when I was growin' up. They just came along and we dealt with 'em, and everybody did, and we had a very peaceful and harmonious ha-ha time together." Arnold, 80s, gave a similar portrayal about friendly interactions across the color line, but he also included an acknowledgment of the structure of segregation: "I never *heard* much black hate talk or anything in my family. . . . There's the black people and they're (pause) maybe not on the same level as us, but then over here is all us white folks. And we got along, I think, for the most part." Arnold hinted at the Jim Crow racial hierarchy ("they're maybe not on the same level as us"), but pointed out that blatant racial animosities were rare (people "got along" "for the most part"). Harmony and Arnold represent well the two major ways that participants portrayed Jim Crow race relations as friendly—either with (like Arnold) or without (like Harmony) an acknowledgment of the unequal structures imposed by segregation.

Some people went further as well, speaking favorably specifically of how African Americans displayed deference to whites through following Jim Crow norms. For example, Mae, 70s, recalled: "The people that we had contact with were of the older black generation, and they knew how things were. I don't really know their feelings, but they would not push themselves on you. And the ones that we knew were a joy to be around, but they always stayed in their place at that time. You know, they didn't push themselves." Mae explained that when African Americans "stayed in their place" and "didn't push themselves," it made things easier for whites, and she positively recalled interacting with black southerners who "knew how things were." Saying, "I don't really know their feelings," Mae did also acknowledge that black southerners' perspectives on these kinds of interactions may have differed from her own. Much of this chapter explores this kind of nuance and complexity in which participants indicated some level of awareness of racial inequalities and black perspectives under segregation but frequently de-emphasized those aspects. Much regarding racial oppression was hinted at, left unsaid, rationalized, or denied.

White violence, and the threat of it, was a constant reality for black Americans throughout the Jim Crow era.[18] However, no participants for this research told a story of a time when they had antagonized African Americans. There were a few stories told about *others*, though. For example, Chuck, 70s, recalled that "there was a segment of contemporaries of mine who were pretty violent toward the blacks in the forties. And they used to go over on Summit Avenue where there was sort of a boundary of black–white residences and throw rocks and occasionally shoot air rifles at the black kids. And I was *really* offended by that." Chuck said that not only did he not participate in racial harassment, he remembered being strongly opposed to it. In sharing this account, Chuck constructed himself as nonracist in contrast with some of his white peers.

The lack of white racial antagonism stories from the interview participants is noteworthy. Jim Crow whites who eventually developed an antiracist perspective and, like Lillian Smith, wrote their own "racial conversion narratives," often recounted having been involved in altercations with black youth. For example, writing in 1958, James McBride Dabbs gave an account of having encountered an African American girl in the street "much larger than I" who looked like she was not going to move out of his way so that he could pass. He recalled his actions, "I drew back and hit her hard in the stomach," and he remembered his feelings, "I wasn't ashamed, but I didn't tell Father or Mother."[19] In his memoir of growing up white in rural North Carolina, Melton McLaurin told of a deeply memorable incident that occurred while playing basketball with black and white boys. McLaurin was shocked when he realized an error he had made absentmindedly: he had licked the needle of an air pump after a black boy had done the same. McLaurin recalled his visceral reaction that manifested as an uncontrollable rush of intense disgust and seething anger.[20] And, in her 1962 memoir, Patty Boyle included a recollection of her manic reaction when her maid got "out of her place" by calling Boyle by her first name.[21] These kinds of shocking incidents registered forcefully with these individuals and were seared into their memory. For white southerners like Dabbs, McLaurin, and Boyle, who went on to transform their racial consciousness, these memories became vital in their forging of a new racial identity, critical of white racism. Key to their gaining awareness of how deeply they had been socialized by Jim Crow was to recall how emotionally attached they had been to white supremacy and how visceral and uncontrollable this attachment was.

Elder white southerners' nostalgia in general is understandable, for it is common for people of any living U.S. generation to reflect on the simplicity and innocence of their childhoods, when the pace of life was slower with less inundation by contemporary social ills, such as media, technology, and consumerism. However, this particular nostalgia was asserted in the context of an interview explicitly on the subject of race during an era now marked as racially oppressive. Nostalgia can work against an acknowledgment of that fundamental reality.[22] The more I heard people talk about how pleasant childhood was, the more I wanted to know if people were merely omitting from their childhood memories a consideration that this was a time of racial segregation and clear oppression, or if they actually associated *racial* segregation with a *better* society. How did they incorporate the *racial* past into their lived experience?

Some participants did incorporate an acknowledgment of racial oppression under segregation when they reflected on their happy childhoods. For example, Gertie, 70s, asserted that the comfort of her childhood may have been linked to her whiteness:

> I feel very, very fortunate, and most of my friends feel pretty fortunate. Maybe this is what everybody does, but we think we grew up in a *wonderful* time and not because it was segregated, but because neighbors knew each other . . . people didn't have a lot of money and no one worried about the lack of it because you were just friends

with a lot of different people. And when I think back I'm sure that even though I had a wonderful life, there were a lot of black children that were *not* having that wonderful life. So, it's a two-edged sword. But I've had a blessed life, I really have.

Gertie associated the Jim Crow era with a better way of life, but she did not claim that segregation was an unequivocally better time period, particularly for African Americans. As she explained it, when she looked back and considered racial inequalities, she acknowledged that her wonderful childhood was, in part, made possible by her whiteness. This kind of insight was fairly common among participants. Most expressed in some way that segregation was an era in which blacks were unjustly disadvantaged.

For Carla, 60s, on the other hand, general nostalgia and Jim Crow was not merely a correlation, it was a causal relationship. She lamented her concern over several current social trends and directly attributed the rise of these "problems" to racial integration:

> There are no role models. The children don't really have parents. And that's what I think about. We talk about, like the welfare society, it perpetuates itself. They were born into welfare, and they *live* in welfare—you know, they just perpetuate it. Unless somethin' breaks the cycle. . . . [Kids] need to find a positive role model. People are saying you can't do it, but if you *want* to do it, you've gotta be the one to say, "This is what I want, and I'm willing to go for it." But where do they get their role models? And that's everybody now; it's not just black society. But why has it come to that? I guess I wanna blame a lot of it on integration, but not because of the blacks, but because somewhere down the line when integration happened society started letting down the guidelines.

When looking back, Carla saw serious social problems, such as the "welfare society" and lack of positive role models, as arising from desegregation. In her view, society as a whole was truly *better* during the segregation era.

INTERPRETING SEGREGATION'S SIGNS AND MEANINGS

In the interviews, participants shared memories of childhood encounters with the signs of segregation in public—labels on water fountains and restrooms, separate entrances to places of business, all-white schools, and so forth. Many said they recalled having been curious about the phenomena and seeking explanations from their parents. A typical kind of portrayal came from Gertie, 70s, who remembered her curiosity over the segregation of the downtown theater:

> I remember my mother showing me the balcony in the Carolina Theatre where the black children had to sit and I said, "How'd they get up there?" because at that time, there was no way, there was a barrier. And she said, "Well, they have to come in a different door" . . . and I remember thinking that I thought that was pretty bad. You know, I didn't see any reason why that would be.

Gertie recalled this conversation with her mother and her confusion and bad feeling upon realizing that black Americans were being treated differently in the local theater. According to historian Jason Sokol, most white southerners accepted the system of segregation as a fact of life and were not motivated to reflect on its contours or logic.[23] Most participants' narratives corroborated this through recounting how they had noticed the strangeness or unfairness of segregation in certain places and that they had been rather unaware of the full scope or meaning behind it. People most often portrayed those public markers of segregation as something they were aware of by early childhood but did not understand until later, with hindsight.

Like Gertie, several participants said they had felt bad knowing that African Americans were treated differently, while others claimed to have attached no such meaning to segregated facilities. Some argued that they paid little attention to it, or that there was no real way for them to have fully comprehended segregation. For example, John, 70s, claimed to have been unaware that a lunch counter he frequented served whites only: "I've eaten in . . . the service bar there many a day 'cause [I frequented] downtown for [several] years. . . . And I honestly don't *remember* whether there were any blacks sittin' there or not. (chuckling) I mean, I just don't sit down and eyeball everybody in the place and say, 'Oh, he's white, he's black, there's a Chinese.'"(chuckles)

Here, John implied that it would have been unnatural for him to take note of the racial identities of customers in a restaurant. Gracie, 80s, offered a slightly different explanation for whites not noticing the realities of segregation. She argued that, like "most of us," she was too focused on her own experience to consider that of African Americans:

> I think *probably* I became most aware when I realized that black children were havin' to take long bus rides, yet they were within walking distance of a white school, and I mean anybody could know that that was unfair. (chuckles) I think most of us, we're just so engrossed in our own daily livin' that we don't spend a lot of time thinkin' about how other people are managing. (chuckles)

Here, Gracie indicated that day-to-day life was so all-encompassing that the injustices of segregation became apparent only if one became privy to information such as black children having to travel long distances, passing white-only schools, in order to reach black schools.

Darla, 70s, recalled encountering separate water fountains, but mused without much clarity as to how she interpreted them at the time. In response to follow-up questions, she tried to explain what was behind her vague sense that whites preferred their own separate facilities:

> Darla: I'm sure there were an awful lot of black people who probably drank of the white water fountain just for spite. (laughs) Ah, I don't know that for a fact, but . . . that to me probably was the most unusual or impressive thing about it as a child, 'cause I can remember exactly where they were and standing there and looking at 'em, and in a way just thinkin', "Golly, I'm glad I'm white, I don't have to worry about drinkin' out of the black fountain." But I wouldn't have minded maybe.
> Interviewer: Was it different? Was it not as nice?
> Darla: No, they were the same. . . .
> Interviewer: So why would you not want to drink out of the—?
> Darla: Well, maybe you would have this idea that maybe black people had more germs than white people and (pause) I really don't know. Like I say, I guess you felt like black people were not as privileged as we were, and maybe they didn't have the health advantages and that type of thing. And of course I think a lot of people were concerned about their children bein' associated with blacks because of the mixed race situation.

Darla tentatively guessed that white southerners' perceptions of blacks as less hygienic and their aversion to "the mixed race situation" undergirded their acceptance of and preference for segregated facilities. She was not sure *how* as a child she had come to understand that the white water fountain was better.

These were accounts in which people explained what they knew, thought, and felt about segregation in the midst of it, as children and young adults. Given how thoroughly white southerners were socialized to the norms of segregation and that those norms reinforced notions of white goodness and superiority but not always in overt ways, it is understandable that whites who came of age in that time would have questioned those norms only in limited ways and would have rarely received a critical perspective from the white adults in their lives. And then, after more than forty years have passed, how did these white southerners interpret the meanings of segregation? We turn our attention next to how people explained segregated facilities with hindsight, as elders.

Many participants acknowledged, in quite matter-of-fact ways, that the Jim Crow era had enabled privileges and advantages for whites. Mack, 80s, asserted his understanding that whites got a head start in life and could achieve success much easier:

> I would say how *fortunate* I had *been* just to have been born white. . . . I mean (pause) black people who succeeded that were born the year I was born—and when I say succeeded, I mean in whatever honorable profession that they chose to do—*far* exceeded what I did. 'Cause I hit the ground running with a head start. And I know that. I mean, to say that I didn't would be ridiculous.

Mack argued that it "would be ridiculous" for someone today to claim that there was equal opportunity across the color line for his generation. Mack spoke from hindsight (saying "I know that" rather than, for example, "I *knew* that"). Similarly, Gracie, 80s, pointed out that she only understood, much later in life, that African Americans were denied opportunities, such as in higher education:

> I feel that since I *was* white that I probably did have more opportunities than a black person growing up at that same time. And I know that I got a scholarship to go to college, and the college scholarship was one that was given by the state . . . and it was done by competi-

tive examination. Now, I doubt that there was a program like that for blacks. I doubt very much. And I *know* that they didn't go to [my college], because—see, now, I don't know why. You know, you'd think I—that a person who was interested in justice would be outraged that they weren't allowed to go. But they didn't go to [my college] for a *long* time.

As she reflected back on her racial consciousness, Gracie made the case that even a person like her, who had long claimed a social justice orientation, was not at the time appalled by Jim Crow structural inequalities that should have been quite noticeable. She believed that the reality of unequal education did not capture her full attention until later in life.

Because, under segregation, white southerners existed on the advantaged side of the racial divide and rarely interacted with black southerners within black communities, few would have been aware of the full extent of racial inequalities. Many people described their awareness as having been quite limited and indicated that when confronted with a shocking incident, a clear contrast, or with hindsight, their consciousness around racial domination was elevated. Several people shared moments that they saw as epiphanies about segregation. For example, a married couple in their 60s recalled that hearing about white racial violence elsewhere in the South enhanced their understanding of, and dismay toward, the extremes of white animosity. They spoke of the impact of hearing about a lynching in Mississippi in the 1960s:

> Husband: That right there brought everything to—it brought to light what a lot of white people had been doing to black people and—
> Wife: And we didn't even realize it, because it—
> Husband: No, because we—I guess we were like a horse with blinders on. You didn't see anything off to the side except what was right in front of you. And plus, at an early age you don't pay much attention to these things because if it doesn't affect you, why worry about it that time? As you get older that changes and you think about it more. You get concerned about it.
> Interviewer: Yeah. Do you remember how you felt the first time you heard about that?
> Wife: Terrible. I couldn't imagine somebody doing something like that. I thought it was horrible.

Husband: And me either, because I've never actually—I haven't been abusive to a black unless it was directed at me first, and then I can get very angry.

Wife: I couldn't imagine how—you know, why anybody would do that to another person. Just because they hated them. I didn't understand.

Husband: You know, even though sometimes we didn't get along with them when we played ball and all [as children], still they were— you know, they were humans. They were just a different color than we were. But still, you just, you don't kill somebody just because of the color of their skin. I didn't like the fact that it had happened, but . . . one thing about it—it did bring it all to light—the hatred that a lot of people had for the blacks. And I couldn't understand that, because I was probably more southern than some of these people that were directing this hatred towards the blacks. I never understood it.

As the man described, being white and living under segregation was like being "a horse with blinders on"—immersed in a culture of white supremacy, but not aware of its full reality on a day-to-day basis. In this excerpt, as they both claim they "didn't understand," this couple also constructed a distance and a difference between themselves and those who carried out heinous acts of racial hatred, and the husband suggested that acts like lynchings were not in fact the southern way, saying that he did not understand, "because I was probably more southern than some of these people." In this way, he constructed true Jim Crow southernness as that which did *not* facilitate anti-black oppression and violence. This couple's exchange demonstrates that even when consciousness raising occurred, it did not necessarily inspire a critique of white southern culture as a whole, or even of the self.

Other participants, however, shared memorable experiences that had enabled them to comprehend the systemic racial injustices in the segregated South that they had otherwise failed to recognize. Several people described those moments as having occurred when they traveled away from their hometown. Lynna, 70s, told of an epiphany she had about Jim Crow when she left the South and got away from her taken-for-granted everyday life:

I just think that when we were growing up, the black people that we knew . . . you just saw who you *saw*, and growing up, you sort of accept that—you take it for granted. And then, I remember when I was [a teenager] and we took this trip out West, and . . . I kept noticing there were no black people. And then . . . there was a sign that said, "No Indians, No Mexicans," and it sort of suddenly hit me that they were [in] the same position that the black people were here. It was a strange, eye-opening experience really.

Lynna recalled suddenly comprehending the South's racial hierarchy through observing white supremacist parallels in the West. She described seeing segregated signs that were different yet familiar as both eye-opening and "strange."

Patti, 80s, also remembered having an illuminating, and unsettling, experience when traveling elsewhere in the South. In her case, she witnessed her children's caretaker being barred from eating a meal with her family in a whites-only hotel restaurant:

> Patti: I took my children to the beach and wanted Betty who worked for me to go . . . and she wanted to do it. We had to go to Howard Johnson's and the only way they let her eat . . . she had to go to the back door of Howard Johnson's restaurant . . . and there was nothing I could do about it. . . . She takes care of my children—she's, you know . . .
> Interviewer: How did that make you feel?
> Patti: Ashamed, angry, a mixture. Mad at Howard Johnson's, ashamed that anyone would be treated that way.

Patti, like other white domestic employers, likely followed Jim Crow norms with her employee in the home, which often included the standard practice of workers eating in a separate room from the family. We may imagine that, until this family trip, Patti had not been aligned *with* her employee on the receiving end of segregation's restrictions. Patti was suddenly struck by the injustice that "anyone would be treated that way," especially her children's caretaker. She felt angry and ashamed in this moment when she experienced the dehumanizing and limiting elements of Jim Crow regulations in a more personal way than ever before. Patti's story offers a view also of how segregation conventions, although designed by whites for whites, could be unnerving at times to whites as they negotiated them. In confronting Jim Crow, white southerners could experience a sense of powerlessness. This type of jarring realization that segregation could deny even their wishes was likely most common among white elites who were accustomed to a privileged life. An upper middle class couple shared back-to-back stories of how some whites assumed that the rules of segregation would be bent simply if *they* requested it:

> Husband: My mother called me . . . to say that this black man . . . was sick and she wanted . . . for me to come . . . take him to the hospital. And I said, "Mother, you can take him to [the black hospital]. "He's not *going* to [the black hospital]! . . . He is going to [the white hospital]!" I said, "Mother, we can't *do* that." "What do you mean *we* can't do that?" I said, (chuckles) "Just what I'm telling you, [that hospital] is *segregated*." "Not as far as Carter is concerned." I said, "Yes ma'am as far as Carter is concerned. (chuckles) You can't *do* that."
>
> Wife: Okay, I did the same thing [on a road trip with our child]. . . . And we needed to stop for lunch. . . . I had the lady that worked for him, and I thought, "Well, we'll just go in this restaurant for lunch," and it dawned on me we weren't gonna be able to go into that. I think I must've asked. And I thought, "Well surely since she's *with me*, she can come in for lunch," but no, she couldn't. . . . But we had that attitude of, if *I* did this, they'll allow it. I guess we didn't really realize how much segregation there was.

In these stories, this man's mother and wife had assumed that whites could overrule anti-black regulations in individual situations by vouching for African Americans. As the wife in the above example explained, she did not "realize how much segregation there was." Apparently some white southerners were shocked with the realization that the system of Jim Crow did not guarantee that they would be able to acquire "white" treatment for black southerners. Undoubtedly an aspect of this misperception was the paternalistic way in which more elite white southerners were accustomed to negotiating the color line. Note the wife's explanation that "we had this attitude of, if *I* did this, they'll allow it." Clearly, through previous experience, these women had come to believe that, when it came to segregation, whites like them got to do whatever they wished.

ASSESSING STRUCTURAL ADVANTAGE
AND DISADVANTAGE

During the nearly one hundred years of legal segregation, virtually all white Americans received racial privileges in the economic realm due to the exploitation, marginalization, and exclusion of African Americans or other non-white groups.[24] But my interviews included very little acknowledgment of Jim Crow's systemic discrimination and economic exploitation. Sociologist Joe Feagin uses the terms "unjust enrichment" and "unjust impoverishment" to capture the material privileges afforded to whites and the systemic disadvantages accrued by people of color over generations via racially exclusive access to wealth-generating assets, employment, and education.[25] This material reality lays bare the superficiality of white southerners' assertions that the racial arrangement under Jim Crow was pleasant and comfortable. As Feagin explains, "At the core of the relations of exploitation under legal segregation was continuing unjust enrichment . . . for each new generation of whites and a corresponding unjust impoverishment for each new generation of blacks. What were portrayed as 'good race relations' . . . by whites were usually extremely oppressive for blacks."[26]

As we have already seen, most interview participants acknowledged segregation inequalities, but they did not portray Jim Crow as a time of overwhelming racial discrimination. And when prompted specifically to comment on patterns of institutional discrimination, many people expressed uncertainty, or revealed an assumption that discrimination was not widespread. Clarence, 60s, guessed that a farmer's race would not have affected the rate of pay received: "I remember black farmers coming to the market . . . and them representing their tobacco the same way that, say, my [family] did, and seemingly they were treated the same way, because they had the same commodity and they were on even footing with us as far as the product goes." While Clarence assumed that black farmers probably received equal compensation, Mack, 80s, animatedly told a story that hinted at Jim Crow whites' widespread expectation that their wages were, in part, guaranteed by their whiteness:

> I heard one of the white men fussin' about him one day and granddaddy turn on him just f- f- furiously. He said, *"You do the work that Henry Jones does and you'll get Henry's pay!"* And happened to have

been a white man, and he retorted to my granddaddy, he says, "Well, *you* sayin' I don't do as much work as a—?!" He said, "Yes I *am*. And he will make more money than you make." Well see, in that day and age that didn't set well with people. But that's the family I grew up in and that's the way they were.

Mack's story pointed out that, "in that day and age," white laborers never expected that their pay would be lower than a black laborer's. On the other hand, for Mack, this story was invoked also as a self-presentation strategy; at the end of the account he concluded that this was evidence of the kind of people he came from. Mack was making the case that his family did not acquiesce to (all) Jim Crow conventions (using more logical reasoning instead) or succumb to peer pressure from other whites.

A few participants notably argued that the socioeconomic inequalities between whites and blacks were not a result of overt racial discrimination or exclusion. Hope, 70s, who grew up working class in the rural outskirts of the city, claimed that class, rather than race, determined what kind of treatment people received:

> Interviewer: So up through the fifties and sixties, was there mistreatment of black people? Did white people get better treatment?
> Hope: Well, I guess if they had more money they did. But it was some people, white and black, that didn't have no money, that couldn't do what some of the rich ones did. And we have some pretty well off black people in this United States.

Hope argued that discrimination followed social class lines but not necessarily racial lines. In another example from a working class participant, Ava, 60s, argued that segregation in housing was "more economics than it was race":

> Black people lived in a certain part of town. White people lived in a certain part of town. Rich people lived in a certain part of town. (pause) It did not have to do with race as much as it had to do with economics. If you happened to have parents who were educated, or for whatever reason were able to provide you with more, then you lived in a different neighborhood to people who were uneducated and could not provide their families more. That really was more economics than it was race.

Together, the quotes from Ava and Hope offer an illustrative contrast to Mack's and a lens on social class divides among southern whites. Mack, a man from a fairly prominent local family, acknowledged unequal, race-based wages paid to manual laborers in the segregated South, but asserted that his own family bucked that trend. Ava and Hope, from working class backgrounds, asserted that racial discrimination per se did not disadvantage African Americans or privilege whites; rather, socioeconomic status was more important than race. By dismissing the notion of widespread white privilege, working class whites like Ava and Hope can construct themselves and their families as nonrecipients of race-based advantages. On the other side, more well-to-do whites like Mack can acknowledge anti-black discrimination but present themselves and their families as exceptions who wielded their power and influence to diverge from the racist norm. For each party, the perspective enables the speaker to distance themselves from racial discrimination.

We can see how these perceptions are intertwined with a social class standpoint, but downplaying or failing to comprehend the extent of racial oppression under segregation is not limited to working class or poor whites. The following exchange illustrates well how racial discrimination can be explained away and downplayed by someone from a middle class background. Bernice, 80s, claimed that it was a lack of education, not racial discrimination, that kept African Americans (satisfied) in low-wage jobs: "The . . . ones that came to your home to work, they were glad to get the work, because that was the only thing that they could do to make any money. They had no education or anything." She cursorily attributed African Americans' poverty to their lack of educational attainment. I attempted to get her to explain her perspective more fully:

> Bernice: Well, most of the blacks that *we* knew were poor people, and I remember thinking, "Well, why can't they have what I have?" . . . I remember thinking, well, "Why can't she have a dress like mine?" You know, or something like that. But, like I said, that's just the way things were. . . .
> Interviewer: Why were the black people poor?
> Bernice: Because they didn't have an opportunity to have a good-paying job. They didn't have the education. . . . Very few of 'em ever finished high school even, much less going to college.
> Interviewer: So why do you think that was?

Bernice: Because (sighs) they may not have been encouraged, or they didn't have the money to go. 'Cause I didn't have the money to go to college either, but I borrowed it and paid it back. Ten dollars a month. (laughs)

In explaining African American poverty in the Jim Crow South, Bernice argued that low educational attainment limited their job opportunities. Then, in explaining the low educational attainment, Bernice guessed that lack of encouragement or financial means was to blame and implied that more black students could have, like her, taken out a loan for college. Through her reasoning, Bernice posited that high poverty conditions were a product of black southerners' suboptimal choices regarding the pursuit of education. Thus, Jim Crow's structural racial inequalities were presented as resulting, essentially, from race-neutral forces and from African Americans' own decisions.

Some participants, often from working class backgrounds, had a quite critical view of the class structure and saw that privileges came readily to people of high socioeconomic status. Marginalized people often foster a critical viewpoint of those phenomena that disadvantage them. We can expect many working class and poor whites to acknowledge and critique class privilege more than upper class whites, just as we can expect people of color to acknowledge and critique racial advantages to a greater extent than white Americans. However, within the context of an interview asking about race throughout the past, *not* noting that there was white supremacist ideology or practice, or going so far as to deny it, is not necessarily indicative merely of lacking awareness. Rather, it can also be read as an act of resistance by not acknowledging a fundamental truth about the legal segregation era.

Ava, 60s, working class, is a case in point. She was adamant that today's standards have imposed improper and inaccurate judgments on the past. She argued that Jim Crow was simply an accepted "way of life" and that "nobody" at the time condemned its norms:

It might have been racism, but that's not the way people *thought* then. There was a place for blacks, and there was a place for whites. Yes, I can remember goin' in restaurants where they had colored bathrooms . . . and I can remember when . . . we'd go into restaurants, and they were given food out the back because they were black, but they were not *mistreated*. Back then, that was a way of life.

Like now (pause) it's considered all wrong. Nobody ever even thought that they were really doin' anything wrong.

Ava disagreed with engaging in moral judgment on Jim Crow segregation. She clearly spoke from a white perspective exclusively through her claims as to "the way *people* thought then" (my emphasis); certainly African Americans and their allies fostered both private and public critiques of segregation practices. Ava overstated the universality of her perspective, arguing that blacks and whites were equally satisfied during segregation:

> Interviewer: Since you've lived through it, do you feel like it's important to tell people . . . what it was like back then? It was a little bit different, right? Different bathrooms, and different schools. Do you feel like it's important to even talk about it today?
> Ava: It was different (pause) as in the way of life was different. . . . You know, to tell them what happened during this time sounds like to *you* who've never lived through it that these people were *really really* mistreated. But that's *not* the way it was at all. That was a way of life at that time, and *this* is the way of life that you see now, and people did not scc that as being wrong.
> Interviewer: Any people? Or white people, or—?
> Ava: Black people *or* white people never felt like that was wrong. *You* had friends back *then* because they were your friends. You did *not* have friends because of the color of their skin.

In a didactic tone, Ava argued that there were virtually no southern criticizers of Jim Crow—white or African American—during segregation. She asserted also that race played no role in interactions, friendships, or perspectives on the status quo. Ava maintained this line of reasoning, that black southerners in general were satisfied with segregation, throughout her interview; she claimed also that civil rights protestors followed self-interested, exploitative leaders rather than being motivated by their own moral and justice orientations.

Ava adamantly denied that white supremacy was a significant driver of ideology, structures, or interactions during Jim Crow. Frances, 70s, used a far milder approach, but reached a similar conclusion. She indicated that the interracial norms under segregation were determined by the actions of deferent blacks rather than dictated by whites individually or collectively:

Interviewer: Like you say, you didn't like, *see* a difference between white and black but—
Frances: Well of course I *saw* a difference.
Interviewer: Okay.
Frances: But, as far as *treating* them, or them treating *me*, I don't know. (pause) When *I* was comin' along though, the blacks—I don't know whether they were intimidated by whites [but] they were not as open to conversing with whites as they are now. . . . When I was small, I think they liked their groups, because there are still a lot of black churches that don't want—that are not integrated. You know, whites don't go to their church. So (pause) I don't know how long it's gonna take to be really fully integrated.

Frances implied that interracial interactions were rooted in blacks' own preference for exclusivity, or discomfort in the presence of whites. For evidence that "they *liked* their groups," she pointed out that "there are *still* a lot of black churches that don't want—" (my emphasis). In drawing this connection to current black spaces, Frances implied that African Americans' preferences drove the level of racial integration, past and present. She gave no hint that white southerners were the primary players who created and fought hard to maintain segregation and to subordinate African Americans.

Mysterious Origins: Explaining the Creation of Jim Crow

Just as some participants denied or omitted mention of the inherent white domination of the segregation era, numerous others discussed the creators and enforcers of segregation in strikingly opaque terms. Rarely naming people at all, much less *white* people, the language used often consisted of vague pronouns like "they," or nebulous wording like "the ones who made the laws." For example, Sharon, 60s, used "they" to refer to those who enforced segregation: "It was just what society expected. You know (pause) they also looked down on *white* people that went out of *their* place. It wasn't just that they looked down on black people that weren't doing what was expected of them." Sharon spoke of an anonymous group of people who "looked down on" anyone, regardless of race, who broke segregation expectations. As the ambiguous "they," Jim Crow's enforcers were presented as powerful and ever present, but not embodied or racialized.

Along similar lines, several participants spoke with vagueness and uncertainty regarding the original creation of Jim Crow laws and regulations. Harmony, 80s, tried to answer a question about why there was segregation: "I think way on *back* for a while it was kind of a *law* or somethin'. I've never known what kind of a law, but they kept sayin' . . . that restrooms have to be segregated— (pause) the water fountains and the restaurants and stuff." Unsure, Harmony mused that segregation was "kind of a law or somethin'" that she had learned about informally. Mae, 70s, responded thus to the question: "Do you feel like you had any responsibility for the way things were, like whites sitting in the front or blacks sitting in the back of the bus?"

> No. I don't, personally. Because that was just the law then, and I don't [know] where that actually started, the law. And even . . . the beach, it had a sign on the door, "whites only" . . . and that just came from authorities—ordinances and all—before we were old enough to realize what was going on. I don't know when all this stuff was enacted. . . . Well, I don't know whether there were times we had a say-so and a vote to even integrate the schools or what to do. I think probably that was made by the school board. I don't know, I don't remember.

Mae said that she was unaware of when or how segregation laws had begun, other than at the hands of "authorities." In Mae's memory, regular people never seemed to have had a "say-so" about segregation statutes. Mae was correct that ordinary people of her generation did not enact Jim Crow laws; most were created a couple of generations before her. However, the laws and norms required constant acquiescence and enforcement by officials, institutions, and ordinary people. The laws and norms were steeped in the white supremacist ideology that rationalized their existence.

Thus, beyond demonstrating a limited historical understanding, these examples illustrate how vague language avoids naming white ac- tors—elites as the creators and ordinary people as the condoners of segregation. For Harmony and Sharon it was a nebulous "they" who made sure segregation was followed, and for Mae, "authorities" and "ordinances" enforced segregation. None clarified that white southerners were the ones so heavily invested in maintaining Jim Crow. Sociologist Glenn Bracey has argued that "rescuing whites" is a common phenomenon in racial discourse whereby whites are let off the hook for building white dominant structures. Bracey identifies "personification" as a maneuver whereby a speaker or writer erases white actors by describing patterns of oppression as carried out by institutional forces.[27] In this section, many participants' use of vague language appears to be a personification maneuver.

Participants demonstrated a lack of historical knowledge, as they ruminated over the origins and forms of segregation—unsure of when it was created, by whom, and for what purpose. One participant who did claim to have clear historical insight into the origins of segregation was Kenneth, 80s. He made the case that it was a response to abuses of power by black Americans during the Reconstruction period (mid-1860s to late 1870s):

> Interviewer: Did you have an understanding of *why* things had been made separate in schools and . . . why the different water fountains? Kenneth: A lot of it goes back to the Civil War, back to the days of slavery. . . . It started during Reconstruction and we had all these free blacks. They sorta took over and it's just now really comin' out about how poorly the (pause) whites were treated during that time of Reconstruction in the South. . . . The victor writes the history books.

Kenneth asserted that, because the "victor writes the history books," the true story of how African Americans "took over" and badly treated whites during Reconstruction has only recently begun to be revealed. Kenneth likely drew his reasoning from the white supremacist reaction to the abolition of slavery and the expansion of some rights and opportunities to the most disadvantaged citizens. In fact, the basic historical reality is that segregation laws were enacted by southern Democrats and local elites as a backlash to political and social gains made by African Americans and poor whites alike during the brief Reconstruction period, and new segregation statutes were supported by many white southerners—and practically no black southerners—and enforced by federal, state, and local governments as well as by Ku Klux Klan terrorist cells.[28] Through invoking erroneous history, Kenneth justified the creation of Jim Crow laws.

Another theme in participants' explanations of the origins of segregation was to discuss the Jim Crow period as a curiosity and holdover from an earlier time. In this way, segregated spaces and norms were

presented as natural phenomena rather than encompassing intentional-
ity or active (white) agents. For example, while discussing how a small
black community was located in the heart of a white neighborhood,
Arnold, 80s, portrayed racialized housing patterns as something that
"just happened": "In our neighborhood, maybe two blocks from our
house was this little black enclave of families. . . . I don't know how
those houses got in the middle of this white section. It just happened
(chuckles) before I came along." Bernice, 80s, spoke about "white
flight"—a common phenomenon nationwide whereby whites react to
the racial integration of neighborhoods by fleeing to whiter areas and
causing often rapid depreciation of property values. While Bernice
clearly acknowledged white flight (saying, "whites didn't wanna live
beside the blacks"), she portrayed their motivation as a simple matter of
people following old traditions:

> Bernice: I remember when we lived in south Greensboro and . . . a
> member of our church, he sold his house to a black family, and
> everybody thought, "Why did you do that?" and 'course once you do
> it, the whole block follows, 'cause whites didn't wanna live beside the
> blacks.
> Interviewer: Why was that?
> Bernice: (pause) I don't know, I guess it's just a carryover from years
> that you just didn't associate with 'em, you didn't live next door to
> 'em or anything.

Arnold and Bernice used naturalistic reasoning to explain residential
segregation: "it just happened" and was "just a carryover from [earlier]
years." Arnold's portrayal missed the reality that white domestic employers often preferred to have employees nearby and thus relatively
integrated housing patterns, or small black neighborhood enclaves,
were common throughout the segregated South. Neighborhood location and composition were determined by whites, particularly those of
influence and higher socioeconomic status. Bernice's explanation of
white flight did portray whites as agents, although without consciousness ("whites didn't wanna live beside the blacks" . . . "I guess it's just a
carryover").

In another historically limited and naturalistic explanation of segregation, Joe, 70s, went even further back in time, reasoning that Jim
Crow was rooted to biblical times thousands of years ago:

Joe: There's only one race, and that is the human race.
Interviewer: Given that you think that, what is it like to look back on how people used to be much more separate along race? Like the neighborhoods, you know what I mean? If there's only one race, why were we separated?
Joe: Well, I guess it goes back to in the Bible time, the tower of Babel. That's when they had the different tongues, the different languages, and I think that's the way it came about.

Joe's origins reasoning essentially erased the agency of whites during the Reconstruction backlash period that fueled the creation and en-trenchment of segregation laws and norms and re-institutionalized white supremacist ideology. In each of these excerpts, white Americans were stripped of some or all responsibility for creating and enforcing segregation. White southerners, rather, were portrayed as following tra-dition and dealing with a societal structure that had come about long before their time. As such, white southerners were conceived of as rather inactive and uninvested in white exclusivity.

Similar to Joe, Ellie, 70s, described legal segregation as an inevitable period—a natural and necessary step from a slavery society to an inte-grated, more equal society:

> Interviewer: So, was segregation good, bad? Can it be spoken about in those kind of terms? How would you describe it?
> Ellie: Well that's a strange question-—was it bad. My feeling is if I had known of the inequalities in the schools that would really have bothered me. I didn't know it. That someone wasn't getting the same kind of education I was getting, I didn't know that. . . . But I would never say that segregation was good, because that's separating peo-ple. But it was historically, I guess you'd say, what happened next. It was what we had to live with. We had to go forward, we had to be shown the way to go forward, which was what integration came about to do. . . . But I think it had to be that way. I mean there was no going back and fixing that part of it.

In responding to a prompt asking about making a value judgment on segregation, Ellie asserted her in-the-moment lack of awareness of the extent of racial inequality and, looking back, reasoned that segregation was simply "what happened next" and "had to be that way." In each of these examples there is the naturalization of segregation as an inevitable phenomenon and the stripping or reduction of agency of white southerners reinforcing segregation and black southerners fighting it. In Ellie's words, "we had to be shown the way to go forward, which was what integration came about to do." By not clarifying who is included in "we" (white southerners, or the entire South?) and saying that "integration *came about*" (my emphasis), black Americans were not constructed as the primary proponents of desegregation and not presented as aligned against an entrenched white power structure.

Additionally, these excerpts demonstrate an absence of an accurate collective memory of the Reconstruction period and reveal Woodward's *forgotten alternatives*—that southern segregation did not in fact *have* to be created and did not have to take the forms it did.[29] The progressive changes that were being made under southern Reconstruction—such as the expansion of voting rights, the creation of public schools, and access to political offices for black southerners and poor and working class whites alike—*could have* continued. It was not inevitable that Reconstruction be dismantled and replaced with stringent Jim Crow laws. Forgetting the alternatives to Jim Crow enables white southerners to view a period of overt white racist oppression as happening long ago for innocuous reasons and being simply a taken-for-granted reality.

Next we investigate the meanings behind participants' ubiquitous use of the explanation that the segregated racial past was "just the way it was."

Unquestioned Acceptance: Unpacking "Just the Way It Was"

In the interviews when people talked about segregation, various versions of the phrase "just the way it was" were uttered innumerable times. Finding the phrase less than explanatory, I wanted to understand what specifically it signified for people. Was it a mere cliché used casually, a best effort at explaining segregation, or were they explaining it away? As the following excerpts demonstrate, "just the way it was" encompasses multiple meanings. Sometimes the phrase was wielded in ways that avoided contemplating or discussing more deeply segregation's inherent injustices. It was used also in support of an ahistorical perspective on the racial past, implying that contemporary society is not linked to the racial past. It was used to justify why (white) southerners followed Jim Crow norms without question.

First, John, 70s, tried to explain why he had been unmotivated to engage others in dialogue about segregation in his youth:

> John: I have to admit, on occasion, I *began* to question in my own mind *why* were they treated the way they were. I mean, why did they have a separate entrance into the movie theater. . . . And to see water fountains and stuff—colored and white—it bothered me a little bit, but as a teenager, what was I gonna do about it? I accepted it. It was just the way of life.
> Interviewer: Do you remember talking about that?
> John: No. I mean, who would I have talked to about it? Would I have gone to one of my white friends and say, "Hey, look at the colored guys?" Or go on to a colored guy and say, "Why are you drinking that?" It was *just the way of life*. No, it didn't affect me particularly, because I wasn't black. I am sure it affected them, but it didn't particularly affect me.

John quickly dismissed the suggestion that he would have spoken with others about segregation. Although he said that it "bothered" him "a little bit," he reasoned that he did not feel enough discomfort to begin a conversation. He rationalized his lack of action and more in-depth thought by asserting that segregation was "just the way of life." Essentially he presented inaction and not questioning as the only logical response a white southerner would have had.

Similarly, Ellie, 70s, used "just the way it was" when explaining her apparent lack of awareness of racial inequality in her younger years:

> The thing that I found interesting as I got older is that I was not aware—and I've thought a lot about this—at the theater, when we would walk downtown to the theater I was not aware that they were coming in a different door of the theater. I just wasn't aware of that. I probably paid no attention to the fact that a lot of the department stores, there were different water fountains. You just sort of did your thing and you really weren't questioning what they were doing or what we were doing. It was just the way it was. . . . But in my [church] it was, all people wherever they were, were equal in God's eyes, but what was happening was they were not equal in opportunity, and that's what I think is hard to look back and realize that you lived through that and nobody realized that.

Ellie reflected thoughtfully while recalling her minimal awareness of the extent or meanings of segregation. Like John, she invoked "just the way it was" to reason as to why she did not question segregation more. She asserted also that "nobody realized" the contradiction between teachings of equality and segregation—an assessment that does not apply to black southerners.

In another usage, Patti, 80s, employed the phrasing to dismiss the idea that living in the segregated South had affected her in a long-term way:

> Interviewer: So, how do you think growing up during segregation affects you today, if at all?
> Patti: (pause) Well really not at all, because that was then and this is now, and (pause) it's just the way it was. (laughs)

In dismissing the notion that a Jim Crow childhood and young adulthood would have affected her into the contemporary era, Patti constructed a distinction between the past and present ("that was then and this is now"). In this case, "just the way it was" was invoked in a way that prevented a consideration of the potential impacts of a segregated childhood, including a person's perspective, life chances, or experiences.

Within its different forms, "just the way it was" worked often to shut down discussion and more in-depth explanations. Another illustrative example is from an exchange with Bernice. Bernice, 80s, had said that she was taught to respect African Americans equally to whites, so I asked her to explain the unequal standard for terms of address for whites and blacks:

> Interviewer: I've heard that in many places that white people didn't call black people by "Mister" or "Miss," "Missus"—
> Bernice: Well, we usually called 'em by their first name.
> Interviewer: Why was that, why do you think that is?
> Bernice: I don't know. I don't know. Now, the big fat one I was telling ya that stayed with mother, she was Corina. I don't think I ever knew Corina's last name. . . .
> Interviewer: Mm-hm. But, would they call your parents "Mister" and "Missus"?
> Bernice: Uh, you mean the blacks call my parents?
> Interviewer: Mm-hm.

Bernice: (pause) She used to call [them] by *their* first name, but [she] put mister in front of it.
Interviewer: So, was there a different expectation then, if you're talking to a black person or a white person? Use "Mister" or "Miss," "Missus" with a white person and first name with a black person?
Bernice: No, like, again I say that's just the way things were back then. (chuckles)

In her response to this last clarifying question, Bernice either somehow did not understand what I was saying (because I was attempting to summarize what she had just told me), or she was avoiding acknowledging the double standard of personal addresses. Her "just the way things were" usage, followed by a chuckle, shut down what was already a rather stilted exchange.

Significantly, Arnold, 80s, recognized that explaining segregation as "just the way it was" was an inadequate portrayal, but he struggled to formulate something more descriptive. In this excerpt, he was attempting to explain how segregation laws, such as separate waiting rooms at doctors' offices, got their start:

> I don't know how that happened. . . . It's just the way things were. I know that's not a very good explanation, (chuckles) but you know, I don't think it's thought about by many people. We were talkin' about hate while ago, I never heard hate preached. (long pause) But some things get in you, the practices, and then for several generations this way, it just sort of gets accepted. And I don't think that excuses improper behavior, so I'm not trying to say it's not our fault.

Arnold indicated that, although he saw the issue with explaining segregation as "just the way things were," he had no better explanation. He implied that because "it's not thought about by many people," including himself, and "some things get in you," (white) southerners never developed an accurate, critical commentary on Jim Crow. However, a novel thing Arnold did in this excerpt was to allocate responsibility to white southerners, and he used we/us language ("I'm not trying to say it's not our fault"). This kind of admission was rare.

Clarence, 60s, revealed that the "just the way it is" explanation was used *during* segregation as well, to shut down discussion and criticism of Jim Crow:

Interviewer: So, you remember wondering about the signs in the office building. Do you remember ever asking about them? People talking about them?

Clarence: Um (pause) yes, but as far as a definitive response, it was more just, well, that's the way it is. And they have their own place, and we have our own place as far as drinking facilities. But nothing really made of it. Other than just that's the way it is.

Clarence's observation indicated that "the way it is" operated as a justification for segregated facilities. "Just the way it is" was a way, during Jim Crow, to end the discussion before it started, to effectively avoid addressing the core intent or meaning of legal segregation—white dominance, exclusion, and subordination of people of color. The "just the way it is/was" phrasing accompanies an acceptance of the racial status quo and provides people a ready rationale for not questioning even very blatant inequalities. In contemporary usage by elder white southerners, it furthers the notion that there *continues to be* no effective way to explain or understand the structure and racial dynamics of the Jim Crow South.

Indeed, a few participants corroborated this conclusion. As one of the most racially progressive participants, Ingrid, 60s, asserted matter-of-factly that "just the way it was" can serve as an escape route for those who did/do not wish to criticize segregation:

Interviewer: A lot of times when people talk about the past, like segregation, they say, "That's just the way it was." What does that statement mean to you, "That's just the way it was"?

Ingrid: That they didn't care enough to do anything about it, the same way I was. And I'm not proud of that.

Ingrid acknowledged the power play embedded in the phrase—dominant group members (white southerners) invoked it in order to *not* critically assess or work against the structures, ideology, or norms of segregation.

The majority of participants justified or explained their lack of action against, or critique of, the blatant inequalities of segregation. Many did not conceive of there having been any other possibilities for their own thinking or actions, and they saw it as inevitable that segregation would come into being and then come to pass—that they were caught in a moment of history. This perspective is not wholly inaccurate. At very young ages, white southerners were socialized through subtle and overt messages to accept that black southerners were "beneath" them and that any criticisms they may have of "the way things are" would fall on deaf ears. As journalist W. J. Cash argued in his influential book *Mind of the South*, during segregation the white South became increasingly resistant to criticisms of the status quo and held to a "savage ideal" that transcended class barriers, a milieu "whereunder dissent and variety are completely suppressed and men become, in all their attitudes, professions, and actions, virtual replicas of one another."[30] Jim Crow socialization, then, by suppressing dissent and baiting whites across the socioeconomic spectrum with notions of racial superiority, ensured that nearly all whites would come to embrace segregation and its white supremacist logic.

Chuck, 70s, illustrated this point well. He said that he "felt pretty bad" about separate facilities in the local theater, but Jim Crow expectations were "too ingrained" for him "to want to take it on":

> Chuck: One thing that always *bothered* me, we had a mezzanine . . . we had a balcony, then we had a *second* balcony. And the blacks sat in the second balcony, *never* anywhere else. And they had a separate entrance, and a separate concession stand very much smaller than the main one. And if they made any noise up there, the usher went up and called them down about it. . . . There was something about that—that even in my youth in those days seemed very, very wrong to me.
> Interviewer: Was it something you could talk about or express?
> Chuck: No, it really wadn't anything people talked about much. I just felt like it wadn't *fair*. And I gave [an out-of-town friend] a tour of the Carolina Theatre . . . and I took him up to the second balcony, and I showed him where the entrance of the blacks was and all that, and how the seats up there were not comfortable . . . and he said, "Well, how did you *feel* about that?" And I said, "I wadn't *bold* enough to fight it. It was too ingrained to want to take it on. But I felt pretty bad about it."

Chuck revealed that he did have some negative feelings associated with comprehending segregated facilities, but he had been socialized thoroughly enough to keep his feelings to himself. Segregation was a hegemonic system, created by the ruling class to maintain the dominance of white elites and racial divisions within the poor and working classes. It was a system that constantly sought buy-in from all citizens and was especially successful at doing so with members of the dominant racial group—whites.

Lillian Smith argued in her memoir that, despite their in-depth socialization to segregation, white southern children were burdened by a deep sense that Jim Crow was immoral. And yet, there was much that remained unquestioned due to the completeness and normality of the status quo: "We worried about things close to home but I don't think we noticed the signs. Somehow we seemed always to walk through the right door. People find it hard to question something that has been here since they were born."[31] Even though many participants shared that they had felt shock or discomfort at certain times when confronted with the realities of racial inequality under segregation, few claimed they did much if anything to challenge it. Gertie, 70s, was one who did. She said that early on she had a sense that segregation was unjust and she tried to challenge it in her own small and safe way: "I noticed that they were at the back on the bus . . . and I know that I remember thinking, 'That's not fair,' and sometimes I went back there and sat sort of at the dividing line." In her mind, Gertie worked against Jim Crow by sitting *near* the back of the bus—a mild challenge indeed—but she explained that the southern way discouraged disagreement over "unpleasant" things:

> Sometimes I've chastised myself for not standing up and speaking out . . . and it sort of goes back to that southern upbringing that you don't rock the boat too much over something that's unpleasant. But I have spoken up at times for the underdog. But to me the underdog can be anybody . . . it's not necessarily just colored people—that's what we called 'em, you know, colored people. (chuckles)

Gertie said that she has felt regret in thinking back to her choice of behavior. White southerners clearly had curiosities and questions regarding segregation, especially during childhood, but few took a strong stand against the norms of their society, either before or—as we will explore in the next two chapters—during the civil rights era.

Certainly there is more that goes into accounting for whites' lack of action against Jim Crow than Gertie's explanation of "that southern upbringing." Undoubtedly, socialization to be obedient to authority was pervasive in that era, especially for young white women. However, we must acknowledge that white southern identity was, in part, built upon a white supremacist ideology and formulated through innumerable interactions with Jim Crow laws and norms. Through learning not to question segregation, Jim Crow's white children were also learning not to question its white supremacist logic. Furthermore, whites' status was not formulated solely by ideology and identity. Whites had material interests in the society's institutions that favored them—in the realms of business, education, politics, criminal justice, and housing. The "unjust impoverishment" of people of color was directly tied to the "unjust enrichment" of whites, especially but not exclusively white elites.[32]

RECONCILING NOSTALGIA AND THE RACIAL PAST

As the analysis herein demonstrates, when this group of white southerners reflected back on the racial era they grew up in and participated in (throughout childhood and also into adulthood for most), they tended to view themselves as people who were not directly involved in enforcing segregation's inequalities and norms. They remembered vividly seeing the signs of segregation—buses, water fountains, theaters, and restrooms—but viewed those structures of inequality as having had little impact in their own lives. Rather, segregation was curious, or "just the way it was"—a way of life rarely questioned or in need of in-depth explanation today. Upon reflection, most people acknowledged that facilities and services for black southerners had been substandard—schools, buses, restaurants, hospitals, and so on. But when it came to the social relations between whites and blacks, typically they recalled their interactions as warm and mutually satisfying, aligning with the notion of "good race relations" in the South that white political leaders insisted were characteristic of the region up through the 1960s, even in the midst of the civil rights movement.[33]

All of the interview participants grew up in an era of overt anti-black discrimination and white privilege. While many explained they were not fully aware of inequality and exclusion during segregation, this reality was revealed extensively through the campaigns of the civil rights movement. So it is significant that Jim Crow's living witnesses would not construct the era as a time of racist belief and action on the part of mainstream, white society. I make the case throughout this book that elder white southerners today are not simply attempting to interpret the past and suffering from a lack of effective analytical tools, they are invested in a positive portrayal of themselves and of white society generally, an investment that hinders a more accurate and comprehensive assessment of the southern racial past, their black neighbors, and even their own childhood experiences.

Nostalgia for the joys of one's childhood or for a bygone, simpler way of life is not necessarily an indicator of resistance to reality. During the course of my research, I encountered an older African American man I overheard saying at a coffee shop, "I would love to go back to 1958." My ears pricked up, and I listened as he launched into an oratory about how people are not safe anymore to leave cars unlocked, media is too violent, children have no good role models, low-wage labor could ensure a decent standard of living, and so forth. In other words, life was altogether simpler *and* better back then. He said, "I always live in the past. I want to remember the good part of life." I was struck by how similar he sounded to some of the people I had interviewed. But there was more to come, which distinguished his perspective. He began talking about the troublesome racial past, weaving it into his arguments. He explained that 1958 was a better time because whites' racism was easier to identify, and that now it had become more subtle and difficult to see: "You used to know your enemy. Now they wear business suits instead of Klan hoods and smile in your face." Ultimately, he argued that because racism had been an ever-present reality across his lifetime it need not cloud his view of the good old days. He claimed that because anti-black prejudice used to be *easier* to identify, he could logically assert that the white supremacy of the 1950s was actually preferable.

The way in which this man incorporated the structural context of overt racist oppression into his nostalgia for the past points toward a potential narrative for elder white southerners. "Black southerners mostly did *not*, and still do not, share such dreamy views of oneness, sharing, and beneficent white–black segregation that have long been part of the white segregationists' version of the traditional racial framing of society."[34] While they acknowledged that the past included some racial inequalities, the elder white southerners interviewed for this book minimally incorporated this structural reality into their portrayals of the legal segregation era. Their nostalgia has not (yet) been reconciled fully with the truth of the racial past.

4

DISTANCING AND REJECTION
The Civil Rights Movement at Arm's Length

For centuries white Americans institutionalized their entitlement to the best of life and marginalized African Americans and other people of color.[1] Throughout the segregation era of the late 1800s to mid-1960s, whites believed in the immutability of differences between whites and blacks and also in ideals of equality instilled through Christian and patriotic teachings. Social scientist Gunnar Myrdal pointed out in the 1940s that whites reconciled those beliefs through mental and emotional contortions that asserted blacks as inferior and thus not entitled to equality with whites.[2] White children who grew up under Jim Crow, including the participants in this research, were socialized to these racist beliefs and practices by their families, communities, and social institutions.[3] As shown in the previous chapter, many participants explained that the Jim Crow racial arrangement was "just the way it was"—normalized but regarded at times with some curiosity.

And then the civil rights movement began. The white South was confronted by the injustices of Jim Crow and forced to rethink its beliefs and practices and, ultimately, to adapt to and participate in desegregation. Today mainstream American society interprets the civil rights movement as a period of moral struggle that ushered in a time of greater racial equality.[4] Activists who employed nonviolent strategies of civil disobedience and who braved violent racist backlash are afforded a place of respect. However, as will become clear in this chapter, elder

white southerners do not share fully in this consensus. Rather, many of
their narratives are constructed in ways that devalue the movement and
downplay the extent of Jim Crow white supremacy at the same time as
they claim to support, and to have long supported, the end of legal
segregation. This is the key complexity highlighted in this and the following chapter: expressing both agreement with the movement/deseg-
regation and resenting the experience of it.

   Additionally, in this chapter there are four intersecting themes about
civil rights movement storytelling—two ways of constructing whites and
two ways of presenting the movement. First, the white southern self in
the civil rights era was constructed as racially enlightened and equality
minded. Second, whites were portrayed as innocent bystanders and
potential victims of a chaotic and troubling period brought on by
African American activism. Third, the movement was devalued through
trivializing activists' organizing efforts. Fourth, Greensboro's identity as
a key site of civil rights activism was rejected or downplayed. I argue
that together these portrayals work to diminish the importance of the
black freedom struggle and to construct white southerners as nonracist
and innocent; the Jim Crow South and white southerners are excused of
responsibility for upholding white supremacy. Connecting to the analysis in the previous chapters, I argue also that these perspectives on the
civil rights era help white southerners to maintain nostalgia for the Jim
Crow era.

   A related phenomenon was people's frequent inaccurate recall of
major events and misuse of basic terminology (such as "integration" and
"segregation"). Interestingly, recent survey research has demonstrated
that, more than any other group of Americans, white southerners who
were young adults during the civil rights era (in the same cohort as the
younger segment of my participants—those in their 60s to early 70s)
rate the movement as one of the most memorable events of their lifetimes.[5] This seems to conflict with many participants' errors in basic
recall of the time period and their misuse of terminology. To explain
this seeming mismatch, I propose that many participants have built and
maintained a *selective detachment* from the civil rights movement.
 Much of the clarity and vividness they retain toward the civil rights era
was expressed through stories of themselves as enlightened moderates
or potential victims and of African Americans as threatening. In
contrast with their narratives of the Jim Crow era, they rarely men-

tioned beloved black acquaintances/employees when they spoke about the civil rights era. Instead, the movement was portrayed as a phenomenon that disrupted much of the stability and "good" interracial relations of segregation.

This chapter will analyze how participants associated "racial problems" and "racial violence" with the onset of the civil rights movement rather than with the Jim Crow era that was inherently dehumanizing and dangerous for black southerners. This association is illustrated well in an exchange in which a married couple explained that segregation entailed harmonious racial relations and that the "trouble" began with civil rights protestors:

> Husband: I remember the Wilson family. I was their boy. They were African Americans. [The father] said he raised me. And we thought that way about 'em, played with 'em, didn't have any problems. 'Course we didn't go to church with 'em, didn't go to school with 'em—it was segregated there. But (pause) didn't have any real problems. Rode the bus all the time, and 'course they sat in the back of the bus. I never saw the bus driver ask one to move. You really didn't see much controversy until World War II.
> Interviewer: So things seemed to be easygoing between people?
> Husband: Yeah.
> Wife: Oh yes! They didn't cause trouble. I mean, we all got along! . . .
> Husband: Now it wadn't all roses— every now and then there'd be somebody stir up something. Back in—when was it? In the sixties, I guess, when we had most of our race riots here. And most of that, I think, started (pause) in the schools and in the universities—A&T [North Carolina A&T State University, a historically black institution].
> Wife: And the integration of the city schools too.

As this couple looked back across the racial past, they presented a distinct contrast between segregation as a time of easygoing race relations when "they [blacks] didn't cause trouble" and the 1960s civil rights era when African Americans began to "stir up something," organizing for change. This couple defined the onset of racial problems as the activism that disrupted Jim Crow segregation. In their view, the civil rights era was an affront to the stability and harmonious race relations of segregated society. Many other participants constructed a similar contrast in their descriptions of these two eras, although rarely in terms quite this blatant. This chapter considers the consistencies and complexities in how elder white southerners remembered experiencing the civil rights era in their home city, Greensboro, North Carolina.

GREENSBORO, THE CIVIL RIGHTS CITY

During the segregation era, North Carolina had a reputation of being the most racially progressive southern state.[6] The city of Greensboro in particular had long prided itself for being a unique space of racial enlightenment in the state, as evidenced by its early settlement by emancipationist Quakers, its numerous local colleges and universities—including two historically black institutions and a Quaker college—and the successes of Jewish textile entrepreneurs. However, as historian Bill Chafe argues in his book on Greensboro's school desegregation saga, *Civilities and Civil Rights*, the city's proud reputation contrasted sharply with its history of white dominance and typical southern-style segregation practices and politics. The city's "progressive mystique" concealed how Greensboro's white elite monopolized power, subordinated African Americans, and resisted changes to the racial arrangement throughout the civil rights era.[7]

Outside of North Carolina, Greensboro registers in contemporary awareness not as a particularly progressive place, but rather as the birthplace of the sit-in movement. Indeed, alongside Little Rock, Selma, and Montgomery, Greensboro is one of the most well-known civil rights cities. It was the "Greensboro Four," freshmen students from the historically black North Carolina A&T State University—Joseph McNeil, Franklin McCain, Ezell Blair Jr. (later, Jibreel Khazan), and David Richmond—who planned and initiated the action to request service at the whites-only lunch counter of Woolworth's five and dime store. Although African Americans had organized and carried out sit-ins protesting segregated spaces in a variety of places between 1939 and 1959, including in Virginia, New York, and Washington, D.C., the February 1, 1960, Greensboro protest is credited with directly inspiring the sit-in *movement*, in which scores of similar lunch counter protests rapidly cropped up across the South.[8] The sit-in demonstrations sent a clear and revolutionary message to the white South that black southerners were not in fact content with Jim Crow as usual.[9]

Despite the glare of a national spotlight on Greensboro's racial inequality—dissonant for white Greensboro's progressive mystique—city
elites did not welcome the challenge to segregation, and the integration
of whites-only facilities became a drawn-out struggle. Citing alliance
with local custom, Woolworth's management refused to serve sit-in protestors and opted to close down the store to avoid dealing with the
matter.[10] Several times over the following months, activists acquiesced
to business and political leaders' requests for the protests to end so that
private negotiations could be held with the aim of reaching a mutually
agreeable arrangement.[11] Time and again, activist leaders realized that
negotiations with white powerholders were not going to achieve a favorable result and resumed their actions and replicated them at other
whites-only spaces.[12] Woolworth's management finally acquiesced and
served its first seated African American lunch counter customers—in a
strange twist, its own employees—on July 25, 1960, almost six months
after the initial demonstration.[13]

Greensboro's civil rights story neither begins nor ends with the 1960
sit-ins. In 1958, Dr. Martin Luther King Jr.'s attempt to visit and preach
in Greensboro was nearly thwarted; only at the last minute did a ve-
nue—historically black and female Bennett College—agree to host
him, risking economic reprisal.[14] By 1959, just prior to the sit-ins, enrollment in the local chapter of the NAACP rocketed past previous year
counts, to 2,300—about 8 percent of the black population.[15] Furthermore, the city has one of the most fascinating school desegregation
sagas—again revealing a contrast between its progressive mystique and
white supremacist norms. It was a process that began before the sit-ins
and lasted to 1971. Just after the 1954 *Brown v. Board* Supreme Court
decision that deemed segregated schools unconstitutional, Greensboro's school board publicly announced it was ready to comply. But comprehensive school integration was not implemented for another *seventeen* years.[16] (Most of the participants I interviewed were married with
children during the school desegregation process, which hit their lives
hard; chapter 5 deals exclusively with their memories of school integration.)

Although they professed racial progressiveness, whites' attachment
to white supremacy had long provided fertile ground for antiracist activism in Greensboro. As Chafe states, "the sit-in demonstrations repre-

sented a dramatic extension of, rather than a departure from, traditional patterns of black activism in Greensboro."[17] And, after 1960:

> There was almost a pendulum motion in the history of Greensboro's civil rights struggles. Blacks wanted to trust in the good faith of whites. Only after frustration reached a peak did overt rebellion occur, to be followed again by quiet and patience when promises of change were offered. Then the spirit of rebellion would rise once more, set in motion by yet another betrayal of promises made in the heat of crisis.[18]

In 1962, a new local chapter of the Congress of Racial Equality (CORE) organized daily picketing demonstrations at whites-only cafeterias in downtown Greensboro.[19] The following summer saw unprecedented levels of protests at white businesses, and thousands were arrested, filling all available jail space.[20] Amid continued demonstrations, many Greensboro whites clung to the belief that African Americans in their city were accepting of segregation and that "outsiders" were instigating the protests.[21] In June 1963, at the height of nonviolent protest actions, Mayor David Schenck stated that the protests had "caused a serious erosion of the mutual respect and friendship that has existed between the races in Greensboro. This . . . will cause all our citizens of all races to be the loser, and Greensboro's progressive spirit to be replaced by animosity and bitterness."[22]

Greensboro's progressiveness was not a complete façade. Greensboro had many white liberals who favored desegregation. Even Mayor Schenck favored integration.[23] But the city's white leaders consistently supported the rights of white business owners to maintain segregated facilities and white residents to have continued access to whites-only spaces. This chapter will reveal how some Greensboro whites who witnessed the civil rights era locally have reconciled over the long term with what happened in their city. I will show that the participants, for the most part, constructed their civil rights–era selves as racially progressive and portray civil rights protests as a fuzzy memory or as moments of danger to whites individually and to the stability of Jim Crow society.

CONSTRUCTING THE ENLIGHTENED WHITE SOUTHERN SELF

As they were asked to think back about their civil rights–era selves, most interview participants portrayed themselves, and often other whites, as racially enlightened people. They did this through positioning whites as passive bystanders during civil rights actions, claiming that they had deemed segregation immoral and contrasting themselves with other white southerners. I argue that these constructions work to assert white southerners as racially innocent—faultless for enforcing Jim Crow norms and inequalities and made vulnerable by the social upheaval introduced by civil rights protests.

A primary way that participants constructed the civil rights–era enlightened white southern self was to portray white southerners as passive bystanders, uninvolved and uninvested in protecting segregation. Whites were cast as people waiting and watching from a distance and then accepting the changes that came to pass. Darla, a woman in her 70s, explained that white people may have had opinions about civil rights, but they were mostly bystanders: "I was not actually affected by it like maybe some people were. I think maybe blacks were probably a lot more affected by it than the whites in the change that was happening, because whites more or less just went on about their business and either they hoped the blacks would stay in their place or they wanted them to have equal rights." Other participants also indicated that white southerners were somewhat opinionated about the movement and reticent about what might happen to the racial arrangement, but they stayed uninvolved and calm during protests. This type of portrayal both illustrates the everyday normalcy of Jim Crow, where whites were accustomed to ignoring and stifling black dissatisfaction, and also denies white southerners' ideological, material, and emotional investments in segregation.[24]

A second way that respondents presented themselves as racially progressive was to claim that they had fundamentally disagreed with the morality of segregation. Often, participants' statements indicated that they were using post–civil rights logic instead of sharing their in-the-moment reactions. For example, several people made statements like, "it should never have been that way" and "it needed to change." In his presentation of the Woolworth sit-ins, T. J., 60s, wove a claim of enlightened antisegregation belief in with his negative feelings toward protestors:

> Here I am from the South and I said, well, gosh, I think they ought to be served, but I also think some of them ought to get up and let people sit down and eat. That was my feelings. . . . I mean here it didn't make any sense that a black person could work in the kitchen and prepare the food, but yet he couldn't sit down and eat it. [Traveling outside the Deep South], I saw [integrated restaurants] and I came back home and said, god, I can't believe this, you know. But I think I felt angry at first in the respect that they wouldn't let other people sit down and eat.

T. J. claimed to have held these two views simultaneously: he disagreed both with segregated restaurants and with the protests against them. T. J. indicated that traveling outside the South had raised his critical consciousness toward Jim Crow ("I came back home and said, god, I can't believe this"), but revealed that his immediate reaction to the protests was not in solidarity with activists. His quote reflects a trend across participants' civil rights narratives in this and the following chapter: how claims of enlightened thinking commingle with displays of racist reactions.

Like T. J., Harmony, 80s, claimed to have been opposed to segregation on principle. She went further, claiming that she was not of the same mind as employees who obeyed their segregationist bosses' orders during lunch counter protests: "I didn't see any reason to have all that [sitting in]. Well, I did see the reason, because they didn't allow it. Whoever that managed the Woolworth's store down there and the eating area, [I] guess they were bein' told by their bosses what to do and all, and I couldn't go along with that." Since Harmony implied that she would not have followed the bosses' orders, I presented her with a concrete scenario: "What if you had been working there and you had been told to—?"

> Oh yeah. That would be a different story, you're right, 'cause I've always felt like you're supposed to obey the *law*, and that in a sense was a law of *management*, and I couldn't do a whole lot to—I mean, I guess you're thinkin', "Well you could have quit if they said you couldn't serve them." And knowin' me, I probably would have. *But* I don't know that that would be a general thing to think, you know.

When asked to elaborate, Harmony admitted that she would have respected segregation statutes as a law-abiding citizen, then moved immediately back to an assertion that, "knowin' me," she "probably would have" sacrificed her job in protest against a segregationist boss. Harmony thus portrayed herself as a good person in two ways—as a citizen obedient to laws and conventions and as a person willing to stand up for her principles no matter the personal cost. Harmony's last statement seemed an attempt to reconcile the contradiction: perhaps actively supporting civil rights protestors would not have been, for whites, "a general thing to think."

A respect-for-law perspective and a hesitancy not to offend other whites strengthened white resistance to the civil rights movement and discouraged fairly liberal whites from opposing staunch segregationists and segregation laws.[25] It bears noting that law is not neutral and certainly was not when enforcing Jim Crow. Since the founding of the United States, the law has been created by white elites and interpreted and enforced in ways that privileged whites.[26] Law continues to be theorized and interpreted in ways that reinscribe white privilege, deny systemic racism, and delegitimize challenges brought by people of color.[27] Thus, the notion of the law as good and just has been a powerful tool for white supremacy, exacerbating and justifying the inequalities imposed upon people of color.

A third, and related, way that respondents established their civil rights–era selves as racially enlightened was through contrasting themselves with segregationists. For example, Burt, 80s, said he was not upset by desegregation, but he knew white people who were angered by it:

> Interviewer: What did you think about integration when it started to happen?
> Burt: (long pause) It didn't bother me a bit in the world. I was glad to see it 'cause I thought it ought to be, just by a question of right and wrong. . . . I knew a lot of people that thought that it was bad for both races—bad for the blacks to try to be like the whites—instead of advancing on their own, they was copying white ways.

Burt combined an assertion of the immorality of segregation with a claim that he was not like the whites who struggled to accept integration. Mack, 80s, went further than Burt, telling of how he argued with white friends about their uncritical agreement with Jim Crow norms, such as inviting African American customers to do business but only in limited ways:

> Woolworth asked black people to . . . buy everyplace else in that store but you can't buy anything at lunch counter—that seemed to me to be totally asinine, and I verbalized that to all my white friends. And I said, "Come on. Be real. If you don't want black clientele at all, *fine*. Put a sign up saying, 'No blacks admitted.' That's your store. Okay, I'll go with that. At least a black person would know they're not wanted there and their money's no good there . . . but to say, 'Come on in and spend your money at the jewelry counter and at the perfume counter and at the candy counter and all these counters,' but then I can't go . . . sit down and eat lunch?" I said, "That dudn't even make *sense* to me."

Interestingly, Mack presented himself not as more racially enlightened or empathetic than his white peers, but as a more logical thinker. He contrasted his civil rights–era self against those who thought segregationist policies were rational.

On the surface, these examples verify that among white southerners there was a range of responses to civil rights activism and impending desegregation, with most folks placed somewhere on the spectrum between outspoken segregationists and white antiracists.[28] However, these narratives cannot be used to place individuals along a racism–antiracism spectrum. In fact, while some, like T. J., admitted to have responded negatively to civil rights actions, none contrasted themselves with other, more racially progressive white people. Thus, their narratives demonstrate efforts at positive identity construction. These narratives of the enlightened, rational self exemplify white southerners presenting themselves as uninvolved in the maintenance of Jim Crow and the vitriolic resistance to civil rights activism.

SYMBOLIC DETACHMENT FROM THE MOVEMENT

While participants established themselves as racially progressive at the onset of the civil rights movement, they overwhelmingly demonstrated a long-term detachment and persistent distancing from civil rights actions and outcomes. The detachment came through in respondents' vague and inaccurate memories as well as their misuse of key terminology of the era. Thereby they revealed a disconnection from the movement and the people involved—civil rights was a "black" thing and did not resonate with them enough to be integrated into memory alongside other events of daily life at the time. Indeed, as I will discuss later in this chapter, participants' memories of civil rights seemed to be especially associative with blackness and criminality, where peaceful protests by black students in the early 1960s were conflated with "riots" and "violence" perpetrated across the nation by African Americans over the past several decades. Much of the social detachment that white southerners fostered at the time between themselves and the events and participants of the civil rights movement appears to have been preserved.

"Sixty? Late as That?" Faulty Memory as Detachment

One manifestation of white southerners' detachment from the civil rights movement was faulty recall of major era events. Several respondents had trouble determining when the lunch counter sit-ins happened and had to ask me for assistance. This memory gap is particularly noteworthy because the 1960 lunch counter sit-in movement by college students is the event that makes Greensboro a city known to the rest of the country (although some respondents boasted of other prominent local events, such as having been the site of numerous "decisive" American war battles and the boyhood home of news anchor Edward R. Murrow). As the following examples will demonstrate, some of the city's white elders have failed to remember the sit-ins and do not embrace them as part of their own history.

One woman found it surprising that the sit-ins were as late as 1960. "When were the sit-ins, '51?" She asked. When I told her the correct date, she remained confused: "Sixty? Late as that?" she mused. Another woman asked for my assistance in determining which came first, the sit-ins or a deadly shooting in town that occurred nearly two decades later, in 1979.[29] Mae, a woman in her 70s who had long patronized Woolworth's, got two vital facts of the Greensboro sit-ins wrong—the rather well-known date of the first sit-in (February 1) and the way in which

Woolworth's lunch counter was segregated (African American customers could get take-out but were not served seated):

> They changed the name of the street [downtown] to February Thirteen—that was the day they went in . . . Woolworth's had a lunch counter, and I would go in there to eat lunch, and blacks would always have to sit at the very back. And so this particular day they went in and sat down up at the front. And servers were not going to serve them, and they just sat there until they did, and I think [that] was the beginning of the integration here in Greensboro.

When people became aware of inaccuracies in their recall, a typical way they responded was to rationalize the error as due to how busy their lives had been during that time. For example, after Bernice, 80s, and I discussed the sit-ins at length, I asked her if she had been married at that time:

> Bernice: No, I didn't get married 'til 1940, '41.
> Interviewer: Um, the sit-ins started in 1960.
> Bernice: Mm-hm. (pause) Oh yeah, I was married at the time of the sit-ins, yes. But I was busy raisin' my family and didn't think too much about things like that.

Similarly, Verna, 80s, used the excuse of her busy family life to explain her lack of memory of the sit-ins:

> Interviewer: How old were you when the sit-ins started?
> Verna: I don't even know when it was. When was it?
> Interviewer: 1960.
> Verna: 1960, let me see. (pause) I was born in [the 1920s]—and you said 1960?
> Interviewer: Mm-hm.
> Verna: Okay, I was about 30, 40 years old and [had several] children. So you see, I was pretty occupied with my own children.

In another similar example, Sally, 70s, rationalized why she could not remember the date of the sit-ins:

> Interviewer: So what were you doing during the sit-ins here when it started?
> Sally: When'd they start? I don't remember the actual date.

Interviewer: Well the one at Woolworth's, the first one—
Sally: It was in the fifties, wasn't it?
Interviewer: '60, February '60.
Sally: 1960? We were just comin' back to Greensboro [after living away for a few years] . . . I was nursing a baby (laughs loudly) . . . and my husband was just coming back and going to work here. So we were not politically involved and not very aware at that point. We had our own issues. (laughs loudly)

In each case, it was only after I helped Bernice, Verna, and Sally place the sit-ins in a particular year that they constructed a reason for their failure to remember the chronology or details of the sit-ins—they must have been too busy with motherhood and daily life. The sit-ins were not available in their minds as a temporally orienting event. They could recall their lives based on the prompt of a particular year, but not on the prompt of a prominent civil rights event in their city. Their lack of memory is arguably connected to a lack of investment in the civil rights movement; if the sit-ins had resonated with them, we may surmise that some of their attention would have been dedicated to integrating memories of the movement into the narratives of their lives.

Arlene, 70s, alluded to this alternative explanation for the lapse in memory. Saying that she could not recall when the sit-ins occurred and reasoning that she must have been too busy at the time to pay attention, she said she was absorbed in her own life and not in tune with what was happening around her: "That would have been my first year of [a new job], and there again (pause) I was busy doing something else (pause) and if I was aware of it, I don't remember. I don't remember discussing it with my parents or my siblings. (pause) Oh my life musta been sort of self-centered!" (laughing) As Arlene indicated, being busy at the time may have been only part of why she did not remember the sit-ins well. She laughingly hinted at another reason—being "self-centered" and not attentive to the concerns of the black community.

This explanation is further evidenced by participants' excellent memory of other events during the same era. For example, in the interviews I often asked people to comment on the assassination of President John F. Kennedy (November 1963). Their responses were not at all typified by the vagueness in their recall of events associated with the black freedom struggle. Mostly they remembered exactly where they were and what they were doing when they heard the news of Kennedy's

shooting, and they remember how they *felt* about the tragedy as well—
devastated, patriotic, and deeply worried. On the other hand, as we will
see later in this chapter, Martin Luther King Jr.'s assassination five
years later, in April 1968, was not a particularly resonant event for most
of the participants. Memory is bolstered when there is a link to emotion
and empathy.[30] This lack in the participants' recall of civil rights activism is indicative of the symbolic distance separating segregation-era
whites from their black neighbors and the movement.

Segregation–Integration: Misuse of Language as Detachment

A second phenomenon illustrating white southerners' social detachment from civil rights–era black concerns was the misuse of era terminology—particularly confusion around the words *segregation* and *integration*. It was common for people to misuse, transpose, or stumble
through the two terms. These errors indicate a lack of fluency in the
language of the racial past of their own lifetimes. For example, John,
70s, struggled to come up with the word *integration*: "The only thing I
remember basically about it is what I saw about it on the news or the
television, the occurrences down in Selma, Alabama, and places like
this where the National Guard had to, in a sense, force other—uh, what
am I'm trying to—can't even say the word—uh, force integration. My
mind went blank."[31] Additionally, when speaking, several respondents
confused the terms *segregation* and *integration*, often without catching
the mistake. They did this despite the fact that integration—school
desegregation in particular—hit close to home and they had had strong
feelings about it and much dialogue about it with others at the time.
Arnold, 80s, flubbed on the terms: "It's hard to think back . . . it's hard
to think that we even thought about living in an integrated—in a seg—a
segregated society." Also, with some help from me, Trudie, 60s, realized that she had used the wrong term:

> Interviewer: You would have been [in your teens] when the Supreme
> Court decided the *Brown v. Board of Education* decision. And that
> ruled separate schools unconstitutional—
> Trudie: Oh. Yeah, uh-huh.
> Interviewer: So that was, I think, sort of the first news that—
> Trudie: You had to segre—
> Interviewer: they were integrating—

Trudie: *Integrate* the schools.
Interviewer: Yeah.
Trudie: I'm using the wrong word, I'm sorry, okay.

Jolene, 80s, had a sense that she used the wrong term and asked me to correct her:

Jolene: When I was going to school we didn't have black children in our school. . . . I don't know how long it's been segregated, or what you call it?
Interviewer: Integrated?
Jolene: Integrated. I don't know how long that's been.

Darla, 70s, got the terminology right, then wrong twice a few minutes later in the interview, then finally self-corrected (transcript page numbers roughly represent time lapses):

It seemed at that time, they were more interested in integration than they were in education (p. 18). . . . The first year he went to a segregated school, the principal there was a black person. . . . 1970 he went to uh, the first segregated school (p. 19). . . . Until the schools are, um, segrega— uh, uh integrated and, um, everybody was concentratin' more, and of course I think that integration was a good thing (p. 20).[32]

Often respondents would make these errors at a point in the interview after we had both correctly used the terms. When I was speaking I used the correct terms, so they received accurate prompts, but it did not always affect their own use of the terms. For example, Delilah, 70s, thought I was referring to the integration of her neighborhood in this exchange:

Delilah: At night we'd play on the curbs 'til it got dark, games and— (long pause)
Interviewer: And I guess the neighborhoods were segregated?
Delilah: Not then.
Interviewer: Not then?
Delilah: We had no blacks livin' in our neighborhood from the time I was born until (pause) mm, 1980.

It was clear that these people knew what they intended to say, but the terms *segregation* and *integration* were not well assimilated into their language.

Why did they use the wrong terms? Certainly the words *segregation* and *integration* have some phonetic similarity, and, as semantic opposites, the words are linked conceptually. There may also be a temporal linkage, meaning that both terms became prominent in white southern discourse at the same time, because of the civil rights movement. Many said that they conceived of their way of life during Jim Crow as normal life and did not question the racial arrangement much until forced to by the movement. If we take this claim at face value, then these two words—*segregation* and *integration*—may have emerged together in their conscious awareness and, without consistent accurate usage, became muddled and conflated. Ava, 60s, helps lend some support to this idea. When I asked her if she found it difficult to remember the racialized aspects of life under segregation, she fired back: "Well you see, I never *knew* segregation *as* segregation, so therefore I don't *remember* it as segregation!"

However, there is another way to interpret these language lapses—as part of a larger *unknowing project* around Jim Crow. Whites were invested in maintaining their way of life and seeing themselves as good people. Even during segregation, ethics of equality and liberty and justice for all were deeply held. The contradiction between those ethics and Jim Crow was reconciled to the extent that it could be with notions of white superiority. So, for white southerners, denying the full reality of the Jim Crow system—including failing to remember key dates and correct vocabulary terms—would have been one way to not "see" the contradictions all around them.[33]

PERSISTENT DISTANCING FROM THE MOVEMENT

Some participants more actively distanced themselves from the civil rights movement, downplaying its importance and rejecting it as part of their identity. Even though many claimed genuine appreciation toward some of the changes made possible by the civil rights movement, such as being able to eat at a restaurant with a black friend, very little gratitude was extended to the movement activists and organizers. Instead, people mostly portrayed the movement as something done by blacks for blacks. Several people belittled and criticized Martin Luther King Jr. Many rejected aspects of contemporary civil rights celebrations, such as commemorations of key events and activists, preferring to deemphasize that history or at least keep it segregated in the black community.

Downplaying Civil Rights Organizing

Several participants downplayed or trivialized African Americans' efforts at organizing and implementing civil rights protests. This was evident in descriptions of how demonstrators carried out their actions haphazardly and in lighthearted portrayals of protestors that belied the serious hazards risked by activists. Mae, 70s, flippantly described lunch counter protestors: "They didn't make any fuss or anything. They just got together and they just ambled in to Woolworth's and asked to be served." In actuality, Greensboro's sit-in movement was intricately planned and lasted for several years at numerous places of business; eventually thousands of people, young and old, participated. Such steadfast organization was necessitated by resistance from white business owners and city leaders. But Mae characterized the activists dismissively, stating that protestors "just got together" and "just ambled in to Woolworth's," as if the act had been spontaneous and its implementation lackadaisical.

Other respondents dismissed the courage of activists and the strength of white resistance by criticizing black Americans for waiting so long to start the civil rights movement. Florence, a woman in her 80s, said: "Had I been born black, I would've protested before *they* did. I would have. I have never understood how they had the patience as long as they did." Florence reasoned that African Americans' patience delayed their challenges to Jim Crow, while her own spirit for liberation could not have been contained. Similarly, John, 70s, said that he would have fought segregation forcefully if he were African American: "I remember Rosa Parks who refused to move to the back of the bus. And bless her heart, more power to her. I mean, I can't imagine being black and having somebody tell me where I had to sit. I'd be just belligerent enough, we woulda had a contest I think. (laughing) I mean, I am no great big and powerful built [man], but I can be mean as hell." (laughing) John laughed while telling of his imagined black self getting in physical altercations over segregation. He gave no indication that African Americans and movement activists risked enormous short-term and long-term consequences when they challenged Jim Crow laws and conventions. As is clear in these examples, when considering black protestors' experiences, the participants indicated that the activism was fairly easy, without serious risk, and could have been undertaken much earlier. The portrayals severely downplay the extent of white supremacy throughout the society.

Even those participants who claimed to have had very favorable views toward civil rights protestors downplayed the antioppression goals of the movement. Instead, their accounts tended to have congratulatory or patronizing tones. One couple complimented the student sit-in protestors for dressing well and being studious:

> Husband: I thought it was *great*—
> Wife: They really did flock to be a part of it . . . and the students were all studying—
> Husband: As it should have been.
> Wife: That's the interesting part. And they came to the counter looking nice.

The wife was most impressed with the calm demeanor of the protestors. Notably, the couple did not allude to the purpose of the sit-ins: to challenge racist policies. As the wife said, she felt "the interesting part" of the sit-ins was how college students were studious and well dressed.

These are all subtle ways in which participants downplayed the key role that civil rights organizers played in furthering human rights and social justice in the United States. Crediting protestors for being nonviolent, "looking nice," "just ambling in," and finally becoming impatient and standing up for themselves disregards the fundamental realities that movement activists put their lives and livelihoods on the line to challenge the Jim Crow system, and that they maintained the movement against sustained white resistance and backlash at interpersonal and institutional levels. Thus, many of the most positive portrayals of the civil rights movement diminished the value and worth of the activism and the activists.

Disowning Greensboro's Civil Rights Identity

Many people I interviewed seemed to resent Greensboro's identity as a key civil rights city. Several participants pointed out that Greensboro was not in fact the site of the *first* sit-in, and some argued flatly that their city did not warrant the title of "birthplace of the sit-ins." Sally, a woman in her 70s, said she heard it said "many times" that Greensboro did not spearhead the sit-in movement: "Actually they say somebody out in Ohio did it first." Florence, 80s, placed the "real" birthplace in Nebraska: "I thought it really started out in Omaha, Nebraska, is what I heard and that they did not get the publicity Greensboro got. That's what I've *heard*. Now I don't know how true that is. I've tried to look it up on the computer and I hadn't been able to trace . . ." Florence indicated that although she unsuccessfully attempted to use the Internet to verify that Greensboro did not spearhead the sit-in movement, she nevertheless thought this likely true.

Similarly, a married couple argued that Greensboro's sit-ins were nothing special and should not be regarded as "the model":

> Husband: Well it was advertised as being one of a kind, which is far from the truth. There were sit-ins all over the country. People have just recently come to realize that. . . . And I think there were sit-ins that happened before ours did.
> Wife: Oh, well, they had 'em before. There were other sit-ins. Greensboro likes to say that it was the model.

Indeed, there were instances of prior sit-in protests in the United States, dating back at least to the late 1930s. However, the "Greensboro Four" are lauded because their act on February 1, 1960, rapidly inspired a wave of similar protests across the South and ultimately led to the dismantling of segregation policies at thousands of white-owned businesses. The people quoted above, however, indicated that because Greensboro was not the site of the very first sit-in, their city deserved no special acclaim.

Patti, 80s, told a story of being flabbergasted by some northerners who came to visit years after the sit-ins and insisted that they go downtown to see the Woolworth's building:

> When [my friend got married] every Yankee friend of her sweet Yankee husband decided they were gonna come. . . . And the first

thing *anybody* wanted to do was go to Woolworth's. And, "*Why do you want to go to Woolworth's?*" "For the sit-ins." Uh, (laughing) "You want to go to *Woolworth's*? It's *closed*! You can't get in there!" "Well, we just want to see it, and we'll all go down there and stand on the street and look at Woolworth's." . . . I haven't gotten over that yet! (laughing) You just gonna go stand on the street and look at the closed-up building?! (laughs) And these were all white people who were doing it, you know.

Patti went on to reason that out-of-towners are naturally more interested in notorious local sites than community members. However, her astonishment reflects something more—that not all of Greensboro has embraced the sit-ins as a point of pride or identity. She found it laughable that anyone would view the Woolworth's site as an important historical marker.

In the following exchange, a wife and husband spoke of how the sit-ins have been commemorated in the city. The woman argued vehemently against the city identifying with the event:

Wife: That museum should be on the campus of A&T, where the students came from, not in downtown Greensboro. . . . And I'm not against the museum . . . but it should be down on the campus where the A&T students were and have it as a commemoration to *them*.
Husband: Isn't that statue of the four down on campus?
Interviewer: Mm-hm.
Wife: You see, put the museum down there with that.
Interviewer: Do you have any pride that the sit-ins happened here and that they started sit-ins all over the South?
Wife: . . . No, I'm not proud of that, no. No, we have other *things* to be proud of. O'Henry was born here, Dolley Madison was born here. Okay? Yes, Edward R. Murrow was born here. We are *very* proud of those citizens, absolutely. I admire these four young men that took the initiative for the sit-in. I admire their courage for it—
Husband: Took a lot of guts.
Wife: But these other people are to be admired more for what they did and the legacy that they have left for us.
Interviewer: Why is that?
Wife: Well, Dolley Madison was the wife of our fourth president! . . . O'Henry is known for his short stories. They've been translated into many, many, *many* foreign languages . . . Edward R. Murrow, who was the *leading* commentator and correspondent during the Second

World War . . . *These* are the people that really accomplished an awful lot. We had other people that accomplished things. We had another black man who did an awful lot for the city of Greensboro, Charles Henry Moore, who is not very well known, but he was a teacher and professor at the colleges here. He was instrumental in getting Bennett College established in Greensboro. He was instrumental in raising money for the black hospital, L. Richardson Hospital. He opened the door for a lot of the blacks and unfortunately he is not remembered like these other people, but he contributed a lot to *improve* their way of life.

While this woman claimed to admire the courage of the sit-in protestors, she resented that sit-in demonstrators had gained notoriety in her city above and beyond other individuals. The sit-ins all occurred at white-run segregated businesses and facilities and led to the permanent desegregation of those spaces, but she preferred acknowledgments of those sit-ins sequestered "where the students were," in the black community. In her view, the larger Greensboro community should instead recognize individuals who left a "legacy" "for us." The first individuals she named—O'Henry, Dolley Madison, and Edward R. Murrow—were born in Greensboro (and were white), but none of their key accomplishments occurred in the city. Nevertheless, she believed the city should identify with them and not with the Greensboro Four. Moore, the one black resident she thought worthy of Greensboro's praise, worked to expand African Americans' access to segregated educational and medical facilities (a black women's college and a black hospital); he thereby "improved their way of life," in contrast with civil rights activists. Undergirding this woman's arguments is a denial of the importance of dismantling segregation, for she found those individuals who inspired a key submovement of the civil rights movement unimpressive relative to a U.S. president's wife and an author of short stories—people who "really accomplished an awful lot."

To interpret this perspective, we start with the fundamental reality that the sit-in protests were aligned against segregation and therefore against the mainstream white society that enforced and condoned Jim Crow. Downgrading the importance of organizers and protestors diverts attention away from criticisms of white racism. To embrace the Greensboro Four and the thousands of other activists would be to acknowledge that there was injustice built into white institutions that

required sustained protests to dismantle. Dismissing the actions that
exposed Greensboro's systemic racism enables a perception of (white)
Greensboro as a "good" city. Further, it is likely that a key factor in this
woman's protectionist view of the city is her upper middle class status.
It has been people like her—possibly including political officials, pro-
fessionals, and business owners in her own social network—who have
run the city and who were confronted most directly with civil rights
activism. We can understand why this woman would perceive attacks on
segregation rather defensively—likely more so than those of lower-income backgrounds, who could more readily claim to be mere bystanders to the movement. (We will see in the next chapter how school
desegregation cut across all socioeconomic categories, indeed affecting
wealthy whites least; it was an issue that felt like an attack or trauma to a
great many whites in Greensboro.)

    In a final example of how the participants demonstrated active dis-
tancing from the sit-in demonstrations for which the city is famed,
Grant, 80s, argued that African Americans' protests were an offensive
affront to the progressive white leaders who had proven themselves to
be concerned with implementing racial equality:

> What troubled me in those days was that Greensboro . . . had been
> very progressive in trying to help this social dilemma of blacks and
> whites in the elimination of segregation. . . . People *wanted* to help.
> Leadership wanted to help. . . . And yet, when that confrontation
> occurred, there was total disregard for what the community had tried
> to do. It was almost like a war between the blacks and the whites,
> supported by the inordinately large population of students. And as an
> individual student, I suppose I would like to have helped the cause
> along. As a *community*, and being involved in the community, I
> found myself saying, Where is the respect for all that's taken place,
> and can we work this out amicably? And it was that the advance-
> ments that had *been* made were not respected, and that troubled me.
> (pause) Did it take an event such as the sit-ins to advance the cause?
> I suppose it *advanced* it. . . . If you'd asked the blacks, they'd say it's
> too late. If you ask me, I'd say it was too early. The cultural differ-
> ence . . . those who had been denied . . . by politics and laws—were
> they really ready to accept their position of responsibility within the
> broader community? Had they advanced their culture, their learn-
> ing, their practices? And I'm now distinguishing—sounds prejudicial.
> It *is* prejudicial, because there were differences. The differences

were *wrong*, no question about that. Every effort was being made to right it in an orderly and timely basis.

Similar to the woman in the previous excerpt, Grant's perspective is aligned with the city's white elite. As Grant saw it, the sit-in protests attacked Greensboro's leaders and their good-faith efforts to improve the status of African Americans—at a pace deemed appropriate by whites. With paternalistic reasoning, Grant constructed segregation-era white elites as the benefactors of blacks who were not "really ready to accept their position of responsibility within the larger community." Above, Grant exemplifies the "personification" maneuver through pointing out that African Americans were denied advancement "by politics and laws."[34] Grant subverts the reality that it was white elites—whom he cast as blacks' benefactors—who in fact held the institutional power to create and enforce discriminatory segregation laws.

As the interview quotes here demonstrate, few of Greensboro's white elders have embraced the city's identity as an important site of the civil rights struggle, for that identity challenges their notion of white Greensboro as having long been a place of good race relations and progressive whites. As William Chafe observed, Greensboro clung to its "progressive mystique"—its claim to fame as a place immune from hatefulness and overt racism—throughout the Jim Crow and civil rights eras.[35] To maintain a grasp on this idea of a never-racist Greensboro, some white elders resent their city's title as the birthplace of the sit-in movement.

Dethroning King

Few specific civil rights figures were discussed in the interviews, because I was interested in people constructing an autobiographical narrative, not in quizzing them on history. However, nearly all participants were asked about how they remembered Martin Luther King Jr.: Did they remember him having visited and spoken in Greensboro in 1958? (Virtually no one did.) How was he regarded in their social circles? How did they remember his assassination? Through their responses, many people diminished the movement by trivializing and denigrating King. Numerous portrayals denied King status as an American icon. Overall, people tended to acknowledge King's leadership and appreciate his emphasis on nonviolence, but they demonstrated a lack of knowledge about him and a lack of a personal connection. Even among those who claimed to have always thought highly of King there was a marked dispassion when discussing his assassination—especially when compared to their emotional and detailed memories of John F. Kennedy's assassination. In addition, quite a number of people criticized King for being a lackluster leader, a troublemaker, a self-serving man, and an immoral husband.

Among the people who were most sympathetic to King's life work and his murder, social distance was evident in their inaccurate, vague memories and their unemotional delivery. Frances, 70s, remembered having had no awareness of King until his murder, and when I asked her how she had felt about him being assassinated, she answered tersely: "Well just like anybody *else* being killed who was an important person." She offered no further description of her reaction, merely claiming that she would react appropriately to the death of a person of stature. Darla, 70s, spoke in lengthy detail about how deeply she had been affected by John F. Kennedy's death and what a terrible a moment it had been for the whole country. A bit later she shared a vague and brief description of King's assassination:

> I remember hearin' that on the news. He was on a balcony, I think, when they shot him. Or, somebody shot him from a balcony . . . and I was really sorry about that, 'cause I *did* feel like he was tryin' to do the right thing. But I think you're fearful for somebody like that, who is so opinionated and who just idn't afraid to just say what they think and live by what they believe. I mean, you're gonna have a lot of people who are gonna be unhappy with you.

Darla was unsure of the exact conditions of the assassination. She said she was "sorry" about the murder and identified King as on the side of justice, "tryin' to do the right thing." However, Darla did not emphasize the assassination as a tragedy like she did when recalling the deaths of both John F. and Bobby Kennedy. Instead, she reasoned out why King had enemies.

Frances and Darla expressed no close connection to King's life work or sudden death. Even those who claimed that they highly regarded King typically tempered their praise in some way. For example, Ava, 60s, claimed that, upon King's death, she "sat down and sobbed like I did when the president died." However, she shared that she did not agree with everything King stood for:

> My feelings about Martin Luther King was that this was one of the greatest men that I had ever seen, as far as how smart he was and what his thinkin' was. . . . When he said things like "One of these days we'll all be known as the same" and that kinda thing, to me that's the way it always shoulda been. And I admired him greatly because he thought a whole lot the way that I thought, except for the fact that he felt like that blacks were being mistreated.

Ava's comments indicate that she admired the idealistic King who yearned for an equal society, but rejected the activist King who identified anti-black oppression as a social problem. She could not agree that African Americans faced "mistreatment" during segregation.

Others' sympathy for King extended only to his nuclear family—to the wife and children who were abandoned and bereaved. In this way, participants disregarded King's status as a key leader of a social movement, relegating him to the individualized, family roles of father and husband. For example, after she talked at length about how deeply she was affected by the deaths of John F. Kennedy and Bobby Kennedy, Trudie, 60s, said she felt sorry for King's family after the assassination:

> I guess bein' a family person, I thought of it more on a personal basis, of his family, what have you done. . . . But I thought, "Man, he shot a young man with a wife," and if I'm not mistaken he has four children, and I thought, "This is such a terrible tragedy, and the man is just tryin' to do what he feels is right and he has a right to speech and whatever he wants to say" . . . but I think I felt more for the family than the movement, 'cause the movement was people I didn't *know*. Martin Luther King you *knew*, and you knew him more or less in your heart, and I really felt sorry for his family.

When describing what she admired about King, Trudie spoke of his moral principles and rights to free speech, which emphasize him as an individual rather than as a leader. She implied also that her individualization of King as a family man reflected her positive regard for him; she preferred not to consider him the head of an impersonal social movement: "The movement was people I didn't *know*." For Trudie, civil rights activists were foreign to her, even though thousands of residents from her home city—mostly African American, but also some white—had participated in movement activism for close to a decade prior to King's death.

It was common for people to deny King status as an American hero and to sanitize his message. Florence, 80s, argued that Booker T. Washington did "so much more" for African Americans than King ever did, but that his "dream" was commendable:

> He seemed to be a good leader that *inspired* a lot of people. I felt like if they *really* wanted a *real* hero, they could go back to Booker T. Washington, who did so much more or made a bigger contribution with his work with the peanuts and all that stuff. But I felt like that he was of a different generation and of a different *time*, and that the time that Martin Luther King lived they needed a leader to look up to. Of course they overlook all of his philandering. I think that the blacks have a way of doing that anyway—I mean, they overlook Jesse Jackson's love child and things like that. But I think his speech that he had a dream, that was a commendable thing and for them to think about that, and for every black child as well as white children to have a *dream*, a *goal*, something to strive for and to try to achieve.

Florence first acknowledged King's leadership, then argued against idolizing him, then criticized African Americans for not condemning King (or others) for adultery. Last, she misrepresented and trivialized King's "I Have a Dream" speech, indicating that his message was about inspiring youth to set personal goals rather than an indictment of racial oppression.

Burt, 80s, expressed an even more disparaging perspective on King and the movement, admitting that he was "no great admirer" of King, a man he regarded as a philanderer, opportunist, and unworthy hero:

> Burt: I learned that Martin Luther King was not the good Christian man—he had a lot of girlfriends 'round here and there. . . . My opinion of Martin Luther King was really they sort of made him a hero. They didn't pick the right person. I could have picked a lot of better heroes for the blacks, but let it be.
> Interviewer: I was going to ask you who you would have chosen.
> Burt: I don't have anybody just—just—
> Interviewer: What were your feelings when he died in 1968?

Burt: (pause) I thought it was a shame that he was shot. It didn't disturb me a great deal. I didn't jump for joy, I didn't say the assassin was a hero, I didn't say we've lost. I said to myself, "The blacks have lost a leader." I didn't think that the country had lost anybody great. My own opinion was that he latched on to an ideal and played it for all it was worth and I was no great admirer of him.

Interviewer: When you say he latched on to an ideal, what specifically do you mean?

Burt: I mean, he was preaching racial equality, racial acceptance, there should be no segregation at all, and he made a lot of money, in my judgment, being paid for speeches and working on that. If he really believed it, I don't fault him for it. I think he figured he had a good thing going.

In addition to criticizing King for not being a "good Christian man," Burt painted King as an opportunist who engaged in civil rights activism for the money and fame.

Across the narratives it was clear that Martin Luther King Jr. is, to this day, not universally embraced as an American icon, at least not on his own terms. The participants downplayed or whitewashed King's activism and his actual messages, or they rejected King outright, giving him over fully to African Americans who accepted him as a leader. Heroification is a political and patriotic act that inevitably simplifies the individuals being praised. Nevertheless, King is one of a handful of African Americans who have been granted this status in contemporary American society. To put it in context, monuments and commemorations that glorify proslavery whites, whites who fought to end Reconstruction, and white racist terrorists are still common in the South and across the United States.[36] And the way in which King has been memorialized for the American public disregards his firm antiracist, anticlassist, and antigovernment standpoints; he has been watered down from a radical activist to a man who preached nonviolence and brotherhood.[37] Thus, that many participants rejected King on some level despite his having already been significantly "whitewashed" and made palatable to mainstream white Americans is even more noteworthy.

In a final example, Suzanne, a woman in her 60s, expressed confusion over why King would be worthy of American commemoration more so than other prominent, less controversial individuals, like Elvis Presley:

I don't feel today it's right because *he* was assassinated—and dedicate all this stuff to him, or highways or buildings—and a holiday! I mean, why wasn't Elvis Presley Day a holiday? (laughs) He never hurt anybody, he stayed out of religion, but yet he brought a lotta enjoyment to millions. We didn't declare his death a holiday. . . . There's just a imbalance in things we go after. What makes that one more important than the other one?

It is clear that Suzanne and numerous other participants missed or rejected the contemporary American consensus that Martin Luther King Jr. was a key leader in an American struggle for human rights to dismantle oppression and to fight for the American ideal of "liberty and justice for all." Their trivialization and rejection of King, as well as their downplaying of civil rights organizing and disowning Greensboro's sit-in identity, reflect a persistent distancing from the civil rights movement.

Five days after King's assassination, two letters to the editor about his death ran in the local newspaper, the *Greensboro Record*, one suggesting that if the American flag was to be flown at half-mast for King, then it should also be flown for troops "dying for a cause" in Vietnam. The other letter was more blatant in its resentment of King's memorialization: "I'd like to say the flag flying half-mast for King is wrong because I don't think he deserved it."[38] The interview excerpts indicate that some white southerners who lived through the civil rights era have maintained anti-King sentiment for over four decades and have not accepted contemporary mainstream commemorations to King and his legacy. Despite the fact that memory is in constant flux, people can maintain perceptions across time, even while the broader society is recrafting the national narrative.

WHITE VICTIMHOOD: TENSION AND DANGER IN LOCAL CIVIL RIGHTS ACTIVISM

The final theme apparent in participants' narratives of the civil rights era was of *white victimhood*. In defining victimhood, I draw from James Holstein and Gale Miller's call to see victimization as an interactional and descriptive process of labeling and meaning making, where we should "examine the practices through which a sense of 'victim-as-a-fact' is achieved."[39] Holstein and Miller argue that victimhood has four primary objectives: deflecting responsibility (asserting innocence), assigning causes (identifying the victimizer), specifying responses and remedies (for example, compensating the victim or punishing the victimizer), and accounting for failure (explaining away the victim's flaws).[40] Thus, key to the victimhood process is the creation of a blameless victim as well as a victimizer. And implying that something ought to be done to right the wrong, victimhood works to construct what injustice and justice look like. Victimhood claims "are not disembodied commentaries on ostensibly real states of affairs. Rather, they are reality *projects*—acts of constructing the world."[41]

By *white* victimhood, I refer to the phenomenon of whites constructing themselves as racial victims. In the interviews it was common for participants to portray themselves as racially vulnerable during the civil rights era—either made real victims or potential victims via targeting by African Americans (e.g., dangerous protestors) or impersonal institutional forces (e.g., school desegregation). Because white victimhood implies white innocence, the threat-victimization theme supports the first theme discussed—the construction of the perpetual nonracist white self. Constructing white southerners as racial victims in the midst of the civil rights era diverts attention away from the reality of Jim Crow structural racism. Indeed, white victimhood redefines the civil rights era as a period in which whites were unjustly targeted, rather than a period of challenge and triumph over long-standing injustice.

During the protests at segregated businesses that began in Greensboro in February 1960, my participants ranged in age from youths to adults and parents in their 30s and 40s. In the interviews they portrayed protestors as mostly nonviolent and possibly easily provoked, and the milieu as tense and potentially explosive. White bystanders were portrayed as being subjected to moments of inconvenience, tension, and likely violence due to protest actions. People sometimes characterized nonviolent protests as actions hostile toward white southerners' sense of safety and normalcy. Many people said that they attempted to steer clear of the civil rights protests in Greensboro. Several recalled that white business owners feared vandalism and robbery, and parents kept their children at home, trying to avoid exposing them to anything dangerous.

Nevertheless, downtown Greensboro remained a major site of city commerce throughout the civil rights era, and several interviewees witnessed protests firsthand. In their descriptions, they recalled the palpable tension, and often they cast themselves as victims or potential victims. They remembered being uncomfortably unsure as to what would happen in the short term: Might there be skirmishes? Might a spark set off an explosive chain of events? In a typical portrayal, Sharon, a woman in her 60s, went against the wishes of her protective parents and saw a sit-in protest at Woolworth's lunch counter: "I remember [my dad] asked me not to go over there because it was very tense and people just *didn't* know what would happen. And whites were especially tense. And I *didn't* go inside the Woolworth but I *stepped* into the vestibule area in there and saw it, and (pause) I remember that being very big, very tense." As Sharon indicated, the white community feared the protests. Many forbade their children from being near them. Sharon still recalled the tension.

Kenneth, 80s, talked about having witnessed a protest and his relief at coming out unscathed:

> There was a mob—I don't know how many, but I know the street was full of blacks, and (chuckles) [the owner] was standing in the door of his cafeteria and he said he wouldn't let 'em in. And just as I got outside . . . down to the corner across the street where I'd parked, they rushed him. (chuckling) And here I am almost in the middle of this crowd of upset people, and I just got out and just kept going.

Kenneth described his avoidance of the black "mob." Like Kenneth, several participants used loaded terms like "mob" and "riot" to describe nonviolent protestors—dehumanizing terms that also imply disorganization, unruliness, and intent to cause harm. This language situates protestors as attackers and Kenneth as a likely target as well. This portrayal goes against a key detail he shared about the scene—that the restaurant owner was managing singlehandedly to hold back a whole "crowd of upset people." Thus, they must not have been physically aggressive, and it is no wonder that Kenneth easily slipped away.

In a description of danger and fear more nuanced than many others, Suzanne, 60s, acknowledged that black Americans may have been fearful also during the sit-in protests. And then she transitioned to complaining about political correctness:

At that time . . . my mother'd take us downtown to shop every weekend, and that was just our highlight of the week to get to go downtown in peanut shops down there and get to go to the luncheon counter, and we felt we were really in the world then. And after that sit-in I can remember my mother sayin', "We aren't going. We can't go anymore." . . . She was fearful of what was going to happen. One of us would get hurt, we would get caught up in something, a fight that would develop, or somebody would lose control and we'd be in their path or something. And we felt fear. And I didn't say *blacks* didn't feel fear. I think maybe they felt like they had to do what they were doin' no matter how they got there. But like I said, it shouldn't have been that way in the first place, but it was, and it did need to change, but I don't think either side should have to fear. But I can remember being very fearful to speak up and say how I felt about something. I think we fear that *today*. . . . You can't say I'm gonna eat more chicken without being in trouble. You can't say I love water-melon without being in trouble. Why?

In her comments, Suzanne did something that few other interviewees did: she acknowledged the danger that protestors faced and expressed empathy for their situation. Nevertheless, she went on to argue that whites are unfairly scrutinized for saying things that African Americans might find offensive ("we fear that *today*. . . . You can't say I'm gonna eat more chicken without being in trouble"). In her portrayal of the sit-ins, she constructed both whites and blacks as threatened, and she built upon her point by constructing whites as victims, people whose speech is curiously and unfairly targeted today.

On the other hand, Gracie, 80s, claimed that whites and blacks were both apprehensive regarding the protests, but she focused on the danger to black protestors at the hands of white police and white suprema-cists (although it is difficult to posit why she chuckled):

Gracie: I think some of the black people were apprehensive, because they realized that there was a real danger to them.
Interviewer: Danger of what?
Gracie: Well, I mean, of being mistreated by the police, or white people goin' after 'em. (chuckles) And 'course the Ku Klux Klan—it hadn't died out. (chuckles)

Overall, people portrayed the period of civil rights protest in Greensboro as a time of uncertainty and fear, and very few (such as Gracie) indicated that African Americans were likely to be victimized or targeted by white vigilantes or white institutions. White southerners were portrayed as innocent bystanders and potential victims of the chaos being created all around them. This perspective lends support to the notion, detailed in previous chapters, that the segregation era was a peaceful time, when life was predictable and calm and when whites and blacks got along well. I focus on Trudie's narrative below, because it demonstrates how closely "racial violence" is conflated with the civil rights era in some white southerners' minds.

Trudie: Associating Protests with Violence

It was common for participants to conflate African Americans' peaceful civil rights protests with danger and violence toward whites. Trudie's, 60s, narrative provides a vivid illustration of the implicit association between black protests and violence, danger, and whites' compromised safety. The first time Trudie's fear of civil rights protestors came up was when I asked if she had been aware of any "racial violence" in her younger years; at this point in the interview we were focusing on the segregation era and her childhood. She responded, "I had [an] incident that scared me half to death. It was scarin' me when they would lock the doors of [my downtown workplace] and tell us to go home. I thought, 'You still puttin' us in danger, 'cause they could still be outside.'" Trudie said she was scared "half to death" at being expected to travel in downtown streets where protestors might be present. Notably, my mention of "racial violence" prompted that emotional account of her fear of black protestors, even though we had been discussing segregation and had not yet broached the subject of the civil rights movement. She constructed "racial violence," then, as her own potential victimization by black perpetrators.

Later in the interview I asked Trudie to clarify the extent of her exposure to actual violence. She elaborated on fearing for her own safety during civil rights protesting and the violence that she assumed was happening and that she had been lucky to avoid:

> Interviewer: So have you *seen* any violence?

Trudie: (pause) Well, I can remember goin' to the *bank* with all the money [from my workplace] to deposit it by myself all the time. But the minute the riots started and everything started bein' stirred up by the colleges and whatever here, then I could not go to the bank alone. I had to have . . . someone to go with me and *that* used to really scare me . . . and I guess in a way I was a little bit . . . naïve due to the way I was brought up. I was just either kept in my house or at work and so I didn't really see probably a lot of the violence that did go on.

Trudie positioned African American college students as antagonists who "stirred up" "riots" and caused her to fear being robbed as she traveled, even with an escort, the downtown streets. She bolstered the validity of her fear by implying that there was even *more* violence than she had been exposed to due to living a cloistered life ("I was a little bit naïve. . . . I didn't really see probably a lot of the violence that did go on").

Trudie's use of the term "riots" piqued my curiosity, for Greensboro's sit-ins are known generally to have been nonviolent. When I asked Trudie to clarify what she meant by "riots," she referenced the peaceful sit-ins and then finally admitted that she never knew of a riot that happened in Greensboro:

Interviewer: So when you talk about riots that happened, what kinds of things were happening?
Trudie: Well, it would be like everybody out of curiosity would naturally go to Woolworth's, see what was goin' on and how many were sittin' at the counter, blah blah blah. Waitresses were so nervous servin' these people because they didn't know what was happenin'. Blacks were happy, the whites you could tell were unhappy. And then I would go back down to Kress's and wouldn't be too long before they'd fill up Kress's lunch counter. But I really couldn't say I saw a riot. The riotin' I did see would have been on TV, but as far as bein' in and around a riot, no. I wasn't allowed to go outside my home. Usually during those times, we pretty much stayed at home, and of course there was church, church, church. (laughs)

So Trudie felt the tension as she witnessed sit-ins and believed there were violent riots in Greensboro set off by the demonstrators' actions. Again she implied that if her life had been less cloistered, she might have seen bona fide riots. It appears that Trudie closely associated black protests of any form with black people committing violence. Given her explanation that "the riotin' I did see would have been on TV," it seems likely that Trudie's association between black protestors and violent riots was formed in connection with mainstream media coverage, such as news of urban riots in the late 1960s, several years after Greensboro's sit-in demonstrations.

Nora: Constructing the Volatility of Peaceful Protests

Of all the people interviewed, Nora, 80s, had the most firsthand exposure to African Americans' protests in Greensboro. She worked downtown during the 1960s and encountered protest demonstrations as she carried out her business during the work week. She described witnessing four significant events: one of the first days of the Woolworth's lunch counter sit-in, a group of African Americans attempting to gain entry to a whites-only cafeteria (possibly the same one described above by Kenneth), picketing on the sidewalks, and a large prayer demonstration by students in front of city hall. Primarily, Nora's stories of these encounters positioned black protestors as dominant and potentially volatile figures, while whites were positioned as innocent bystanders and fair-minded people trying to avoid conflict.

First, Nora described seeing one of the initial days of the famous Woolworth's lunch counter sit-in:

> I've been at the restaurant there at the Woolworth's dime store, talkin' to [the] manager of it when the four black boys walked in and sat down at the counter. I didn't get to stay—my lunch hour ran out. I didn't see anything . . . other than that [the manager] told one of the clerks to go ahead and wait on them, said, "Go ahead and *serve* 'em." The [server] was wantin' to sorta back off. I guess she was afraid to get that close to 'em, but they were nice looking, well-dressed African American young men. And they never did serve 'em, but [the manager] did ask them to.

This was Nora's most favorable portrayal of protestors. As her narrative progressed, she increasingly described protestors and the situations they created as potentially violent and anti-white. Next she told of encountering a group of people being barred from entering a whites-only cafeteria:

> Nora: And then the *next* day when I was going to lunch, I decided I'd go to the cafeteria . . . and when I went by, [the owner] who had been our mayor just a coupla years before, he had backed up, put his hands on the doorknobs and was standin' there, and some of 'em wanted to come in and he said, "I'm sorry, I just can't serve you." He didn't raise his voice at 'em or anything . . . but he didn't give in. And I thought, sooner or later somebody's gonna get *hurt* with this, because one of 'em go off sorta halfway hit an officer or something . . .
> Interviewer: Did you go in to eat that day?
> Nora: Oh yeah, I went on to eat that day. Shoot yeah, I'm not gon' miss my meals! (laughs) No, I'm not gonna let any of 'em cause me to miss my meals.

Nora portrayed the owner as firm but calm and the protestors as the potential creators of a violent altercation, possibly assaulting police officers ("one of 'em go off sorta halfway hit an officer or something"). She also laughingly characterized the protestors as a nuisance that she was able to circumvent in her quest for lunch as usual. Next, Nora recalled picketers on the sidewalk:

> It would be aggravating sometimes if you were on your lunch hour and there's a dozen going down the street walking three abreast! . . . It could be a big hindrance. . . . Sometimes they'd stop with their placards on and naturally you weren't gonna say, "E*xcuse* me, sir!" and step up in *front* of 'em. But unless it was something like that, I just ignored it. . . . They've got as much right on the sidewalk as I have I guess, so I tried to sorta wiggle in and out and not bother them.

Although Nora here said that she was able to navigate through the demonstrators, she believed that it would have been a major error to speak to them ("naturally you weren't gonna say, 'E*xcuse* me, sir!'"). Nora was convinced that there had been serious danger of volatility to avoid.

On this same theme of blacks' sensitivity and potentially explosive retaliations against white bystanders, Nora's last story of encountering African American protestors positioned herself as having luckily emerged unscathed from a peaceful prayer demonstration. She continued to believe that she had placed herself in serious danger by cracking a mild joke within earshot of black high school and college students who knelt in prayer on the steps of city hall:

> They had a long walk of students . . . I mean, a *parade* of them, and they came to city hall and . . . they were all knelt down and going to have prayer for the American people . . . And I was just having to step around wherever I could to get down between the people and . . . [a male acquaintance] said, "How long are they planning to stay here?" And I said, "They'll leave when the pigeons come to roost." 'Cause I mean (laughing) we had pigeons by the *hundred*—they'd roost up on the ledge. . . . [And] about six heads (laughing) popped up and . . . it was all I could do not to laugh. But I would not have laughed and given them any reason to have gotten up and hit me or anything like that. And [the man who was with me] got afraid that one of 'em would get angry and would get up and start a fight or something. . . . And when I got home my husband agreed with him! (laughing) . . . He said, "If you have to, walk all the way around the block! But don't make any comments." . . . Now that everybody's telling me about how quick I could've set off a fight or an uprising, I said I would not *do* it again! And I *wouldn't*!

Over forty years later, Nora perceived her joke as a very close call, although—notice how often she laughed while telling it—she recalled it also as a funny story. She clearly regretted having made the flippant remark, not because it was disrespectful or unkind, but because it could have sparked an "uprising" by angry black youth in which she would have been the target of their aggression. This interpretation defies rationality, for it was a prayer demonstration by African American youth. However, long ago others—her husband and another white man—convinced her that she should view the incident with fear.

Indeed, Nora maintained a whites-as-potential-victims, blacks-as-aggressors perspective on this event. When I inquired about the purpose of the youths' demonstration, she did not believe that they had a legitimate one, perhaps other than to gain visibility or to taunt white adults:

> I think that they just wanted to be seen. . . . When they came to the city hall that day and knelt down as if they were in prayer, I felt like that they were just trying to make a . . . statement to us that "One day

I may have your job." . . . I don't think that *any* of 'em were *prayin'*. I don't think it was a thing about Christianity or anything like that. . . . It did not make any sense . . . to me.

Not only did Nora perceive of African Americans' protests as volatile situations in which whites were prudent to tread lightly, she also read aggressiveness in protestors' intent, as she believed that they used spirituality to mask a hostile message to whites about blacks' impending dominance. Notice that Nora presented black protestors as threatening both physically and economically. African Americans were presented as antagonists carrying out a vendetta against whites, making it difficult for ordinary, innocent citizens like her to go about their business. Overall, Nora's portrayals of her firsthand experiences with civil rights protests denied the reality of systemic anti-black oppression under segregation ("It did not make any sense to me"), as she indicated that their protests must have had superficial targets or ulterior motives.

As many of the interview quotes here show, when recalling the civil rights era, many people remembered it primarily as a time of chaos and vulnerability for whites. For numerous individuals, the fearful memories were not simply what they witnessed, but were infused with imagery of African Americans as violent and unpredictable. By constructing themselves as vulnerable bystanders amid dangerous civil rights protests, participants delegitimized the civil rights movement.

FOR THEM, BY THEM: NOT OUR MOVEMENT

These white southerners' portrayals of the civil rights movement and the large-scale changes it rendered were complex—a combination of positive and negative, both within and across interviews. On the positive side, people presented the civil rights era as important due to its bringing integration, which they said—almost to a person—was a change that needed to occur. Looking back on the era, most acknowledged on some level the utility and worth of civil rights activism and often favorably referenced the nonviolent protest strategies. But, overwhelmingly, they presented the time period as unfortunate and troublesome by causing whites to feel fear, bringing chaos into daily life, and instigating unnecessary racial animosities. When reflecting on what it was like to experience the 1960s firsthand, they emphasized whites' feelings of hardship and victimization and decontextualized the movement from its goals and strategies. That larger context that they knew intellectually (i.e., this social movement brought about greater equality and opportunity) all but disappeared in their storytelling.

Certainly the civil rights movement challenged the accepted way of life whites had found rather comfortable and predictable during Jim Crow and, as such, few white southerners could fully embrace it as a movement that benefited all of society. Interestingly, very few mentioned the reality that there were white participants in the movement, an omission that reinforces the notion that this was solely an effort *by* blacks *for* blacks. Social distance had typified white southerners' relations to black southerners during the segregation era, regardless of their sometimes intimate relationships with black individuals.[42] Thus, civil rights–era white southerners were virtually unpracticed in aligning their perceptions, interests, or empathy with African Americans in the quest for civil rights.

5

WHITE VICTIMS

Trials and Tribulations of
School Desegregation

The history of public education in the United States has been rife with racial struggle.[1] Enslaved African Americans regularly risked severe penalties to gain even a modest amount of literacy and education, and, in the wake of emancipation, African Americans and other groups of color, with much personal and financial sacrifice, opened their own schools and fought for universal education.[2] Great efforts toward creating a quality public education were pursued during the brief Reconstruction period in the South (1865–1877), but, as the white elite power structure became reestablished, resources were reallocated away from black schools for other uses.[3] By the early decades of the twentieth century, segregated schools institutionalized enormous racial inequalities:

> No matter how it was measured—by the quality of the facilities, the length of the school term, financial appropriations, student–teacher ratio, curriculum, teachers' preparation and salaries—the education available to black children in the New South was vastly inferior to that available to white children. At least twice as much was spent on white students as on black students. . . . The minimum salary for white teachers was nearly twice as high as the maximum salary paid black teachers. Few books or supplies were available in black

schools. . . . No one pretended to take seriously the Supreme Court decision commanding separate but equal schools.[4]

Despite the glaring inequalities, whites consistently fought to keep their schools with superior funding and resources, and only when under great political pressure acquiesced to changes that would bring greater equity in schooling.[5] After many decades of unequal segregated schooling, the U.S. Supreme Court handed down its landmark *Brown v. Board of Education of Topeka, Kansas* (1954) decision, which asserted the unconstitutionality of racially segregated school systems. The decision sent ripples through the nation, and immediate and severe white backlash ensued.[6] Throughout the South, much of the white resistance to the prospect of school desegregation invoked "states' rights" discourse and fanciful notions that Jim Crow's pleasant race relations would be devastated by integration.[7]

This chapter analyzes how the interview participants remembered the school desegregation process in Greensboro. The theme of white victimhood that we explored in the previous chapter is highlighted again here, for it was especially prominent in people's storytelling around their children's experiences in transitioning schools. Through accounts of arbitrary school assignments, "forced" busing, chaotic classrooms, and even African American bullies, many narratives painted a portrait of school integration that constructed whites as the pawns of impersonal mandates and as victims of a traumatic ordeal. While virtually all participants readily acknowledged that segregated schools had been unequal for black students, many nevertheless focused heavily on the myriad ways in which they perceived that white children and families had been done a disservice by integrating schools. Again I highlight the tension between people stating that they agreed with the principle of desegregation and resenting how it occurred. I argue in this chapter that white southerners' remembering themselves as vulnerable and/or victims during the civil rights era facilitates a certain kind of identity maintenance in which they are able to preserve their perception of themselves, and the white South, as largely nonracist.

GREENSBORO'S SCHOOL DESEGREGATION SAGA

Greensboro, North Carolina, was the setting of a fascinating saga of school integration. The night after the Supreme Court ruled on *Brown* (1954), finding segregated schools unconstitutional, the Greensboro school board gathered for their scheduled monthly meeting. The chairman presented a new item of business—a resolution to proactively carry out the Supreme Court's desegregation ruling. After a brief debate, the board (composed of six white males and one black male) voted six to one in favor of the resolution.[8] True to its progressive reputation, Greensboro became the first city in the South to publicly state its willingness and readiness to comply with the *Brown v. Board* decision.[9] "Greensboro's decisive response seemed a good omen to those who perceived the city as a leader of the modern South."[10] However, Greensboro wound up being one of the very *last* school districts in the South to implement a comprehensive school desegregation plan—a full *seventeen* years later, in 1971.

According to historian William Chafe, despite their promising resolution in 1954, the Greensboro school board adopted "the most minimal steps toward desegregation, and then only under pressure."[11] A handful of black students were allowed to enroll in white schools in the late 1950s, and it was years later, in 1963, that the school board launched a weak "freedom of choice" integration plan, where African American first graders were allowed to enroll in previously all-white schools. A couple hundred black children made the transition.[12] Then, when Title VI of the 1964 Civil Rights Act mandated that each school district submit a comprehensive desegregation plan, Greensboro responded by making freedom of choice available for African Americans in all grades, but only for the first ten days of the 1965 school year.[13]

These steps produced only superficial integration. By 1967 the proportion of African Americans attending desegregated schools in Greensboro was significantly lower than in other comparable cities in the region.[14] Freedom of choice in Greensboro, popular among whites, was a sham. Through it the school board actually facilitated backward movement in school desegregation. As Chafe explains:

> When white children lived close to a black school, the board of education provided buses so that the children could attend a predominantly white school. When black children wished to attend a

predominantly white school, however, the board offered no transportation unless 50 per cent of the children in the black neighborhood
wished to transfer. . . . Blacks wishing to attend white high
schools . . . had to provide their own transportation. . . . The school
board refused even to provide passes for riding on city buses.[15]

As the sole African American member of the school board later recalled, "the powers that be . . . were determined to fight a last ditch
stand and to maintain the status quo as long as they possibly could."[16]

The Greensboro school board went so far as to take on the federal
government. In 1968 the Department of Health, Education, and Welfare declared Greensboro in noncompliance with desegregation mandates and threatened to revoke more than a million dollars in federal
funding. In response, the school board threatened to appeal to the
Supreme Court to retain their freedom of choice plan.[17] According to
Chafe, the Greensboro school integration issue was an effective indicator of the attitudes of the city's white elite: "Deeply convinced of the
moral virtue of their position, Greensboro's white leaders . . . had
passed—in their own eyes once and for all—the test of moral and legal
compliance with desegregation. . . . No matter what others might say or
do, they had justice on their side and would win."[18] Due to their noncompliance the Greensboro school system weathered the loss of federal
funds and kept fighting in the courts to keep freedom of choice, which
had been in effect at that point for eight years (1963–1971). Twenty-
seven city schools were still effectively segregated, with over 95 percent
either white or black students.[19] Then, a major shift in school board
membership occurred, where three staunch freedom of choice proponents were replaced by more moderate members, and a new chairman
was named. Quickly, in the 1971 summer months, a full desegregation
plan with comprehensive school assignment and busing programs was
submitted and approved at the federal level and implemented at the
start of the 1971–1972 academic year.[20]

Despite its school integration foot-dragging debacle, Greensboro
held fast to its progressive reputation. This is how the city's school
desegregation is described in the book *A Celebration of Guilford
County since 1890*, published in 1980 by the county commissioners:

The completely integrated system began operations without incident. This exemplifies the quality of leadership and the nature of

race relations in the Gate City. While places such as Boston, Louis-
ville, and Flint, Michigan, experienced violent resistance to busing,
the citizens of Greensboro placed education and community spirit
above other considerations.[21]

This glowing portrayal ignored Greensboro's slow pace of integration
and highlighted instead how smoothly and cooperatively school desegregation occurred compared to areas outside the Deep South, implying
that Greensboro's racial progressiveness exceeded that of much of the
nation. Rather, only a few school districts in the United States took
longer after *Brown v. Board* to implement public school integration
than Greensboro did. It is true that the city's 1971 comprehensive integration plan was not met with violent resistance, but white city leadership spent nearly two decades shrewdly avoiding large-scale desegregation efforts, and significant opposition emerged from the white community.[22] White Greensboro's progressive mystique was a cherished conviction that was able to thrive despite much contradictory evidence.

Opposition Movements

Greensboro residents did not all embrace the comprehensive school
integration plan mandated in 1971, even in the black community. From
the city's Black Power faction, a school integration opposition movement emerged among some young leaders who did not want to suffer
the loss of all their majority-black schools and who argued that school
desegregation was being promoted as the city's cure-all for institutional
discrimination.[23] One black community leader advocated "natural desegregation" via economic development in black communities that
would decrease racial inequality, leading to open housing and viable
neighborhood schools.[24] However, most of the high-profile African
American leaders in Greensboro had either served as plaintiffs in the
original court cases or had long been advocates for school desegregation; the black opposition movement quickly acquiesced to the pru-
dence of black unity in supporting school integration.[25]

White residents' vocal resistance to comprehensive school desegregation was more significant and sustained. White parents formed a new
organization, Americans Concerned about Today (ACT). The group
organized a boycott of the school reassignment procedures by asking

parents to try to enroll their kids in the schools they would have attended under the prior year's freedom of choice plan and to "sympathy
boycott" by keeping at home children whose school assignments had
remained unchanged.[26] Hundreds of parents attended meetings of
ACT in late summer 1971, just before comprehensive desegregation
was set to occur, but interest in participating in boycotts and legal
actions waned. As the school year began, some white parents accepted
the changes. Others chose to flee quietly rather than fight: enrollments
outside the city public school system soared. Several new private
schools were established in Greensboro and serviced the approximately
2,000 mostly wealthier and white students who left city schools, and the
predominantly white county school system gained 500–700 students.[27]
One of the new private schools, Vandalia Christian Academy, which
promised to emphasize discipline and Christian teachings, enrolled
over 300 students for the first day of the 1971 school year and was
"besieged for days by others trying to get in."[28]

The pastor of Vandalia's sponsoring church was quoted in the newspaper as saying the school was restricted to white students because
"Negro children would cause us problems in that tensions would develop."[29] Coded, rather than overtly racist, language was laced throughout
Greensboro whites' public opposition to school integration. Several
antidesegregation letters to the editor appeared in Greensboro's (white)
local newspaper at the onset of the 1971 academic year, with most
employing rhetoric of "tyranny" and "communism" threatening to de-
stroy "liberty" and "freedom."[30] One passionate letter, written by
Greensboro resident Patsy Jarrett, a member of ACT, invoked notions
of patriotism, morality, and victimization to attack school desegregation:

> What has happened to America? A nation that has always been
> superior to all nations. A nation the people have always been proud
> of. A nation of the people, for the people, by the people. A nation
> where the majority ruled, not the minority. A nation of high morals.
> A religious nation; a nation that stands for freedom. What is free-
> dom? The right for nine men to tell you that your child is going to be
> bused across town to another school, for the benefit of a few people,
> knowing that it is not for the health and welfare of our children, who
> are so innocent. . . . When did our country become so weak that we
> allow communists to come in and tell us how to live and bring the
> American people down to their level? . . . Have our forefathers, who

have fought with their lives to keep this a free country, died in vain?[31]

Jarrett's letter did not even mention race. Another letter to the editor did address race and racism explicitly, but to argue that "segregation should by now be a dead issue":

> What in the name of common sense has gone wrong when a child is denied the right to attend the school across the street or down the block and forced to be bused across town in busy traffic to a strange school all in the name of some will-o'-the-wisp ideal of proper racial balance? Have children become political pawns to assuage the guilt of years of de jure segregation? It would appear so.[32]

Pitting politics against innocent white people and children, this writer suggested that, by the early 1970s, any action aimed at addressing the legacy of segregation was unnecessary, driven solely by guilt, and grossly unfair.

Explanations of Opposition

I asked the interview participants to recall the *Brown v. Board* decision, but most could not. They recognized it as an idea, but it was not part of their recalled experience of school integration. For many, memory of school desegregation began hazily with Greensboro's early, minimal integration (starting in 1957) and crystallized with the implementation of busing and school assignment programs (beginning in 1971). Nevertheless, I asked them to comment on why Greensboro took seventeen years to fully integrate, after the school board had announced so early that the city was ready. Bernice, 80s, offered a best guess: "I don't really know. I guess maybe they wanted to see how it worked out in other places, maybe (laughs) before they started doing it around here." Bernice gave no indication that school desegregation had been a polarizing issue—that whites, or any people for that matter, had fought against it.

Darla, 70s, used vague language in her response to the question. After my probing, it became clear that she recognized that white people were the primary actors fighting school integration:

Darla: I guess they just couldn't come to terms with how it was gonna be handled and they couldn't *agree* and—
Interviewer: Who? The school board or the—
Darla: Well, I think the *parents* were the ones who were so up in arms over it, and the school board too, to a degree.
Interviewer: Would that be the white parents, or was it black parents too?
Darla: Well, I really think the white parents would have been the ones who were most opposed to it. And I don't know that the black people would have been as opposed.

Darla finally clarified that whites were primarily the ones who worked to prevent school integration. But, elsewhere in her interview, she portrayed whites as people who embraced school integration with a positive spirit:

I think that integration was a good thing to the degree that a lot of white parents became more involved and were tryin' to make it work. I know that's the feeling I had among the parents that I knew when we first started that. I mean, you just need to go ahead and make the best of it and just do what you can to make it work and (pause) I don't remember there bein' a whole lot of—well, there was a whole lot of unrest, and there were some parents who were just very unhappy about the situation.

In this part of her narrative, Darla stressed how amenable and instrumental white parents had been to desegregation efforts. Notice how she corrected herself when she started to claim that whites embraced school integration without "a whole lot of unrest" and acknowledged that there was significant white opposition. By distinguishing herself and "a lot of white parents" from "some parents" who opposed school integration, she implied that there was a white majority that embraced desegregation and that she had been a member of it.

On the other hand, Gracie, 80s, presented a different perspective when I asked how whites in Greensboro reacted to school desegregation: "Well, they resisted it. (laughs) A lot of people resisted it. I guess there were some people, maybe, who welcomed it." Gracie was a person who had been actively involved in integration efforts through her work in the school system. In her view as a school insider rather than as a parent, the overwhelming response among whites was one of resistance, not of cooperation. Trudie, 60s, a working class woman who, as we will see, was not an advocate of school desegregation, astutely noted the social class dynamics of whites' resistance. She argued that white elites were the ones who fought school integration most effectively because they had the power and resources to transition to the private school system:

> Oh, I think some whites *really* resented it. And if they were rich enough, that's why they moved . . . a lot of home schoolin' and sendin' your child to . . . private schools. But the rich ones, to me, really got together and started their own private schools, and I don't know if they would allow blacks in it, or only the rich blacks, as I call it. So, blacks were sorta left out in the cold I feel. . . . I didn't *know* this for a fact, but I sometimes wonder if white people kept holdin' back as long as they could hold back because they didn't really want this, and if they were rich enough to hold back, they could hold it back.

Although Gracie described herself as a longtime proponent of school integration, Trudie maintained a quite critical opinion of school integration. However, they both acknowledged the widespread pattern of whites' opposition to school desegregation.

Although white resistance toward school integration was pervasive nationwide, the white community was not unified over the issue.[33] Ronald Formisano, chronicler of school integration in 1960s–1970s Boston, argued that social class, ethnicity, religion, and notions of "turf" all played key roles in shaping how whites responded to school desegregation.[34] In the Greensboro context, social class played a marked role. Wealthier whites were able to engage in flight rather than fight maneuvers. County, private, and parochial schools overflowed, and new schools opened, as hundreds of white students were moved away from the integrating city public school system. Above, Trudie indicated that lower-income families had no mobility options and thus no choice but to comply with school reassignment and compulsory busing initiatives. Some of those families would have readily developed a class-based resentment toward wealthier whites.

On the other hand, not all upper-income whites contributed to the trend of abandoning the city school system. Ellie, 70s, provided a perspective on how divisions were created within more elite white social circles over school integration decisions. Ellie and her husband had several children in school during desegregation, and they decided, unlike some of their middle and upper middle class friends, to accept the coming changes and keep their kids in the public school system. She indicated that a rift was created in the white middle classes between those who fled to private schools and those who chose to do "the right thing" by complying with the new school assignment and busing programs:

> My husband and I thought we were doing the right thing to work through this so that it would be better for our children's children. And when we hear some of the things that go on, we question whether we made any impact at all. I mean, we were just one small family, but if everybody had been able to have that feeling that we were trying . . . but there were a lot of people who just said, forget it. And that was hard on us to say, "Why do you think that you're so much better than we are, that your child is more important than ours that they need to get a better education than ours?" And that's hard to live with and to work through.

Ellie felt abandoned by other whites who made the selfish rather than the greater good decision, securing a "better education" for their children than for her own. She expressed resentment that those, like her family, who chose to do "the right thing" would lose out on the educational benefits accruing to those who refused to participate in school integration. Ellie indicated that this difference in response created intraracial divisions among whites that did not exist prior to desegregation.

One other participant spoke to these new rifts. Although Ingrid, 60s, was clear that she had been opposed to busing, she recalled how she had convinced her husband, despite his own views, to end a friendship with a man who emerged as one of the most outspoken anti-integration activists:

> Ingrid: My husband and I had a friend who was . . . so against the busing. And it bothered me that he was doing that, and I didn't want to have anything to do with him anymore because of that. I talked my husband into disassociating with him. . . . I didn't want my kids bused. I agreed with that. But I didn't agree with his purpose in doing it, which, to me, was just because he did not like the blacks.

Interviewer: So what did [your husband] have to—?

Ingrid: He was, of course, on [the man's] side.

Interviewer: But how did you talk him out of having anything to do with—?

Ingrid: Well, I don't know how I talked him out of it, to be honest with you. (laughing) I just said I didn't want to have anything to do with him anymore. . . . We saw him one time after that. He invited [us] to a gathering that he had . . . probably about five or six years after that. And that's the last time I ever saw him, and we were not very friendly to each other.

Ingrid recalled how she and her husband cut this man off from their lives and that this was a permanent development. Ingrid indicated that it was not the man's anti-integration stance itself, for she was also against busing, but rather the feeling she believed was behind his stance that he was publicizing—overt anti-black prejudice. This account speaks to the intricacies in how whites navigated the institutional *and* interactional realms throughout the changes brought on by desegregation.

As will be evident in the pages to come, the interview participants who were connected to school desegregation via their own children remembered the transition primarily as a difficult and even traumatizing ordeal. I will argue that this perception of their own hardship enables them to downplay and rationalize continuing resentment toward school integration. As is illustrated throughout this book, the people interviewed often acknowledged the reality of past racial inequalities faced by African Americans. In this chapter, they agree that segregated schools were inequitable. Nevertheless, their storytelling of school integration focused heavily on the chaos and confusion caused by desegregation and the injustice, danger, and trauma faced by innocent white children. Thus, the overall perception one garners about educational injustice from their narratives is the heavy burden faced by white students and families.

WHITE CHILDREN'S VULNERABILITIES

Excluding the very youngest and oldest of the interview participants, the majority were parents of school children when comprehensive school desegregation was implemented in Greensboro schools in the fall of 1971, and they experienced the transition firsthand. When they spoke of their initial reaction to integration, their portrayals were mixed—some said they acquiesced or agreed due to a sense of inevitability or morality, while others said they were opposed from the beginning. And, for several people, the resentment clearly lingered, nearly forty years later. When explaining their initial resistance to school integration, notably, no one said they opposed it on a racial principle; rather, most said they were displeased with *how* desegregation was designed and implemented and told stories about its causing unjust and unwarranted hardships to children and families—from long bus rides to the loss of a stable learning environment in the classroom to white kids being bullied by black kids. Some people whose children had not undergone any of the turmoil of those first few years of school desegregation nevertheless expressed empathy for white families who had. White children were constructed as the primary victims, while little empathy was expressed toward black children and families.

Darla's, 70s, narrative incorporated several common themes among the interviews. She spoke at length about school desegregation, criticizing how it had been implemented and the problems it had caused. In this excerpt, her language is telling: she described her son as a "guinea pig" who was "thrown with black children" to explain his introduction to integrated schools:

> Our son . . . was the guinea pig of this first busing. He went the first year down to [a formerly white school]. . . . The next year he went to [what] had been a black school. . . . The next year he went to [another school]. And he was thrown with black children. A lot of—well, not only black children but a lot of the white children and black children responded negatively, I think, to the situation. There was a whole lot of teacher discipline, trying to get things under control. He *never* came home and said, "There are six black people in my room," or "I don't like this black person or that black person." He really didn't make any big comments about it.

These themes were quite common among participants: school integration was an unfair, harsh process, but their (white) children responded with an open mind. Note also how, in this excerpt, Darla stopped herself before she claimed that black students were the ones who did not respond positively to integrated schools ("A lot of—well, not only black children . . . responded negatively . . . to the situation"). She presented her own child as accepting and racially tolerant despite being burdened with the inconvenience and unfairness of desegregation.

Trouble on the Bus

Similar to elsewhere in the South, compulsory busing was a lightning-rod issue during Greensboro's school desegregation process. Many white parents deeply resented their children's new, long commutes when they otherwise could have walked to school, and they worried over buses being dangerous and the bus routes confusing. Particularly concerned with the youngest, most vulnerable students, several people argued that riding a school bus imposed an unfair hardship on their young children. Only a couple of people mentioned the fact that for decades a great many black children had been riding buses and walking long distances, sometimes passing white schools along the way, in order to reach their segregated schools. In other words, the "neighborhood school" system that many whites preferred and were accustomed to—especially in the middle and upper classes—did not work as effectively for African Americans who had far less control over their employment and housing, facing racial discrimination in those realms. Black parents (as well as poorer whites) rarely had much choice in their schools, or the ability to relocate to any neighborhood they preferred.

Arnold, 80s, was one such participant who deemed it very unfortunate that his family was unable to capitalize on the choice to live near certain schools. He used victim terminology to describe white children's experiences:

[My children] weren't victims of being forcibly bused, except the one child, my youngest. The others escaped that need and that could have been bad, if they had to be bused someplace. Busing, I thought, was (pause) not a good thing. I know what they were trying to do, but I don't think it was a good thing, because all the people all over town, would have been far better for them to go to a local school. In fact, we'd located our home . . . within short walking distance of three schools . . . so our children could walk to school, didn't have to ride a bus. I felt that was the best way it could possibly be. (pause) But you would never get integration, you would never get the mixing of the races that way. I understand that. (chuckles) It just wouldn't happen. (pause) It's something had to be forced and that's what happened.

Arnold acknowledged that school integration required a mandate or it "just wouldn't happen," but he nevertheless viewed the desegregation process as bad ("I know what they were trying to do, but I don't think it was a good thing"). In his view, a desegregation program was necessary, but white children should not have been made pawns in the process and families should have been able to retain their prior preferences.

Similarly, Trudie, 60s, maintained her opposition to busing at the same time as she acknowledged the importance of integration for the sake of cross-cultural exposure and equity:

> Bein' bused all the way across just to make it equal, I didn't like that . . . because the children, it's like, oh my word, get 'em up, get 'em on the bus by 7:30—*some of 'em* were goin' to [ride] for an *hour*—and I thought it was very unfair to the *children*. As far as the integration, that was *good* that they got to see the other culture. . . . I don't like to hear of, well this school doesn't have hardly enough money to run. . . . It was not fair. To me, the black children should have had the same privileges.

Trudie presented both benefits and drawbacks of school integration. On the positive side, she placed cross-cultural exposure and black students receiving an equitable education. On the negative side, she placed the unfairness of long bus rides for the sake of achieving school integration. In her view, underresourced segregated black schools were unfair, but so was the transport of children to rectify that inequality. This kind of portrayal was very common across the interview narratives. This perspective asserts that the implementation of full desegregation and busing programs addressed the issue of equity, but *created* many new problems that were unfortunately inflicted upon whites.

One person who offered a different portrayal was Hope, 70s. While she also recalled the inconvenience of school assignments and busing, she presented by far the most positive view of school integration among those participants whose children had been bused to faraway schools:

> It was hard to see your child bused all the way, and if she'd get sick, I'd have to try to find transportation to go get her . . . [and] we had a school right down the road that she could walk to, and had to bus her

all the way across town. . . . But they enjoyed getting on that big ole yellow bus and riding. . . . My younger children had black teachers and we just loved them. They was good to my kids, and you know, what could I say—I couldn't be mean. I know some people can, but not me. And my kids never complained about it at all. I guess though that's the way me and their dad was. You know if we'd set around and talked ugly stuff about other people, they would pick up that same thing. . . . But we never did that.

Hope spoke of the inconvenience of busing and school assignments, but she also mentioned her children's enjoyment of bus rides, lack of complaint, and good black teachers. Hope also reasoned that her children's positive experiences were a reflection of her and her husband's good parenting, which we can interpret in two ways: as a move of positive (nonracist) self-presentation, and as an indicator that how parents responded to school integration may have been related to how their children interpreted the experience.

School integration *was* difficult for many families, white and black: arbitrary school assignments, confusing logistics of bus routes, the loss of many neighborhood schools, animosities between students, and overwhelmed teachers. A handful of people, like Hope, expressed no major resentment toward school desegregation. Many more not only described their angst at the time, but demonstrated that they retained to this day significant resentment toward school integration. In what follows we will see the lingering bitterness and disappointment harbored by numerous participants. Looking through the lens of memory, we will consider the functions of this persistence of emotional resentment— how it is related to their sense of self, racial identity, and perception of race in the society.

Trouble at School: Black Bullies

Beyond busing, interview participants portrayed school integration as a racialized hardship through storytelling about troubling experiences in the school and classroom. Two kinds of stories predominated—tales of African American bullies and the incompetence of black teachers. Several people shared vivid stories of how their children, or others' children, were bullied by black students. Frances, 80s, said her children were victimized and traumatized by African American bullies:

Our children had a little bit of problem in *school* with the blacks
stealing their lunch money. Our son told us that he would not go to
the bathroom by himself for fear he would be jumped. . . . And he
quit takin' his lunch because they would steal his lunch or his lunch
money, so he just didn't *eat* while he was in school. He would wait
and eat when he got home. That was what *he* encountered.

In Frances's portrayal, her children were targeted not by individual
bullies but by "the blacks"—groups of African American children.
There were several similar stories told of white students facing debili-
tating fear and restriction because of black students' threatening behavior. One participant said her daughter developed a urinary infection
because of attending a majority-black high school that "was so bad when
my daughter went there . . . that she was afraid to go to the bathroom,
to the point that . . . we had to take her to a urologist." Arnold, 80s, told
about how his daughter said she had been accosted by black males
when she attended a primarily black school: "What a lot of the black
guys would do is they would congregate around a girl, especially a white
girl, and sorta block her in and sorta intimidate her if they could." These
portrayals imply that integrated schools created a forum for white students to be bullied by entire groups of black students.

Ellie, 70s, said her son was the victim of bullying by a domineering
African American boy who targeted whites: "I just will never forget
this. . . . There was a big black boy that sat in front of our son, and
when . . . he got to school, this black boy sort of ran supreme in the
classroom, and he would have our son get down and lick his shoes and
he would say, 'Your people have slaved my people, now I'm gonna slave
you.'" As Ellie pointed out, this was an unforgettable memory for her,
and it is notably vivid, considering that she was not present in the
classroom to have witnessed this kind of incident, but rather likely
heard it from her son secondhand. As we will see later in this chapter,
Ellie harbored a marked level of disappointment over how her family
experienced school integration, and stories such as this one shape and
rationalize her persistent feeling of bitterness.

Taken together, the participants' stories of African American bullies
suggest that white children's psychological and physical health were
threatened by their new black schoolmates. Although we cannot dis-
pute the veracity of each individual's account, it is clear that these
stories do not speak to the reality of black children's—and, by exten-

sion, black families'—often traumatic integration experiences. Black children, throughout freedom of choice trials and later with comprehensive school desegregation, navigated a predominantly white school system, white teachers, and white classmates who were heavily influenced by the persisting white supremacist ideology of the era. While many schools remained predominantly white even when fully integrated (due to population distributions in an area), black communities lost much of their school system and disproportionately lost their teachers and administrators in favor of their white counterparts. In other words, across the South, school desegregation increased black children's exposure to white hostilities and decreased African Americans' control over their children's school experience. Indeed, the opposition to school desegregation within black communities often worried that this aspect of the transition would come to pass.

One participant told a story that sheds some light on how whites, in anticipation of school desegregation, primed themselves through rumor to *expect* racial hostility and physical threat from black students. Mack, 80s, said that an administrator of a white public school privately alerted him that his fair-haired daughter was likely to be targeted and physically attacked if she attended an integrated school:

> [The administrator] told me one day, "Mack, I think if you can afford it you would be smart to send [your daughter] . . . to private school . . . because she has too much visibility." He said, "I'm afraid that some of the black girls would try to cut her face or mutilate her in the girls' room." And he said, "We've had threats of that, especially with pretty white—*blonde* white girls." He says, "Don't spread that around."

In recounting this warning, Mack said that the man told him not to share the information, a note that conflicted with the man's portrayal of the severity and generalizability of the danger ("we've had threats of that"). In the end, Mack and his wife did keep their daughter out of integrating schools. Several participants reported choosing to do so (most common among upper-income families who could afford private school tuition), and their various rationales included fear of targeted racial violence, providing sensitive or gifted children a learning environment in which they could thrive, and avoiding the bus rides that they deemed a hardship. All these rationales constructed white children and families as the unfortunate pawns and victims of the desegregating school system or of black Americans.

Trouble at School: Teaching and Learning

Furthermore, several participants recalled the teachers their children had in integrated schools. Recall Hope's portrayal above, in which she expressed how her family loved their children's black teachers. When other participants spoke of black teachers, however, their stories were disparaging, while stories of white teachers were most often accompanied by empathy. In talking about two integration-era teachers—one white, one black—Patti, 80s, represented themes present in several other participants' portrayals. Patti recounted a skilled white teacher struggling in an underresourced and overcrowded school:

> She was having a tough time. She was one of the few white women there and she's a wonderful, *wonderful* teacher. . . . [I] observed in the classroom on one of my holiday days, and my eyeballs fell out. . . . I don't know whether the integration had gone too fast and they weren't prepared—I mean I can't give you causative factors, I can only tell you what I saw. But there were three children in there that I think you would call special needs who were *so out of control* that they were bouncing off the walls and destroying the educational opportunity of everybody else. . . . It was not the teacher's fault. She was doing *more* than any human—she was skilled. But these three children should *not*—I mean, it was criminal!

Patti indicated that those three students who were "destroying the educational opportunity" in the classroom were African American ("I don't know whether the integration had gone too fast and they weren't prepared"). Patti spoke of the white female teacher who had to deal with the situation with respect and extended empathy to her. In a similar story, Arnold, 80s, empathized with the difficulties faced by a novice white teacher:

> Only one of our children got bused during the forced busing to help integrate the schools. Just one year . . . and pretty well lost the year. I mean, the poor teacher. . . . I think it was her first or second year teaching, and she had a whole classroom of kids, and she had two

little boys who were learning to read with the headset . . . in the sixth grade, they were learning to read! And they were black of course. . . . And I thought, This poor teacher, she's got a terrible situation here. (chuckling) 'cause she doesn't have [but] just a handful of kids that are doin' what she's supposed to be teaching. She's got to bring these others along as best she can.

In Arnold's portrayal, hardship fell on both his child who "lost the year" and the white teacher who had to deal with "a terrible situation" of a wide range of student proficiencies. Notably, Arnold responded to the teacher's inexperience with empathy rather than disparagement. In his view, his son got a subpar education, but he located blame with the lowest-skilled students rather than with the teacher.

While these stories extended understanding to struggling white teachers in integrated schools, Patti told an additional story that portrayed an African American teacher as laughably incompetent:

Part of the dilemma was that the English teacher was woefully unprepared. How she was certified to teach English . . . I have no idea. . . . But (chuckles) it was things like, she would read out a spelling list . . . [and] *this* I remember so clearly. "Flow!" . . . So [my son] had spelled it f-l-o-w. Well he failed his spelling test, and among the many wrong things was *flow*, because you spelled it f-l-o-o-r. (chuckles) . . . It was just a nightmare for *me* because this was *not* what I considered adequate, but that's what I was stuck with.

With vivid detail, Patti illustrated the teacher's incompetence to teach English to her son. She indicated that she internalized her son's integration experiences: "it was just a nightmare for *me*" . . . "what *I* was stuck with" (emphasis added). And, elsewhere in the interview, Patti explained that this educational situation became a key reason behind deciding to remove her son from the city school system.

A married couple shared what they perceived as two of their son's primary school integration experiences, both of which portrayed black teachers as being too (racially) sensitive and unfairly reprimanding their son:

Husband: He came home and he told us of two instances. One was a teacher calling the roll, and she called out [his first and last name],

and he answered that he was here and he says, "They call me [my middle name]." So she took that and turned it into a racial problem.
Wife: A racist issue.
Husband: A racist issue.
Interviewer: Hm?
Husband: He couldn't understand it either. But that's one time—
Interviewer: He got in trouble?
Wife: Well, she kinda reprimanded him because she felt like that he was correcting *her*. . . .
Husband: What was the other one?
Wife: The French teacher?
Husband: French teacher.
Wife: Yeah, she was black and she was tryin' to teach them, and she caught him talking and so he had to write, "I shall not talk in class" a hundred times. Well, he thought if she'd had any gumption she would have had him to write in French.

In this exchange, as the couple interacted and collaborated in storytelling, it was clear that they not only shared these two memories but also associated the two closely (as he asked her, "What was the other one?"). Relative to many of the other accounts shared by people, these moments seem rather mundane—their son being mildly reprimanded by a teacher—and yet the couple remembered them as *important* stories about what desegregating schools were like. Key in these portrayals of integration-era black teachers is the construction of them as ineffective due to their own deficiencies rather than the upheaval of the transition.

Ellie, 70s, offered an illuminating explanation of how white parents set *themselves* up to interpret their children's experiences in desegregated schools in particular ways. Ellie indicated that (white) people assumed in advance that black teachers would be of low quality:

> There were times when the children would start school at the beginning of the year and would come home and you'd say, "Who's your teacher?" And you never let your child know it, but when they told you, you just wanted to go in the other room and cry, 'cause you knew what the year was going to be like. You had lost years because they didn't get anything. But you were still trying to make a system work, and some of them were good, some of them were bad. But you probably didn't maybe watch the white teachers closely. I would

probably say that's true—or expect there to be a problem, where maybe you might expect there to be otherwise.

Ellie recounted her immediate devastating reaction upon learning her child would be instructed by a black teacher, and she recalled also the long-term devastation of "lost years [of education] because they didn't get anything." Furthermore, Ellie claimed that teachers gave special treatment to black students that created unfair standards and/or sent the wrong kind of message about race to children:

> With the children, it was hard. It was a very difficult time for me, because they'd come home and they'd say, "Well, we had to turn in our papers by such-and-such but so-and-so doesn't because they're black." And that was the message the children got. And the teachers did that. . . . So that part of the early bringing together the races to me was not done in the best way. I don't know what I would have done differently, but today I wonder—there's one of ours I would like to have sent to private school, but I couldn't do it and leave the other [children] in the system, so I didn't do it.

Since Ellie elected to keep all of her children in the integrated public school system, she pondered, as an elder with middle-aged children, what could have been different, and better, if her children had not experienced desegregated schools. Elsewhere in her interview Ellie spoke about how her most gifted child may have suffered irreparably from her decision not to send him to private school.

An instructive contrast to Ellie's perspective came from Bonnie, 80s, one of the most progressive participants. She recalled an incident in which her husband corrected her son's complaint about the same perceived double standard noted by Ellie above, where it was thought that black students in newly integrated schools were unfairly allowed more leeway than white students:

> We were in the car and we were on our way to a weekend [vacation] and [our son] said, "Those black kids can get by with anything and they are never punished," and we said, "What are you talking about?" "Well, just let one of us white kids do something and we're hauled right into the principal's office and probably get a paddle; the black kids can get by with anything." My husband pulled the car over, stopped the car, and he said, "Have you ever learned any history in

school? . . . Do you know anything about how blacks have been mistreated all their lives, and they kind of deserve to misbehave every once in a while, but I will have to say that the teachers are probably afraid to correct them because this is such a new experience." I never heard (chuckles) our kids complain again about that sort of thing.

In Bonnie's memory, her husband abruptly pulled the car over in order to teach their son a lesson about the importance of contextualizing with racial history what was happening in desegregating schools. She recalled that her children learned that lesson so effectively that they never voiced similar complaints again.

As much previous research on school desegregation has revealed, there was no consensus among white southerners regarding how to respond to or interpret desegregation. They reached different conclusions, from open acceptance to acquiescence to resentment to staunch opposition, and there were distinct regional dynamics.[35] Numerous southern states engaged in "massive resistance" to school integration, including Deep South states like Mississippi and Alabama and border states like Arkansas and Virginia.[36] North Carolina generally took a less resistant and more gradualist approach.[37] The narratives in this chapter give a view of the range of white responses, although we must keep in mind that these accounts were produced about four decades after the era in question. Bonnie's account stands in contrast to Ellie's account. Again, we consider how white parents' expectations may have affected the way they ultimately interpreted—and remember still today—their school integration experiences. While Ellie maintained that her children experienced losses that were unfortunate and uncalled for, Bonnie pointed out the larger historical context that necessitated school integration and made its sometimes conflict-ridden dynamics understandable and acceptable.

Racialized Empathy

It was apparent in many participants' accounts that their memories of school integration were given shape by things they perceive were done to them as *whites*, either by African Americans directly or by the desegregation process generally. In these stories, the burdens of school integration are presented as falling heavily upon whites: white teachers as struggling with underprepared students and chaotic integrated classrooms, white students as targeted by black bullies and ill-served by black teachers. There was a racialized pattern of empathy, with most being extended to whites. Crafting whites as the vulnerable party during school desegregation implies that whites-only segregated schools and superficially integrated freedom of choice schools were healthy and productive settings for teaching and learning, while fully integrated schools took a severe toll on good teachers, gifted and sensitive white students, and innocent children accustomed to the normalcies of neighborhood schools. In these narratives, segregated schools were constructed largely as safe and positive spaces, appropriate for (white) children's learning, while integrated schools were constructed as damaging. Few respondents acknowledged that school integration was a difficult, much less traumatic, experience for black students, teachers, or parents, who lost their school system due to the 70–30 white–black ratio that was targeted in Greensboro's school assignments.[38]

Several participants told empathetic stories about other whites' troubles with school integration. Sharon, 60s, who had minimal personal experience with desegregation policies, retold her neighbor's story about a combative busing experience where white children were harassed by black children: "Mary Jane told me . . . that she was on the first . . . *white* bus that was shipped into a black school. And she said, 'They were throwing rocks at us.' And I said, 'So they didn't want you there,' and she says, 'No! They didn't want us there, and we didn't wanna *be* there!'" In this story, Sharon indicated that Mary Jane was not only a pawn of busing but also was victimized by aggressive black children. Sally, 70s, also relayed a story an acquaintance told her about African American bullying:

> I heard a woman say not too long ago that . . . she was in a black high school district . . . and her child was in the, like, 30 percent white. And he *was* bullied considerably. And I don't know whether he was bullied because of the color of his skin . . . but she felt like some of it was the color of his skin, and that it was just *the* worst years that she had to live through.

According to Sally, this was a recent conversation with a white woman who, like several of the interview participants, felt decades later that school desegregation had been a deeply traumatic experience both for her children and for her personally ("it was just *the* worst years that she had to live through).

It is unlikely that many elder white southerners have had African American acquaintances tell them personally of the experiences and trauma *they* underwent during school desegregation. Because of the whiteness of their social networks and lingering patterns of racial interactions and social norms, it is likely that most elder whites have had minimal exposure to fully honest black perspectives. Thus, we should not expect in interviews such as these that people would recall a great many stories of black students being bullied by white students or harassed by hostile white teachers, or of black teachers struggling with disrespectful white students or parents. Nevertheless, what is noteworthy is how rare it was for a participant to even mention the possibility that African American families experienced hardship during school integration, or that their segregated schools had been grossly underfunded by white powerholders.

Even a former schoolteacher in her 70s, whose narrative stood out because she did not invoke white victimhood when discussing school desegregation, gave just a brief nod to the trauma possibly faced by African Americans. She pointed out the courage of black parents sending their children into white schools under freedom of choice: "I remember one year we decided that [my grade level] should be integrated . . . and I had four in my room and they were delightful, and the children, they all got along well. But I think the parents had to be really brave to let their little children come to that white [school]. It must've taken a lot of guts. And yet they had a grand time." This woman acknowledged the bravery mustered by black parents, yet she undercut that acknowledgment by asserting that "they all got along well" and "had a grand time." Similarly, Bernice, 80s, affirmed African Americans' hesitancy for their children to enter white schools, but implied that they never encountered any real problems: "The black parents were sort of fearful for their children, which I can understand, 'cause it'd be like sendin' 'em into a hornet's nest more or less. But I never did . . . [hear] that any black got mistreated or, you know, mauled or anything like that." In both of these accounts, the potential for blacks' desegregation hardship is affirmed but then dismissed as unlikely.

One man, Ned, 60s, did speak with some detail about how whites bullied black students as a matter of course. He told of the experiences of Josephine Boyd, the first African American student to enroll at Greensboro Senior High School, as a senior, in 1957:

> Yeah, her name was Josephine. . . . I did hear some of the horror stories that a lot of the white kids put her through that as far as I—I didn't think it was right. Because she had to bring at least two or three changes of clothes with her because they would use water guns and squirt Clorox [bleach] on her, and I mean, she just got—I don't see how she took it because . . . every week she was there had to have been hell.

Ned had been at the time close in age to Josephine Boyd and recalled that it was common knowledge that she was persistently traumatized throughout the school year for integrating the white high school. Ned's memory brings into focus, and critiques, the picture painted by many of the other participants' accounts: that it was primarily white students, teachers, and parents who were made vulnerable and victimized by school desegregation.

It should not be expected that participants would have elaborated on black southerners' integration experiences and interpretations. However, the respondents *did* at times tell the stories of other people, and, when they did, the stories tended to be centered on whites' difficulties, for which they expressed empathy. Thus, their interpretations of school integration were not entirely self-centered on their own personal experience. When describing a transition period that most people acknowledged was designed to address decades of unequal schooling for African American students, participants' narratives largely focused on whites' troubles and expressed regret or bitterness that desegregation had occurred the way that it did. Collectively, their narratives imply that, in a just world, there should have been a way to desegregate schools and bring about equity without whites bearing significant burdens. Again, in constructing the civil rights era in this way, attention gets diverted away from that common acknowledgment of Jim Crow inequality, that integration "needed to happen."

PERSISTENT RESENTMENT

When it came to discussing school desegregation, the interview participants tended to reveal complex views. Many people acknowledged that
segregated schools were unequal, and none indicated that they had ever
strongly opposed the *principle* of integrated schools. However, many
openly resented desegregation and expressed lingering bitterness today
over *how* it occurred, with the implementation of new school assignments and citywide busing mandates, as well as the loss of educational
quality, predictability, safety, and overall peace of mind. We will explore in this section how their construction of white victimhood both
justifies their initial opposition and rationalizes continued resentment
toward school integration.

Certainly some of the lingering frustration that white southerners
hold toward school integration was encouraged by how the Supreme
Court wound up communicating and mandating school desegregation.
In their 1955 decision, one year after the initial *Brown v. Board* case,
the court pushed implementation decisions onto local school boards
and used the vague language of "all deliberate speed" to describe the
rate at which segregated school systems should be dismantled. As Feagin points out, the Supreme Court avoided affronts to white sensibilities
in their rulings: "Neither of the two *Brown* decisions explained to the
general public the anti-civil-rights reality and immorality of racial segregation, and neither decision mandated clearly the steps necessary to
end actual segregation."[39] The lack of a firm judicial finding against the
institutionalization of unequal schooling discouraged ordinary white
southerners from understanding African Americans' experiences with
segregated schools and emboldened them to feel victimized by the
seeming arbitrariness and nonsensical timing of mandates formulated
by local authorities.

And the affront to whites' sensibilities was perhaps especially severe
in places like Greensboro, whose leadership skirted and counterat-
tacked desegregation for so long that they were finally forced by the
federal government to hurriedly design and implement a comprehensive program within the span of a few months. As Sally, 70s, explained:
"I don't think any of us were ready for it. It was very abrupt. They didn't
do it over a period of time, they just (snaps her fingers) did it. . . . They
switched the children all in one year." While black leaders and some

whites had dedicated numerous years to working toward a viable and extensive school integration plan, Greensboro's school board refused to desegregate fully.[40] When comprehensive integration finally had to happen, the majority of white residents, who had sat passively by for years while African American families did most of the work of integrating under the freedom of choice option, suddenly felt put upon and confused: why was this all being *forced*, and why so suddenly?

I present the following profiles of two of the individuals who had the most extended commentaries on school integration. The narratives of Ellie and Carla demonstrate more in depth the reasoning and feelings undergirding white southerners' lingering resentments toward school integration. As we have already seen, Ellie presented herself as progressive through attempting to do "the right thing" by embracing public school desegregation. She also rued what appeared to her as irreparable damage done to her children because of it. Her sense of disappointment and sadness for her own children, decades later, is palpable. On the other hand, Carla offered a more acerbic indictment of school integration as a social ill rather than just a phenomenon that caused problems for individual families. Carla went so far as to blame a host of contemporary social problems on desegregation.

Ellie spoke at length about how her children had unfortunately suffered in integrating schools, and she expressed disappointment toward contemporaries who had chosen to flee the public school system and abandon families like hers. Ellie also indicated that her family shouldered a further major cost from embracing school desegregation, which manifested in her children's negative racial attitudes. She claimed that her children harbor anti-black prejudice as adults today because of the ordeals they endured during school integration:

> And when we were raising our children, we felt we had a responsibility to do what was, quote, "considered right" in the schools to try to fix things. But because of what our children were experiencing, we have children that are very prejudiced, much more than I would say I ever was, much to my sorrow. And they as adults would say, "Mom, you had no idea what it was like." And that's very hard for me, because I thought we were doing it for the right reasons.

Ellie lamented the losses to her children from her choice to send them to integrated schools, and she constructed integrated schools as the cause of her now-grown children's anti-black prejudice. Ellie implied that if her children had not been subjected to integrated public schools, they would not have developed a negative impression of black people— they would be at least as racially progressive as her, if not more so. To this day she questions her decision to comply with school desegregation, wording her initial conviction in the past tense: "I *thought* we were doing it for the right reasons" (emphasis added) and highlighting the unfortunate and disappointing consequences that befell her children.

Carla, 60s, one of the youngest respondents, graduated high school in the mid-1960s and did not experience as a student integration under the freedom of choice plan (it had been primarily implemented in grades below hers during her school years) or under the comprehensive school desegregation program that began in Greensboro city schools in 1971. Desegregation had been in place for several years by the time her own children were of school age, and they attended schools that were not predominantly white. Carla had little good to say about her children's experiences in integrated schools. She also indicated her dismay that city schools, in her view, worsened after integration and continued on that course:

> I don't understand—[my children] were in county schools, and they were fine. But I brought them into the same city school *I* went to, but it had deteriorated so much that [my daughter] was afraid to go to the bathroom. . . . That's been [over twenty] years ago, so I can't imagine what it's like now. In *my mind*, they need to have a police officer in every classroom I think. (chuckles)

Carla directly associated the onset of school integration with the "deterioration" of the public school system. She admitted that many of those who initially opposed school integration likely used racist reasoning, but she affirmed their opposition, claiming that their prophecies turned out to be correct:

> When they integrated the schools, I think the *worst* thing that happened in *my* mind—and I'm sure there were racist comments, and yet, I think it's come true—I can remember . . . [a family member] . . . said, "By integrating the schools, they're not gonna bring the blacks *up*, they're gonna bring the whites *down*." And I think that's what happened. . . . To me, when they integrated the schools, it's

almost like then *all* the standards lowered. And I think it has come *true* that, by integrating . . . the whole level of society was lowered. . . . To *me*, *all* of the standards have been allowed to come down, to deteriorate. . . . I just don't get it. I don't understand *why* they're supporting the welfare system that they're supporting. You know, it's like everything *went* down*hill*. But why did that happen? If we were gonna integrate, why didn't we keep the standards? . . . So I blame a lot on integration—not the blacks, but because what happened to the administration of the systems? I *know* that you can say their level of education had to be brought up, but was it? Or was ours just brought down? I just don't get it. I can't quite understand what happened.

Carla believed that school integration was the beginning of a downward spiral for "the whole level of society" where "*all* the standards lowered" and have remained low. While clearly indicting integrated schools, Carla mused over the root cause, suggesting that it was not African Americans per se that caused the problems she perceived, but rather "the administration of the systems." (On the other hand, she identified black Americans' support of "the welfare system" as a contemporary manifestation of problems brought about by school desegregation.) Although she lacked clarity on the dynamics, Carla was firm in her view that "the *worst* thing" was that school integration did long-lasting damage to the entire society.

MAINTAINING WHITE VIRTUE THROUGH MEMORY

While the civil rights era was remembered as a period that ushered in some expansion of racial equality, by and large the interview participants portrayed both the black freedom struggle and school desegregation as times that, for them, had been replete with uncertainty, heightened racial animosity, chaos, victimization, unfairness, and loss. Some, like Carla above, constructed the civil rights era as the cause or catalyst of persistent social problems. Thus, even though they characterized the most blatant markers of segregation as unequal if not unjust (e.g., separate school systems, separate water fountains), collectively, the narratives focused on the troubles they experienced, within their racial location, that were brought on by desegregation efforts—black bullies, compromised learning environments, and school assignment/busing mandates. While chapter 4 demonstrated how the interview participants distanced themselves from movement activism and downplayed civil rights activists' justice orientation, in this chapter we saw how they embraced school integration as their personal battle and highlighted their struggles to protect their own children from perceived injustice.

Integral in constructing a victim is establishing a person's innocence and vulnerability.[41] Thus, the participants' vivid storytelling around their own vulnerability and victimization work to construct Jim Crow/ civil rights–era whites as innocent racial subjects. Once their racial innocence and goodness are established as inclusive of the civil rights and segregation eras, elder white southerners are given ready access to a lifelong nonracist, positive identity. This positive racial identity can be potentially on the individual and collective levels, for negative portrayals of the civil rights era safeguard elder white southerners' nostalgia for the Jim Crow era. In other words, constructing the civil rights era as a markedly troubling time works to solidify the notion that the segregation era was a stable, pleasant time. While the majority of participants agreed intellectually that aspects of segregation had been unjust, the most vivid storytelling occurred around the themes of segregation nostalgia and civil rights threat and vicitimization.

6

REFLECTING ON A LIFETIME

Views of the Post–Civil Rights Era

Thus far we have analyzed elder white southerners' portrayals of the racial past and have seen how, despite the variations and nuances in people's perspectives, there were patterns in how people constructed the past. Most people readily acknowledged racially unequal structures but often downplayed their severity and pervasiveness. Although they agreed with the contemporary mainstream perspective that the segregation era ran counter to American ideals of equality and justice, this perspective was often undercut by "whitewashing" dynamics unflattering to the white South. Indeed, much of the most vivid storytelling focused on racial harmony during segregation and perceived troubles and burdens during the civil rights era. We have covered two key complexities of the narratives: (1) both acknowledging and downplaying the racial oppression of Jim Crow, and (2) expressing agreement with integration while delegitimizing the movement that brought it about. This chapter analyzes participants' perspectives of the contemporary post–civil rights era, progress in racial relations, and what should be done to move society forward. Here I outline the third and final key complexity: assessing favorably the racial changes witnessed over a lifetime while resenting reminders of unflattering aspects of the past and efforts for further progress.

The final questions of the interview were designed to help participants think about race today, about links between past and present, and engage in deeper reflection across their lifetimes. I asked them to talk about their perspective on the current racial milieu generally and more recent events, such as the 1979 "Greensboro massacre" and its mid-2000s truth and reconciliation effort. I also asked them to weigh in on the importance of remembering the racial past. More than at any other time, frustration and anger manifested when the conversation focused on the current state of affairs, so this chapter highlights further the links between racialized perceptions, identity, and emotions.

ASSESSING RACE TODAY: LINKING PAST AND PRESENT

How we remember the past is linked closely to current social and political circumstances.[1] In each interview session, I asked participants to share their views of contemporary society. This was a subject about which people tended to have clear opinions. In fact, several participants kept drifting into commentary on race today throughout the entire interview, and I had to make repeated efforts to bring them back to discussing the past. These were moments when it became clear that people did not have a clear sense of the chronology of the racial past and that they organized race in their minds in a more associative fashion. For example, recall Suzanne's comments in chapter 4 when she spoke of feeling afraid because of the protests at segregated businesses and then said that segregation

> shouldn't have been that way in the first place, but it was, and it did need to change, but I don't think either side should have to fear. But I can remember being very fearful to speak up and say how I felt about something. I think we fear that *today*. . . . You can't say I'm gonna eat more chicken without being in trouble. You can't say I love watermelon without being in trouble. Why?

Suzanne made a temporal shift from the 1960s to today via the theme of white fear. Suzanne's narrative moved seamlessly from the sit-in movement to a climate of political correctness where she believes whites are afraid of making innocuous statements because they might be interpreted as racial remarks. In this section, I analyze participants' commentaries on the current racial milieu, and I consider how they make use of the past in their interpretations of the post–civil rights era. Some of their assessments were presented as gains (including equal opportunity and the normality of interracial friendships), and others were presented as losses (including unfortunate cultural changes and continuing complaints about racial inequality).

Gains Made since the Civil Rights Era: Equal Opportunity

In speaking of what typified the current racial era, it was common for participants to speak in a positive manner. Numerous people noted that equal opportunity is a reality, claiming that the barriers of the past had been lifted for black Americans. This is a popular view among white Americans but not black Americans. In a recent national survey, 34 percent of whites and only 6 percent of blacks reported believing that black Americans had achieved racial equality. While 19 percent of African Americans believed that blacks would never achieve racial equality, only 3 percent of whites believed the same.[2] It is far less common for African Americans to believe that we have already arrived, or would eventually, at a truly postracial era where racial inequalities are no longer relevant.

Ava, 60s, acknowledged past inequality and asserted that there is now equal opportunity, and then some, for African Americans:

> I think racism was a problem years ago. But I do not feel like racism is a problem today. Because *now* black people are allowed to go to any college they wanna go to. If *anything*, they are allowed *more* grants and scholarships than they have *ever* had in their life—I mean, in anybody's life as far as that's concerned. Any black person who wants to apply themselves has the opportunity to be a doctor, lawyer, Indian chief. They have a choice. And there was a time when in certain areas they didn't have a choice.

Ava argued that black Americans are currently experiencing unprecedented and enviable access to institutional opportunities, such as higher education and high-status professions. In her view, the only hindrance they might experience would be within themselves and their own choices. Ava placed her assessment in historical context, claiming that the era of structural inequality was officially over.

Mae, 70s, assessed the extent of racial progress similarly, by contrasting present opportunities to past restrictions, but she was not as confident as Ava in claiming that equal opportunity had been achieved:

> Well, they say oppressed, but held back or whatever—from my point of view they've come a long way, but I still think there's a long way to go. And at one time I don't think they could even own their own business here in Greensboro, or anywhere really. And now we've got two or three large businesses that these people just got started and they've just boomeranged. And if they're capable I don't feel like they should be held back because of their color. And I don't know how free they feel, but from my point of view they have been free to a certain extent from all this—like not being able to drink out of the same water fountain.

Here Mae commingled her belief in the *ideal* of equal opportunity ("I don't feel like they should be held back") with her assessment of the reality ("they have been free to a certain extent from all this"). Although she equivocated about whether equal access was the objective reality, she nevertheless promoted that notion.

Gertie, 70s, presented an alternative view, more in line with research—that equal opportunity has not become a reality and whiteness still confers advantages:

> I think that being born white certainly has its advantages and I feel *really* bad for many people . . . just being born with their color skin starts them off behind the eight ball so to speak. (chuckles) Whereas being born white just seems to bring certain privileges, all of which is not right, but that's the way it is, I feel. It used to be much more that way. I think it's changing, but it does change slowly.

More than most other participants, Gertie identified white privilege as both a historical and contemporary reality. She did not construct a division between past racial inequality and the current state of affairs. She portrayed the march toward equal opportunity as still in progress and as nearing its destination.

On the other hand, Grant, 80s, argued that whites have done everything in their power to allow blacks full membership in mainstream society, but black Americans insist on maintaining "two cultures" and therefore are the cause of their own lack of progress:

What I observe in places that humans gather . . . blacks tend to gravitate to each other. And whereas *my* perception is that the white population has (pause) tried to make opportunities available. (pause) The African American group is not yet comfortable, and they tend to gravitate to each other. I think we can look . . . at any kind of little grouping. We can broaden that and talk about religious practices. There's nothing more distinguishable than a religious congregation. Why have they not mixed a little better, or is it difficult? Why do we have to make an effort to cause it to happen? . . . As a *group*, that distinction remains. . . . Who's responsible for it remaining distinguishable? *My* observation, individual, is that it's the African Americans more than it is the white society. The white society has (pause) set aside the distinguishing political and legal barriers and yet we still see the tendency of (pause) like social groups to gravitate to each other. It's a comfort level. . . . In one respect I feel very, very sorry and am grieved that the African American segment is maintaining two cultures, because I believe it is *precluding*, or at least *retarding*, the opportunity to assimilate. And what's made this country great . . . is the assimilation. (pause) Clearly there is much to be offered and provided by the African American group, but it is not yet fully assimilated as I anticipated when *I* was younger, that it would be by this time.

In Grant's view, white Americans had done everything in their power (removing "political and legal barriers") to bring about racial progress and integration. He pinpointed blacks as the party who preferred segregation and who needed to make more of an effort. Included in Grant's assessment of the causes and barriers to racial progress were expressions of disappointment: he felt "very, very sorry" and was "grieved" that African Americans were not taking the steps he thought necessary to assimilate and thereby contribute to mainstream society. Overall, Grant portrayed mainstream society as open and equal because of the progressive actions of the white South, while he portrayed black Americans as preventing the realization of his ideal multiracial (but not multicultural) society.

When discussing the contemporary landscape of race and opportunity, participants affirmed the ideal of a nonracist society. As the four quotes above show, participants varied in their assessments of how much progress has been made. Overall, the majority portrayed formerly discriminatory institutional structures as now nondiscriminatory and thought that the final frontier of progress lay in the interpersonal realm. Infused in their narratives were ideological themes that have been identified by scholars of contemporary racial discourse—dominant ideas that organize post–civil rights thinking about race, especially among whites. Sociologist Eduardo Bonilla-Silva has theorized these ideas as *abstract liberalism* (society is fair and open), *naturalization* (racial patterns are natural/inevitable and due to the choices made by people of color), *cultural racism* (inequalities are driven by cultural deficiencies among people of color), and *minimization* (denying the legitimacy of racism claims by people of color).[3] The interview excerpts above incorporated these themes, including abstract liberalism (for example, Ava saying "I do not feel like racism is a problem today") and naturalization (for example, Grant saying, "blacks tend to gravitate to each other" and that "it is precluding, or at least retarding, the opportunity to assimilate").

Gains Made since the Civil Rights Era: Integration (But Not Interracial Relationships)

A second key way in which participants constructed a positive difference between the past and current racial eras was to emphasize the normality of integrated social spaces and interracial interactions. They again invoked the idea of abstract liberalism.[4] For example, when asked whether she believed there had been extensive changes in Greensboro, Ingrid, 60s, said, "Oh, yes. . . like, for instance, if you go to the park there's a lot of blacks and there's a lot of whites. There's a lot of different cultures, with families. That's encouraging. That's a good thing to see. They are doing family things together." Frances, 70s, said that she tended to notice positive changes brought by integration:

> I don't see all of the bad things that are happening in connection with integration. I see the good things that have happened. People accepting other people, which it should it be. And I know that that's the way God intended. But I know there's some bad things have happened, but I think that bad things have happened through *every* generation, from the start. You gon' have some mean people and good people.

REFLECTING ON A LIFETIME

And a married couple indicated that interracial friendships were a clear sign of racial progress:

> Interviewer: Do you think there are things that people like me, or grandkids, great-grandkids—do you think there are things we can learn from your experiences during that time? Is there anything you could teach them, or help them to understand?
> Husband: Well, don't talk about it. So I don't—
> Wife: I don't really think so, because they're so used to being in the situation like it is now.
> Husband: I just think we over the hump with it now. (chuckles) Um, I mean, people have come to accept and it's just not that problems like it was when it first—
> Wife: Like I was saying, all of our grandkids, when they were younger, they just had their friends and they would go to their house and just accepted it like there's no color barrier, you know. So if we sat down and talked about years ago, I think they would just sit there in disbelief that it was like that.

From the perspective of this couple, younger generations have lived such integrated lives that the segregated racial past has become both irrelevant and impossible to comprehend. They presented their grandchildren's easygoing interracial friendships as an indicator of how extensive the progress has been.

Abstract liberalism had its limits. While numerous participants spoke favorably of interracial friendships, only a few people spoke with any positive regard for romantic interracial relationships and multiracial families. For the vast majority, the increase in mixed-race families has been a disconcerting outcome of integration. However, when people discussed their opposition to interracial families, they usually attached to their comments an affirmation of the belief in the equality of all people. For example, Burt, 80s, noted an ideal and reality of social equality within his explanation of his opposition to interracial marriage:

> Black people [are] not segregated anymore even in the schools, or in the restaurants or any theaters. . . . I regard racial intermarriage as a very bad thing for both races. Now whether that means I want to keep them apart, as far as raising children, I do. . . . I don't think interracial marriage is good. But Greensboro has changed just like most of the other cities in the South. We now recognize that the

blacks have civil rights, they have a right to go to our schools, go to our churches. I just sort of wish they'd stay within their own race.

Burt presented the expansion of civil rights and the integration of schools, businesses, and churches as social progress, but preferred that African Americans "stay within their own race" for marriage.

Suzanne, 60s, also affirmed the ideal of racial equality and reasoned out her opposition to interracial relationships:

> I told my grandson a lot of things that I've said to you—that it doesn't *matter* you know, whether black or white, rich or poor. You don't judge 'em by that. . . . And, even at [my age], I would like my grandson to marry white, 'cause *he's* white. And other reasons too. I see a lot of the interracial marriages with children, and I talk to some of 'em that is totally confused. A lot of 'em tell me that they have problems, because if they marry a white, they don't fit in with their black family when they go to family gatherings and things. . . . They're very uncomfortable. They're not accepted by certain members of the older generation in these families. . . . So it causes conflict and trouble.

And Harmony, 80s, said:

> I go way back in my belief in people—I think we're all alike. And we should be all treated alike and all. I mean, I know there are certain things that I—I've never known exactly how—I—I—I *know*, but I can't express it—the feeling of interracial marriages, I don't uh (pause) I just feel like, that uh (pause) it's not that—I won't say I don't *believe* in them, it's just that I think that—(sigh) I'm this way about any kind of a situation that might become a problem. I feel like if you can avoid it, do it. . . . I feel like it's, uh, *my* day and time—and now it's different too, I realize—that we were taught—uh, or not taught, but told that if you had an interracial marriage that the children that you might have were at a disadvantage because they were, uh, never sure of how they were classified, and uh, what they should be doin'. I don't know.

Suzanne rationalized her opposition to interracial relationships with evidence from recent conversations with people about the difficulties of interracial marriages, including, notably, "older generations"—ostensibly her own generation—who are not accepting. Harmony had great difficulty articulating the reasoning for her views. Harmony displayed here what Bonilla-Silva has termed *rhetorical incoherence*, a phenomenon—typified by grammatical mistakes, repetition, and long pauses—that is common when people talk about racially sensitive matters within a social context where such views are not popular.[5]

The post–civil rights context can make it difficult for Jim Crow–era whites to articulate a rationale for any "old-fashioned" views they retain. In saying, "I feel like it's, uh, *my* day and time—and now it's different too, I realize—" Harmony struggled to reconcile the reasoning she had acquired in her past socialization with the norms of the contemporary era. Similarly, Gertie, 70s, claimed that her discomfort with interracial relationships was the racial prejudice that had been most difficult to eradicate:

> I don't remember when I first started noticing that, but I *know* that it was a shock when I first saw it. . . . And then I thought about all the problems that they would have and how hard it would be to be, uh, not discriminated against. And I think probably took me more to get over that prejudice than any other thing. I think I did have some prejudices about that and couldn't understand really why someone would want to. But then the more it happened, I became less prejudice, but I really was concerned about, well, what happens to their children.

In contrast with Burt, Suzanne, and Harmony, Gertie portrayed herself as having gone through a gradual transition during the post–civil rights era, becoming more and more accepting of interracial relationships.

For a small number of participants, the issue of interracial relationships hit much closer to home; they had been confronted with it in their own families. Jolene, 80s, was one of those people. It was not until the end of the interview that she volunteered that information; she was discussing her views of African Americans:

> Just like I say, in the sight of God they're just as white as I am. Their soul is just as white as mine and I'm not going to mistreat if there's any way out of it. And that's the way I feel, but a lot goes on that I don't particularly agree with. Like my [grandchild] is married to a black [person], and that broke my heart, 'cause I feel like God does not intend towards being married like that . . . and I think that whites should stick with whites and blacks with black, as far as marriage is

concerned. I really do. And it just broke my heart when [they got] married but nothing I could do. And the children are beautiful. They're white as I am, and cute as buttons. I hate I don't get to see them [very often]. But that kind of disturbs me. I mean really it does. . . . And I told [my grandchild], I said, "Now I guess you know you're ruining our bloodline . . . 'cause it'll take years for the blood to clear up." You know, that's what I've been told, I don't know . . . I'm just kind of disappointed. . . . I just wish it hadn't happened, but nothing I can do.

Jolene first relayed her belief in racial equality—although by elevating whiteness, saying that blacks' "soul is just as *white* as mine" (my emphasis). Then she shared that she had been heartbroken and remains disappointed that her grandchild married an African American person and had children and thus "ruined the bloodline." Although "the children are beautiful" and "cute as buttons" (and again elevates whiteness: "they're white as I am"), she wished that the marriage had never happened.

As historians and social scientists have documented, whites have long been obsessed with the sexuality of African Americans and have been highly paranoid about the supposed threat black men pose to white women and white racial purity. This concern with maintaining the purity of white blood was the driving force behind laws banning interracial marriages and interracial cohabitation. All southern states enforced a version of such laws through the 1950s.[6] It ought not be surprising that the most visceral taboos of the participants' upbringing would have had the most staying power and resistance to modification, impervious to the decades they have had for reflection and adjustment. Again, the role of emotions (in this case, disgust, disappointment, resentment, and love) in shaping racial belief and identity comes into focus.

Losses since the Civil Rights Era: Black Cultural Dysfunction

One of the key ways in which participants portrayed the post–civil rights era as less preferable to earlier eras was by pinpointing what they saw as cultural dysfunctions within the black community that had emerged in recent decades and/or had infiltrated white culture. The way people tended to describe it was that integration had unfortunately provided new opportunities for black culture to negatively affect mainstream

white culture. Several people also questioned the effectiveness of desegregated schools. For example, John, 70s, identified some concrete
things as negative outcomes of integration—an unimproved educational
system, rap music, and "jive stuff":

> I will say this to *you* personally, the integration part of our schools, I
> don't think, has *lifted* and improved the schools necessarily, or the
> learning of our children. . . . It hasn't happened. I don't like *rap*
> music and some of . . . all this jive stuff that has precipitated primari-
> ly from the black man. Uhh, I think the white man has done more to
> raise the black man up if he's willing to do it. And I think the white
> man adopting more of the black culture has hurt the white man. I
> don't know if I've said that quite the way I mean for it to come out or
> not.

Although John shared his opinions initially with confidence, he then
expressed uncertainty about whether he "said that quite the way I mean
for it to come out or not." John seemed to acknowledge that his statements may be out of alignment with contemporary racial discourse.
However, the essence of John's perspective—that there are major dysfunctions in the black community that negatively impact the mainstream—is common today, especially among white Americans. For example, in a recent online survey, 24 percent of whites believed that
blacks are lazy, 33 percent that blacks are aggressive or violent, and 24
percent that they prefer to live on welfare.[7] A minority of white respondents agreed with positive traits of African Americans: 40 percent of
whites considered blacks law abiding, 48 percent considered them good
neighbors, and 45 percent hardworking.[8]

Harold, 70s, matter-of-factly shared his criticism for black families.
He used abstract liberalism and cultural racism reasoning,[9] arguing that
black parents, not schools, are to blame when black students have low
academic achievement:

> Some of 'em are moving up, but a lot of 'em *aren't* moving up. And I
> think you need to straighten the parents out. To be blunt, half these
> kids are the little bastards of teenage mothers, and when you have a
> baby when you're fifteen and another when you're seventeen, you're
> no *mother*, you're still a child. And if the black leaders wanna shape
> their people up, I think we need to shape the families up. Quit
> blaming everything on the school.

Harold's frustration here is palpable. He indicated that equal opportunity and meritocracy had become realities in the post–civil rights era, such that some African Americans "are moving up." Thus, blame for any unrealized progress should be shouldered by the black community. Harold argued also that black leaders should "shape their people up" rather than hold mainstream institutions, such as schools, accountable. The theme of participants expressing frustration and exhaustion with black activists is analyzed further in the next section.

Like John, Carla, 60s, believed that whites had been negatively affected through their increased exposure to black Americans in a desegregated society:

> I think it's brought society down a lot. I think them walkin' with their pants hangin' down around their knees, I can't understand that. . . . To *me* that was a black thing to start out, and now all the white boys are doin' it. Why do they wanna wear their pants so they're gon' fall down. If they had to run, they'd be in tough trouble. They'd be runnin' in their underwear. (chuckles) I just don't get it. But I think it's gonna all merge together before it's over, I'm afraid. I—well, maybe that's a good thing. You know, we used to say that it would—(pause) that they would breed them *up*, but I think [a family member] was *right*—It didn't bring the blacks up, I think it brought the whites down. I really do, and I think that's happened in the mainstream of society.

Carla was confident in her assessment that integration had brought about some unfortunate ripple effects ("I think it brought the whites down. I really do"). She implied that white culture was stronger during Jim Crow, when they had less extensive interactions with African Americans. However, Carla wavered in her projection for the future and was not sure if the end result of integration would be positive or negative ("it's gonna all merge together before it's over, I'm afraid . . . well, maybe that's a good thing").

Mack spoke at length about his views, with his wife chiming in from time to time. For example, when reflecting on the changes in society, Mack said there was still "a long way to go." His first example of today's racial barriers was that white people were unable to criticize dysfunctions of the black community without being called racist:

Interviewer: So you've seen a lot of changes then in your life?
Mack: Oh my heaven! Absolutely. Tremendous amount of changes.
Um, I think we've come a long way. I think we've still got a long way
to go. And I thi—the thing—the thing that I find disconcerting today
as we sit and talk is that anytime a white person makes *any* criticism
of blacks, he or she are immediately labeled racist, a bigot. And
therefore we just keep our mouths shut while black people continue
their merry way doing things that we think is—is totally disadvanta-
geous to them. For instance, 78 percent of all black children today
are born out of *wedlock*. (pause) [Directed at Interviewer]: I mean,
isn't a black child entitled to a daddy and mother?
Interviewer: Mmm . . .
Mack: I don't understand it.
Wife: And the breakdown of the black family.
Mack: I know that fifty, sixty years ago that wasn't true.
Wife: Absolutely not.

Mack and his wife agreed that black Americans engaged in dysfunctional behaviors and that this was primarily a post–civil rights phenomenon.
They invoked experiential knowledge to back up the assessment ("*I
know* that fifty, sixty years ago that wasn't true"—my emphasis). In
doing this, they drew a contrast between past and present, constructing
a notion of the emergence of new problems within the black community ("the breakdown of the black family"). Mack also resented another
change—not feeling free today to express this kind of criticism.

Another interesting aspect of this excerpt was how Mack asked *me* to
weigh in on his comments. While most participants acted the part of
interviewee and spoke about their experiences and views, Mack was a
particularly didactic participant who also repeatedly solicited my opinion. Given my generally very different perspective of racial issues, I was
rarely comfortable simply agreeing with him when he queried me. In
the above exchange, I doubted the accuracy of his 78 percent statistic.
Indeed, the correct number was closer to 70 percent, and children born
to unmarried mothers have increased at similar rates for all groups over
the past several decades.[10] His question—"isn't a black child entitled to
a daddy and mother?"—indicated the answer that he wanted to hear.
Giving the expected affirmative answer would have validated his prem-
ise that there was something wrong with black Americans; saying no
would have shifted the focus to why I disagreed. To avoid both of these

results and to instead encourage him to continue talking, I offered just a verbal acknowledgment, and they continued the narrative.

In these examples, the speakers used their lifetime of experiential knowledge to bolster their view that black cultural dysfunction has proliferated in the post–civil rights era. In other words, they invoked their personal experience with the segregation and civil rights eras to give context to their assessments. They believed that they had lived to see some unfortunate consequences of desegregation. By constructing a corrupted present day in contrast with the past and portraying the influence of black culture as negative, these narratives undercut the value of the civil rights movement and support the image of Jim Crow as a good or neutral era.

Losses since the Civil Rights Era: Too Many (Unfounded) Claims of Racism

A second way that participants painted the post–civil rights era in a negative light was through expressing frustration with people of color and antiracist activists who call attention to racial injustice. As the excerpts below illustrate, many heightened negative emotions emerged on this topic. When I asked Florence, 80s, to weigh in on whether there are racial problems today, she first affirmed that acceptance and understanding had improved, and then launched into a diatribe about racial labels and claims of racism:

> Interviewer : Do you think there are problems today between races? Are they similar to anything in the past, or are there new problems?
> Florence: Well, I guess there'll always be *problems*, depending on your definition of problems. Okay? I think we have a better understanding this day and time, a better acceptance of each other. . . . We all try to get *along* and not worry about it. . . . And I think it's a shame that they keep tryin' to make an issue out of racism all the time. It's a racist issue. And quit sayin' that they're Afro Americans! Okay! I'm Anglo Saxon, or Irish whatever, you know. I'm an American! They are too. But quit hammering that into us that they're Afro Americans. You know, and quit making . . . racial issues out of things. Get over it! Come on!
> Interviewer: Where do you think we're headed—the future, the next fifty years?

Florence: You've got to be optimistic. . . . I think that we are moving on, and we're forgetting the racist issue, perhaps—if *they* would let it stop. Quit mentioning it! Quit talking about it! We're people! We're people.

Notably, in response to my question, Florence did not indicate that she saw continuity between the racial environment of the past and present. Rather, she gave a positive assessment of racial progress and followed it up with bitter resentment toward those who "keep tryin' to make an issue out of racism all the time." Exhausted also with labels for non-white racial groups, Florence wanted people to do as she chose to do and just call themselves Americans. From her perspective, further racial progress is being hindered by those who refuse to "forget the racist issue." Florence did not state directly who she was referring to, but she implied African Americans generally and black activists specifically.

who gets to call them selves American

Similarly, Ava, 60s, expressed frustration toward news media and those who keep "hollering prejudice": "You know, you can holler prejudice *any time you wanna holler it!* But there was a time that blacks were mistreated. There was a time that blacks did not have the opportunities that they have today, but I do *not* believe that today blacks are (pause) discriminated against as much as the news media says they are." Arguing that equal opportunity is widely available, Ava invoked abstract liberalism. She also employed minimization by asserting that discrimination against black Americans is not as extensive as some people and the news media propose. Carla, 60s, went further in her assessment of racial discrimination. She said that whites now face discrimination, but are unable to protest it:

> It's like society has a double standard. . . . That it's *okay* as long as the whites are being discriminated against, but they're not going to hold them to the same standard. . . . There needs to be one set of standards for everybody. The blacks should have to live up to the standards the same as the whites. And it isn't happening. I just don't get it. And probably whites are so busy workin' they don't have *time* to get out and protest.

Carla asserted that whites experience discrimination in the post–civil rights era, and she offered two explanations for the persistence of this phenomenon: the current social climate gives African Americans more leeway to complain, and whites are so busy with their jobs (ostensibly in contrast with blacks) that they do not have the time to challenge their unjust predicament.

As illustrated in the above excerpts, participants expressed frustration and fatigue with African Americans' claims of racism experiences. Again, their views are not significantly divergent from younger white Americans' views. In a recent online survey of nearly a thousand white Americans (and online surveys are likely to capture a demographic younger than the interview participants), a full 41 percent agreed with the negative character trait that blacks complain.[11] However, what sets their perspective apart is how, many times, they invoked experiential wisdom to bolster their views.

Several participants reserved their most vehement commentaries for contemporary prominent black activists. Jesse Jackson and Al Sharpton were the names volunteered most frequently, and often as a duo. Notably, I did not bring up these individuals in the interviews, except to ask if/how they remembered Jesse Jackson when he was student body president and civil rights leader while attending Greensboro's historically black state university in the early 1960s during much of the local sit-in movement. Most people volunteered their views of black activists when queried in general terms about the current state of racial affairs and how further progress would be achieved. For example, when asked if there were "ways you feel like things haven't changed," T. J., 60s, proposed the "race card," Sharpton, and Jackson:

> Mm-hm. . . . I hate the race card. We play the race card for everything. If there's a figurative person that I would say I dislike, because I think he's way off base—Al Sharpton. He's a troublemaker. He always shows up if it's a black thing, but if a black person killed a white person he's not there to defend them. And Jesse Jackson . . . he denies it, but once he . . . spit in white people's salad before they served it and carried it out to them. And that's cruddy. I hate stuff like that. I guess that yeah we still have racial stuff here, and I think each generation, supposedly it's going to get a little bit better.

Echoing contemporary racial discourse, T. J. portrayed the "race card" as African Americans making unwarranted claims of prejudice and discrimination, with black activists committing the most infuriating infractions. The "race card" narrative assumes equal opportunity as the reality

and disbelieves any charges that whites or institutions enact racist practice. It is also a storyline of white victimhood; it constructs whites as
victims via being called racists and not being able to play a "race card"
themselves.

Several people minimized the continuing reality of racism by portraying black activists as seeking fame or fortune—a perception that
some had of Martin Luther King Jr. as well. For example, Burt, 80s,
said he had "no use" for Jesse Jackson: "I think Jackson was a rabble-
rouser and I thought it at the time and I still think it now. I have no use
for him at all. I think anything—I think he is constantly looking for
some quick—he's been idealized, and been treated as a black hero, and
I think he's parlayed that into a good thing. I don't have anything to do
with him." Arguing that Jesse Jackson had received too much attention
and praise and that he had "parlayed that into a good thing," Burt
implied that African Americans had been duped into seeing Jackson as
a pursuer of justice rather than self-interest.

Early in the interview, John, 70s, brought up slavery and condemned
it, then presented the success of select African Americans as a positive
outcome of slavery. He followed up those comments by criticizing black
activists for the way they keep the past alive:

> I don't know if you wanted to get into this or not, but think about it—
> slavery was probably one of the most dastardly, *horrid* things man
> has ever done to man, but stop and think today—where would be
> prominent black people today in this country right now—let's just
> say Oprah Winfrey or go back to George Washington Carver or Mar-
> tin Luther King . . . where would *they* be today? They would've
> probably never been born if it *hadn't* been for slavery bringing their
> ancestors—forefathers to this country. So people like, uh, Jesse Jack-
> son . . . and Al Sharpton, why do they keep this—they're the biggest
> racists in the world. They ten times more racist than I've ever
> thought of being. And that *galls* me to tell you the truth, because
> they won't let the past *lie*—they keep on bringin' it up, blamin' the
> white man.

John presented some noteworthy contradictions. He did not want activists to allude to connections between the racial past and present, but
he wanted to celebrate how slavery had made possible fame as an
African *American*, including contemporary figures like Oprah Winfrey.

John identified antiracist activists as "the biggest racists in the world" while arguing his own racist opinion that slavery amounted to a favor done to enslaved Africans and their descendants. John's perspective reflects themes we have seen throughout this book: open acknowledgment of past racial oppressions ("slavery was probably one of the most dastardly, *horrid* things man has ever done to man"), but a preference for emphasis on the more positive interpretations of the past (from a white perspective).

In the quotes above, there is much bitterness toward the icons of post–civil rights black activism. Jesse Jackson and Al Sharpton in particular are scapegoats for whites' frustrations with reminders of racial inequality. They have become the "face" of attacks on race neutrality and white goodness. This move is noteworthy because embodying current "racial problems" within a few vocal activists asserts racism as an individual rather than structural problem. Indeed, these men are hated because they will not stop making the case that current incidents are linked to the white supremacist past, that the United States has not in fact arrived in a "postracial" era where people of color are no longer hindered by racial bias and discrimination. In rejecting these activists as self-serving troublemakers, systemic racism is dismissed as a reality.[12]

"YOU CAN'T LIVE IN THE STEW": REJECTING TRUTH AND RECONCILIATION

Near the end of interviews, I asked participants to speak about one important local event that occurred in the post–civil rights era—the 1979 Greensboro massacre and the early-2000s truth and reconciliation effort toward healing lingering community pain and mistrust around the event. This was perhaps the issue of greatest consensus among the participants, as the overwhelming majority rejected the notion of investigating the event and thereby allowing it to linger in the collective memory. Only a handful of participants indicated a belief that anything positive could come from the truth and reconciliation effort.

In 2004, Greensboro, North Carolina, became the site of the first Truth and Reconciliation Commission in the United States.[13] The Greensboro Truth and Reconciliation Commission (GTRC) was formed with the goal of addressing community divisions and mistrust stemming from an incident that had happened more than two decades prior. In November 1979 a group of union organizers, who had recently affiliated with the Communist Workers Party (CWP), planned a rally and march to draw attention to the white supremacist tactics being employed behind the scenes to weaken the local multiracial labor movement. They titled their event "Death to the Klan." A collection of Ku Klux Klan and neo-Nazis from the region organized a caravan to attend the march, with an arsenal of firearms in tow. Through an informant, the Greensboro Police Department knew of the planned counterprotest and had a squad car assigned to follow the Klan-Nazi caravan into town. As the caravan attempted to drive through the march site, shooting ensued, and five labor activists were left dead—four white men and one African American woman.[14] News crews were present for the march, and their video cameras captured much of the event. Chilling footage shows men from the caravan retrieving rifles and handguns from the trunks of their cars and leisurely firing on the scattering crowd of adults and children. One shooter gingerly gripped a cigarette in his mouth while calmly firing his weapon repeatedly.[15] Despite the police trail on the caravan, law enforcement arrived to the scene only after the shooting ended and arrested some Klan-Nazi men.[16]

At trial in downtown Greensboro, a white jury unanimously acquitted all of the white supremacists, finding them not guilty of murder, rioting, or any crime.[17] Shortly thereafter, over concern that the incident increased racial animosities, the North Carolina Advisory Committee (NCAC) to the U.S. Commission on Civil Rights investigated the case and its aftermath. That process was sanctioned by the local political elite, and few CWP voices were given a forum.[18] The NCAC report concluded that Greensboro was polarized around economics and politics and that there was a racial divide in residents' perceptions of race in the city, with whites believing that Greensboro had been making and continued to make good progress toward integration and racial equality.[19]

In 2004, seven volunteer commissioners were elected by the community to head the GTRC, and with a small staff they worked for two years from a grant- and donation-based budget, gathering accounts from witnesses and community members, conducting historical research, and holding public town meetings.[20] The commission sought to include marginalized voices that had never adequately been heard—

notably former CWP members and residents of the predominantly black neighborhood, Morningside Homes, where the incident had taken place. Buy-in by local elite was not secured, as the process was perceived as a left-wing effort. Mayor Keith Holliday, a white man, publicly criticized the process, arguing that "harm can come from an inaccurate truth leading to inaccurate accountability, non-forgiveness and especially non-reconciliation."[21] The Greensboro city council voted on whether to publicly support the GTRC, and the vote fell along racial lines, with all white members officially opposing the commission.[22] In 2006 the GTRC's final report was published and distributed around the city. Its well-documented content strongly indicted the municipal police force who had advance knowledge of a potential violent ambush by the white supremacist faction, yet provided minimal law enforcement presence. Also implicated by the final report was the local mainstream newspaper, the *Greensboro News & Record*, which had systematically portrayed the incident as the inevitable clashing of two equally violent groups of *outsiders*—fringe white racists and indefensible communists—who came to blows only incidentally, and unfortunately, on Greensboro soil.[23]

Although most of the interviews for this book were conducted within a year or two of the conclusion of the GTRC process and public release of the report, few of the participants indicated having a clear understanding of the goals and strategies of the GTRC. They seemed to reflect the lack of buy-in for the process from the broader community. Nevertheless, nearly all of the participants shared their opinions of the commission. Most were negative, showing little appreciation and much resentment that this trailblazing effort toward expanding historical understanding and fostering community-wide communication had occurred in their city. The distancing and rejection that was apparent in participants' portrayals of Greensboro's 1960s civil rights activism was reflected here, but with a thicker layer of resentment.

In a typical example, Darla, 70s, claimed that understanding the past was important, but she disagreed with truth and reconciliation in Greensboro:

> I think children need to know how things were, and [my grandchildren will] say, when I've said somethin' that . . . black people had to sit in the balcony, and they would say, "Well, *why* would they *do* that?" I mean, it's hard for them to understand that that kind of thing

happened, and (pause) I mean, I remember it very vividly, and (pause) I *do* think it's important to tell the children things that have happened and (pause) things that you lived through, because it adds to their knowledge.

However, when I asked Darla about the local truth and reconciliation effort, she reasoned that enough time had passed to make the 1979 incident insignificant: "I'm all for things that are better for mankind, but I feel like it's been talked about and rehashed and rehashed and maybe enough's been said about it. . . . It may help some, but I don't have real strong feelings, thinkin' that it's gonna change anything after this length of time." Darla doubted that the effort could be effective because it had been overanalyzed already and too much time had passed.

Verna, 80s, began the interview with tears over the warm memories of her beloved black childhood nanny, and she ended the interview with sharp criticism of the GTRC—and only on the idea of it, for she said she was unaware of it prior to my brief explanation. She, like many other respondents, argued that bringing up past controversies is counterproductive and does much more harm than good:

> To go back over those things . . . and *scratch* it, it's like you fell down and hurt your knee, and you keep *scratching* at it, and it's never gonna get well. And I think going *over* and *over* and *over* and *over* doesn't solve a John Brown thing. It just festers things. Alright, you found that the Klu Klux, they did this and the other did that, and the newspaper did this, or they gave permission to do this and . . . they want those facts down and that's it, to *shut the door*! Or, if you wanna go find out about it, read about it, read about it, read about it. But as far as just going through digging it up, digging it up . . . You can't live in the stew. You can't always control what happens *to* you, but you can control what you do with it as the result. And as far as stirrin' things up and bringing back the ugliness and the despicable things that we've done, move on to make things *better* not just stay in the *stew* of somebody did this and somebody did that and got to change this and got to get more money for that. Get over with it! *Move* on. And I guess the older you get, you get disgusted at the picky-picky-picky type of things, and you look back and find that they don't work, you know.

Verna's disgust was palpable and was mirrored in other narratives. She made the case that while individual knowledge seeking was acceptable ("if you wanna go find out about it, read about it"), it was highly problematic to engage in more collective or public information gathering, for it represented staying "in the stew." Like several other participants, Verna argued that her age had given her the wisdom to know that these types of efforts were more hurtful than helpful ("you look back and find that they don't work").

Several people vented frustration and resentment over the idea of truth-telling when they believed it had to do with the tumultuous racial past. In actuality, the 1979 Greensboro massacre involved a group of white supremacists (all white) and a group of labor organizers (multiracial); it was not a straightforward black–white conflict or a black activist–led GTRC effort, but several participants described it that way. One married couple, who were also incensed by the GTRC, revealed this perception:

> Interviewer: Have you heard about the truth and reconciliation commission?
> Wife: *Yes*. I think they are a pathetic group of people looking for a cause. That is my opinion of 'em. The people that are on that committee want recognition. You know, it's like beating a dead *horse!* This issue about the Klan and the blacks fighting it out and they're trying to reconcile what happened—*it's a dead issue!* Get *over* it and let's move on! I don't see there's any need of their existence. Find a new issue. Do something productive. Okay?
> Husband: I agree with her on that. I think the thing was taken through the courts. Hadn't it been through the courts? . . . my understanding . . . it was settled in the courts.
> Wife: And let's just move on.
> Husband: It's beatin' a dead horse.
> Interviewer: So in general do you think it's important to talk about bad things that have happened in the past?
> Husband: I think you should. But—but—
> Wife: And build on the mistakes that were made, but don't blame me for slavery. I had nothin' to do with it, my parents had nothing to do with it. It was the *times* . . . but let's build on the past and let's move on and let's remember that we are Americans and *pull together.* Make this country a better place for our children and grandchildren. . . . Regardless of what color you are, or what your race or your

religion is, we are *Americans*, and let's be proud of the fact that we are.

Husband: You won't get an argument with me about that.

This couple interacted and played off one another's comments, building a consensus that truth and reconciliation was a futile effort of "beating a dead horse." While the man gave a nod to the value of discussing "bad things that have happened," he agreed with his wife that it was wrong to blame current whites for past transgressions (i.e., slavery) and it was right to follow ideals of colorblindness and patriotism.

Not every participant was opposed to the local truth and reconciliation campaign. One of the rare positive views of the GTRC came from Bonnie, 80s:

> I'm all for it and if the Truth and Reconciliation Committee could have brought about some healing then I would favor it, but some people think, "Well, there's nothing to heal . . . city didn't do anything wrong," but, you see, it's so hard to put yourself in somebody else's shoes and apparently these black leaders felt there was something to heal and I mean what would it have hurt to have said we're sorry? *I mean yes, do your study*, and if we can heal this divisiveness, let's do it! Didn't happen. (chuckles)

Through her former job, Bonnie had more ready access to accurate information about the 1979 event and the GTRC process. In contrast with the majority of participants, she saw the GTRC not only as valid, but also as a potential positive force for the community at large. She expressed disappointment at how so many (white) Greensboro residents had dismissed the effort outright, and she affirmed the importance of using empathy to understand the motivation for reconciliation.

Many participants believed, theoretically, in dealing with the legacy of the racial past because there was still progress to be made. Overwhelmingly, however, they were opposed to efforts attempting just that. Hope, 70s, revealed this division between theory and practice:

> Interviewer: So if there are any problems today that have to do with race, what do you think they are?
> Hope: I think it's people that's not gonna ever forgive and they just gonna keep stirring and stirring. The more you stir on something that stings it gets worse and worse, you know. . . .

Interviewer: What do you think we can do to make it better?
Hope: I think more people should go to programs that would lift the hatred out of people's heart. . . . I really don't know if they just need to get black and white together and try, but I know that's gonna be hard to do. But maybe one of these days, I hope and pray that it will——that black would care about white and white would care about black. I really do.

On the one hand, Hope believed that talking about the racial past was counterproductive. On the other hand, she wished that people could come together in compassion and goodwill. Hope expressed one of the most hopeful views of the racial future, as she wished for a shift toward racial harmony and understanding. However, her reasoning revealed a contradiction: (1) people should forgive rather than "keep stirring and stirring" and (2) "go to programs that would lift the hatred out of people's heart." This logic suggests that the racial past should be depoliticized and any efforts toward healing should be dealt with in the personal realm and target "hate."

ON THE RELEVANCE OF THE RACIAL PAST

As the conversation shifted to contemporary matters, many participants affirmed with satisfaction that the post–civil rights culture was the only thing their grandchildren had known. Most people spoke favorably of certain aspects of life today, such as integrated social spaces and people's seeming colorblindness. One of the final interview questions asked participants what they would do if they were asked to speak to a group of schoolchildren about the racial past. Again, a divide between theory and practice came into focus. While many people had said they thought that remembering was important, most people were either opposed to more public forms of dialogue or simply at a loss for what they could contribute to the conversation. Most often, participants had to pause and think for some time before they had an answer to the question. It was clear that few had considered the possibility that their experiences as Jim Crow–era white southerners gave them something to share with future generations, that this could be an integral part of their ancestral contribution.

Chuck's, 70s, response was typical—vague and not particularly explanatory: "I guess, to answer the question, how would we . . . describe segregation in our lifetimes, I would say, 'We just did it the way we did it, because that's what was done.' And I don't know that we had any ideas about how we could buck it or change it or anything until late in life." Several people included in their response an assessment of race today, usually indicating that the racial past was irrelevant because so much had changed. Sharon, 60s, advocated for an amoral assessment of segregation, combined with an assertion that the past is truly past:

> (Long pause) Well, (pause) I would have to tell my experiences. But I would explain that it was what society expected at the time, in our culture. And it doesn't mean it was right, it doesn't mean it was wrong, but things have changed. . . . I would certainly gear it along the fact that it's history, it's changed (pause) and that we should respect our diversity. I could tell 'em some experiences, but I would certainly monitor it with (pause) the fact that it's changed.

Sharon also said that "actions speak very, very loudly" and argued that adults role modeling racial harmony would have a more positive and resonant impact than just talking about the past.

For several participants, the idea of sharing knowledge about segregation was acceptable, and even valuable, but they reported rarely if ever engaging in such dialogue. Ingrid, 60s, was typical of people who favored it theoretically but did not engage in it:

> Interviewer: Do you think it's important to pass on your memories of the southern past to younger people who didn't experience it firsthand like you did?
> Ingrid: Yeah. What I know about it. I think it's important for them to know that there was unfairness.
> Interviewer: Do you tell your children and grandchildren about these things?
> Ingrid: Not very often, very little. (laughing) . . .
> Interviewer: Why don't you tell them?
> Ingrid: You know, I don't know, other than when the subject comes up if they want to talk about it, I'm willing to talk about it. But it's not something I bring up to them, because I see in my grandchildren that things are already going so much better in that direction.

Ingrid affirmed that "it's important for them to know that there was unfairness," but she never broached the subject with her grandchildren because "things are already going so much better in that direction." Most participants failed to see the relevance of their Jim Crow experiences in the context of today's society.

Although everyone agreed that history in general is important, not everyone was comfortable with the idea of focusing on racial history. Some felt that today's youth would be unable to comprehend the racial past, with all its nuances, because they had only experienced a patently different racial era. This brings back into focus the third complexity, analyzed in this chapter: participants generally rated integration favorably but were uncomfortable with too many reminders of past oppression and even resented links being made between the racial present and past. Many people had clearly incorporated styles of contemporary race discourse into their narratives, agreeing that historical inequalities had been unjust and that equal opportunity was a post–civil rights reality. The next and final chapter synthesizes the major insights of this book and makes the case that elder white southerners' narratives reveal that the processes maintaining whites' identity and structural racism are interrelated.

7

MEMORY AND WHITE MORAL IDENTITY

People want to think well of their social group, and so even if they are equally exposed to truthful and flattering versions of the past, they may find it easier to understand, remember, and repeat the flattering ones.[1]

Memory is not static and is not located in the past; memory is a *contemporary* process of selecting and interpreting the past.[2] Memory is a process carried out to achieve cultural and political ends. In constant flux and subject to myriad interpretations, memory is perpetually contested terrain, as people and groups battle over how to keep the past alive. Remembering is powerfully shaped by one's perspective and current needs for identity maintenance. The people interviewed for this book—ordinary white, elder, lifelong southerners—offer a unique lens on how people construct the past through memory. As white individuals who outlived an era of overt white supremacy under legal segregation and who lived through the racial justice struggles of the civil rights era, their narratives reveal complexities in how dominant groups interpret social inequality and expansions of social equality. Having had several decades to adapt to a post–civil rights society that professes to be free from the egregious racial problems of the past, elder white southerners occupy a key social location for understanding how memory is linked to identity maintenance.

It is common for individuals and groups to use memory as a tool to positively represent themselves, although this is accomplished with varying levels of consciousness and intent.[3] As psychologists Baumeister and Hastings explain, people's "interpretive needs" rooted in a positive self-image drive their portrayals of and beliefs about the past:

> Like individuals, social groups have important memories that help them define themselves, understand the world, and structure their motivations. Also like individuals, social groups may often find that a literal, objective record of the facts is not always the most helpful way of satisfying those interpretive needs. As a result, social groups . . . will sometimes gradually distort their memories in systematic ways. . . . Most groups, like most individuals, try to maintain a positive image of self. Because the reality of events does not always fit that desired image, it is necessary to choose between revising the image and revising the meaning of events.[4]

When "the reality of events does not . . . fit that desired image" of the self, groups are motivated to distort their memories. In the post–civil rights era where claiming to be nonracist is in vogue, the reality of the racial past does not fit an image of a "good" white South. Thus, while distortions of memory are common among all people to a certain extent, elder white southerners are a group whose identity maintenance impels them to misremember and misrepresent the racial past. Key mechanisms through which people distort memory include selectively omitting unflattering facts, fabricating falsehoods, exaggerating or embellishing certain details, and lessening responsibility through blaming the "enemy" or one's circumstances.[5] From this perspective on memory distortion we can make sense of the myriad patterns in the interview narratives revealed throughout this book, including confusion about dates and events and misuse of important terms, portrayals of Jim Crow interactions as amicable, emphasis on the importance of class inequality over racial injustice, and whites-as-victims of the civil rights and post–civil rights eras.

Although a deeply personal phenomenon, identity maintenance via memory is not merely about the personal. Memory is implicated in the maintenance of social structures. Joe Feagin points out that "how we interpret and experience our racialized present depends substantially on our knowledge of and interpretations of our racialized past. The collective memory of that racist past not only shapes, but legitimates, the established racial structure of today's society."[6] Collective memories help make possible a certain set of explanations for the status quo, enabling dominant groups to justify systemic inequalities from which they benefit. For example, memories that construct segregation as "just the way it was" or Jim Crow whites as people rather uninvested in white supremacy enable a worldview that interprets U.S. social structures as generally fair (not fundamentally oppressive) and dominant groups as neutral actors (not interested in the maintenance of inequality).

WHITE MORAL IDENTITY MAKING: CONSTRUCTING SOCIETY, SELF, AND OTHER

Elder white southerners, like other groups, work to maintain a positive sense of self. They have had to do so by negotiating a historical record that establishes them as people who were favored by Jim Crow inequalities. By highlighting the process of collective and individual identity maintenance, we can make sense of the dominant themes in how people constructed the southern racial past in the ways they did. Context is important: the interviews were conducted four decades into a post–civil rights era that deems multiculturalism and integration as theoretical ideals and the civil rights movement as a redemptive process. In this milieu, publicly praising Jim Crow's racial rules is essentially off-limits. Furthermore, white southerners have shifted their perspectives through interaction with social changes.[7] To establish a positive identity with reference to the racial past, elder white southerners would need to acknowledge segregation's racial disparities. But heavily emphasizing those disparities as injustices might indict elder white southerners as active agents of white supremacy. Throughout the narratives were mentions of Jim Crow inequalities and discussions of rather pleasant racial interactions. Overall, people portrayed the segregation era as complex and redeemable, and they portrayed their segregation-era selves as uninvolved in and unaffected by racism. Additionally, they often engaged in maneuvers of white protectionism, pardoning or rationalizing the racial prejudice that they identified within other white individuals, often family members. Their segregation narratives revealed that participants constructed a positive identity for themselves, other (but not all) whites, and the white South.

When discussing the civil rights era, many people claimed to have been amenable to the activism from the onset, agreeing with the logic of equal access to facilities and services. However, strongly asserting the value of the civil rights movement might indict the white South for having produced an unjust racial structure and fighting to maintain it when challenged. Thus, we saw how participants demonstrated symbolic detachment and distancing from the movement through inaccurate and vague recall of noteworthy people and events and by downplaying activists' efforts and the pervasiveness of white opposition to those efforts. Ultimately, they presented the civil rights movement as a necessary and even "good" thing but as warranting today rather limited commemorations. In the contemporary context, elder white southerners cannot assert a positive identity by outright denying the worth of the movement, but prominent emphasis on the black freedom struggle would lead to questions about the role they and other whites played in resisting it. Thus, we saw how participants constructed white innocence via presenting themselves as vulnerable and targeted by angry African Americans and impersonal social changes during the civil rights era. Their white victimhood narrative skirts the issue of white southerners' culpability in maintaining Jim Crow and passively witnessing or actively resisting the movement. Through claiming a status of racial vulnerability at the onset of the movement, they imply the racial innocence of their Jim Crow–era selves.

As they spoke of the role of memory in the post–civil rights era, many elder white southerners resented continued reminders of "negative" aspects of the racial past, arguing that "moving on" was the best route to racial reconciliation. Although this "forget or at least forgive" ethos was presented as a universal positive, we can see how it builds further their own positive identity. Participants asserted equal opportunity in contemporary society and downplayed the relationship between the segregation era and current inequalities, presenting today's racial inequalities as not closely linked to past oppression. Rather, there were explanatory criticisms of black culture (perceived as more dysfunctional than in the past) and African American activists (perceived as fanning the flames of racial resentment). Although comfortable celebrating racial progress, few saw clear connections between past oppression and present inequalities, and there was heavy criticism of current racial justice efforts. Through their post–civil rights narratives, they portrayed mainstream society as fair and open (or even skewed in favor of nonwhites), themselves as enlightened, and African Americans as problematic.

Through their narratives, the participants were engaged in constructing a lifelong white moral identity, articulating a sense of themselves as good people innocent of perpetuating racial oppression. I argue that white moral identity making consists of (1) asserting the (white) self as virtuous and generous, (2) portraying people of color as deficient in some way, and (3) downplaying the white-dominant racial hierarchy. In other words, whites present themselves as racially innocent and enlightened through direct claims, by denigrating or patronizing people of color, and by presenting mainstream society as not significantly structured by white racism. Through employing these strategies of white moral identity making, whites are able to present themselves in differing ways relative to the context. For example, upper-income white southerners portrayed their families as blacks' benefactors during Jim Crow (strategies 1 and 2), some lower-income people claimed that they had been just as disadvantaged as black southerners (strategy 3), and several people remembered themselves as victims during the civil rights era (strategies 1, 2, and 3). Whether employed in memory narratives or interpretations of contemporary life, white moral identity making is a process that maintains both a personal and collective sense of self through constructing whites and nonwhites.

CONTINUITIES AND ADAPTATIONS: IDEOLOGY AND FRAMING

 Elder white southerners are not "living in the past"; they participate in contemporary culture and discourse. Indeed, there are noteworthy similarities between their narratives and how younger whites interpret the racial past and present. Numerous social scientists argue that racial views are now frequently expressed through ideals of "colorblindness," whereby equal opportunity is assumed and racial inequalities are rationalized in less overtly racist ways than in the segregation era when whites asserted their innate racial superiority.[8] Interweaving beliefs in individualism and meritocracy with culturally based criticisms of people of color, younger whites are dismissive of current racial justice efforts because they believe such things unfairly disadvantage whites.[9] According to today's logic, systemic white racism was eradicated by the civil rights movement and no further interventions are required because people of color are responsible for their own destiny.[10] Racism is now popularly conceived of as a problem consisting entirely of individuals' prejudices. We saw in the previous chapter how the interview participants' views echoed these styles of contemporary ideology—for example, claiming that it was African Americans and antiracist activists who made racial issues worse because they were the ones keeping racial animosities alive.

However, an important way that elder white southerners and younger whites differ is how they situate themselves in relation to the racial past. Younger whites view systemic racial oppression as a historical issue and thus not relevant to their perspective. They distance themselves from segregation (and slavery) as part of asserting both their individual nonracism and the nonracism of the post–civil rights society in which they have always lived—for example, claiming that since segregation ended before they were born, they should not be burdened with white guilt or policies to address past oppression.[11] Because they personally lived through an era of overt white racism, older whites cannot wield the same historical distancing maneuver as effectively as younger whites do, although we did see some such attempts (for example, "don't blame me for slavery" and "our generation had nothing to do with discrimination"). More common was for participants to incorporate their perceptions of the segregation era into contemporary discourse. For example, musing about the "breakdown of the black family" post civil rights (recall the exchange between Mack and his wife in chapter 6) implies that structural racial inequalities existed but have been dismantled and that recent *cultural* dysfunctions explain black Americans' status. Avoiding indicting themselves or the segregation era for white racism, this type of interpretation calls attention to "what went wrong" among African Americans and thus manages to both assert contemporary equal opportunity and subtly construct segregation as a wholesome era. The participants in this study demonstrated that older whites have, to a certain extent, been able to weave their interpretations of the racial past into post–civil rights discourse. Therefore I would emphasize the continuity in the white racial frame across time—that how Americans think and talk about race has shifted in response to societal changes, but the foundational racial logic has remained quite consistent. Whites are in-

vested in seeing themselves as good, and they contrast themselves
against people of color, and sometimes other whites, to do so.[12]

Furthermore, at times the narratives seemed to be in conversation
with current conclusions about segregation. Some of what happened in
the interviews was the attempt to dispel simplistic notions that all Jim
Crow white southerners were driven by anti-black hatred.[13] Recall
June, profiled in the first chapter, who lashed out over the phone,
insisting that the only point worth emphasizing about the South's racial
past was the amicable relations, because all the negative aspects were
not only inaccurate, they had been overplayed. Before I had a chance to
explain the research study, June assumed my agenda must be to make
whites look bad, which she felt, with much resentment, had already
been done. Also, a few participants shared that their children or grandchildren had chastised them for making statements that sounded like
old-fashioned prejudice. They are aware that people of their background are at least sometimes seen as racially suspect. Thus, we could
view their many stories of mutual care and respect between Jim Crow
whites and blacks as inspired in part by perceived attacks on their morality and rationality. Of course, embedded in this perspective is the
inaccurate belief that racism is, and always has been, a problem located
in the hearts and minds of select individuals rather than in the society's
structures.

Many people echoed June's perspective that racial progress would
consist of downplaying racial inequality and emphasizing instead more
positive things. (Alluded to throughout chapters 2–5, this reasoning
emerged plainly in chapter 6.) At issue is what positivity means. Not an
objective assessment, from white southerners' standpoints, being positive involves "moving on" from highlighting history that shows that the
South was a hostile place in which to be nonwhite. For many of the
participants, being positive can include an *acknowledgment* of past injustice, but one ought not focus attention there. Indeed, in contrast
with June, most participants did not deny that legal segregation produced unjust racial inequalities. But there was marked fatigue with
continued reminders and even a near consensus that racial progress was
being thwarted by such reminders. Some would like for their experiential knowledge to be awarded more respect.

June and other participants illustrated an intricately emotional relationship to the racial past. Numerous interview narratives were infused

with strong emotions and opinions regarding the racial past and contemporary racial issues, even though most people claimed that they had
never been particularly affected by race and were not especially interested in the research topic. They largely bought in to the common
notion that being white is being without race—that "race" is something
that whites only experience when interacting with people of color and
bearing witness to nonwhites' lives. This is not an unexpected phenomenon but is noteworthy considering that the participants had spent their
formative years living in a culture overtly shaped by white supremacist
ideology and Jim Crow statutes. These are people who were confronted
with the civil rights movement as a national and local movement that
challenged the racial status quo and, thus, whites' status and sense of
normalcy. Any claims of emotional detachment to the racial past, then,
were belied by the interview narratives themselves and are best viewed
as a strategy of denial.

DENIAL, REMEMBRANCE, AND JUSTICE

In the aftermath of World War II, many non-Jewish Germans claimed,
despite much evidence to the contrary, that they had not been aware of
Nazi genocidal pogroms.[14] They even argued that they were unfairly
being cast as villains, an attack on par with being sent to concentration
camps.[15] When interviewed decades later, former members of Indiana's
1920s Women of the Ku Klux Klan claimed that they had engaged
exclusively in friendship and community building, even though they had
actively supported the men's Klan and created their own white supremacist campaigns.[16] When a past reality comes to be seen as unflattering
to a dominant group's image, denial is a common occurrence. People
who were advantaged in an oppressive society and participated in the
maintenance of that society's norms are invested in constructing a positive sense of self and holding on to their status.

These narratives also shed some light on how oppression can become a rote, everyday normality, especially among those not bearing
the brunt of the oppression. Participants indicated time and again that
they had not been fully aware of the depth of racial inequality during
segregation. They would have rarely been encouraged, in their homes
and social circles, to develop a critical analysis of "the way things were,"

although they had—and continue to have—the potential to do so. They would have also been discouraged from developing genuine empathy for African Americans' racialized experiences, even for those individuals they may have cared for deeply. It is difficult to "see" the suffering or disadvantages of those with whom you do not fully empathize, especially if your status and way of life rely on the maintenance of that oppression. Segregation-era white southerners learned, some with relative ease and some with trepidation, to accept and participate in the white supremacist ideology and practices of their society.[17]

We need not assert conscious intent in the process of remembering and identity maintenance. As sociologist Stanley Cohen argues, members of dominant groups have the ability to shut out or ignore the injustice and suffering around them, not from coercion but from cultural habit.[18] In this view, denial is integral to how dominant groups are accustomed to managing both their past *and* their present. Although denying historical atrocities and misrepresenting blatant injustices may seem like egregious breaks from rational interpretation, denial is *normal*.[19] Even in the early 1960s, at the height of the civil rights movement, a majority of white Americans—between two-thirds and 90 percent—reported in polls that African Americans had equal access to education, employment, and housing opportunities.[20] Thus, even before the transition to post–civil rights discourse, whites were telling pollsters—presumably having convinced themselves—that racial equity, not discrimination, was the reality. Despite the shifting of public discourse across time, the dominant racial worldview—the white racial frame—has long provided the organizing ideas that enable the rationalization of racial inequalities.[21]

Denial by whites in a white-dominant society is readily enabled by prevailing ideological discourse and white racial frame. Furthermore, it has become clear in this book that the current ideology can expect an acknowledgment of past realities *and* provide the tools to misrepresent that past. The current national narrative of the civil rights movement constructs it as a good social movement that ended segregation and brought about true equal opportunity. Elder white southerners have adapted to a changing society and have had to deal with the post–civil rights perception of Jim Crow as a period of racial injustice. At the same time, the white racial frame provides the logic of white normality and virtuousness, black dysfunction, and inaccurate assertions of equal opportunity. Thus we saw, via analyzing the three major complexities in the interview narratives, how participants both acknowledged structural realities of the racial past and emphasized alternative perceptions (for example, of nice Jim Crow racial relations or white victimization in the civil rights era).

Indeed, whites have worked to construct racial realities throughout U.S. history such that their preferred interpretations are recentered.[22] Scholars of the American South have noted that, in the aftermaths of the Civil War, Reconstruction, and the civil rights movement, white southerners asserted notions of white innocence and victimization at the hands of "outsiders" and black activists.[23] Post–Civil War white southerners promoted a "reconciliation" narrative that emphasized, instead of slavery's end and the expansion of social justice, the losses faced by the (white) North and South alike.[24] The still wildly popular film *Gone with the Wind* (1939) exemplifies this cultural shift. As historian David Blight has argued, the white South's narrative of its own loss and recovery won out because the white North bought into it and participated in mainstreaming it.[25] How we are to remember the southern past is in the hands of the entire nation, not just the South.

This book has revealed contours of defensiveness and denial maintained today among elder white southerners through their narratives of the racial past. Denial was demonstrated time and again in the interview narratives, through such things as individualized notions of racism (i.e., "opting out" of racism and identifying racist individuals), expressed obliviousness regarding the origins of white racist segregation statutes, and assertions of African Americans' contemporary dominance of society. This denial fuels resistance against movement toward a society with expanded racial equity. As Feagin argues, the perpetuation of systemic racism in a society requires a "sustained collective forgetting of society's harsh realities" and "selective remembering, most of which abandons white responsibilities for past oppression or glorifies white achievements."[26] By constructing themselves as lifelong advocates of equality and racial goodwill, and even by acknowledging structural racial inequalities, elder white southerners craft a positive identity in the post–civil rights era and downplay the white supremacist realities of their collective past and present. Cohen explains that *not* knowing can be much more complex than a simple act of turning a blind eye: "We are vaguely aware of choosing not to look at the facts, but not quite conscious of just what it is we are evading. We know, but at the same time we don't know."[27] Philosopher Charles Mills asserts that this propensity for whites to *not know* the racial reality—which he calls the "epistemology of ignorance"—is not accidental, but rather is a requirement of maintaining structures of white domination. He argues that whites who buy in to the status quo (who sign on to the "racial contract") are invested in misinterpreting the world and will receive much validation within white society for doing so.[28]

There used to be an official called the *remembrancer*. "The title was actually a euphemism for debt-collector; the official's job was to remind people of what they would have liked to forget."[29] Could a contemporary remembrancer responsible for the U.S. South's racial history be warranted? Could remembrancing be a collective effort? An honest accounting of our racial past *and* present will be essential if we are to move toward true equity and a freer society. As truth and reconciliation efforts emphasize, the experiences, memories, and perspectives of all people—victimizers and victims as well as those who stood by and did nothing—must be reconciled together and with the historical evidence. Collectively we are tasked with determining true stories from false accounts, experiential insight from self-serving logic, liberation ethics from status quo moralizing. As W. E. B. Du Bois wrote nearly one hundred years ago, "A true and worthy ideal frees and uplifts a people; a false ideal imprisons and lowers. Say to men, earnestly and repeatedly: 'Honesty is best, knowledge is power; do unto others as you would be done by.' Say this and act it and the nation must move toward it, if not to it."[30]

APPENDIX
Researching Elder White Southerners

There are numerous debates among qualitative researchers about the methods we use and the impacts of those choices. Should the interviewer be "race-matched" to interviewees?[1] How much of ourselves should we reveal to (or conceal from) participants in order to build rapport?[2] When studying dominant group members, how do we balance a critical analysis and ethical treatment of participants?[3] Is it an antiracist researcher's responsibility to challenge participants who express racism or argue erroneous facts?[4] How can we make sure our work won't be misinterpreted or misused?[5] And how can we manage, and make analytical use of, our emotions?[6]

The first question was by far the simplest for me. My interviews were race-matched naturally, because I am white and wanted to conduct a study on white southerners' memories. In a previous study I had interviewed both black and white southerners. The white participants had less accurate and detailed recall and less evident investment in the racial past, and I wanted to explore white memory and identity more in depth. Plus, innumerable studies have approached race as a people of color issue, and so whites have less often been analyzed. But my research design was not a simple matter for others to understand. Many people, including several of my participants, asked me why I chose to only interview whites or suggested I ought to include nonwhites. In fact, one of the concerns I had to address from the Institutional Review

Board that reviewed my research proposal was the possibility that I was going to "do harm" by not including black southerners in my sample. Race researchers have to deal with mainstream assumptions around race, such as the notions that whites have no race and that whiteness only has meaning when contrasted with nonwhiteness.

For research, the notion of race-matching is often couched in terms of being an "insider" versus an "outsider." It is commonly assumed that marginalized groups (e.g., people of color) are likelier to be forthright with a researcher who is similarly situated in the social hierarchy, especially when they have had bad experiences with researchers in the past. On the other hand, racial insider researchers can be subject to insider talk rife with taken-for-granted assumptions, and they may be restricted by expectations that they conform to in-group norms. Race-matching does not guarantee better data.[7] Additionally, even if a researcher believes she has an edge on establishing insiderness, there is no guarantee that participants will interpret her that way. Charles Gallagher said that white southern respondents othered him when they perceived him as a northerner, overeducated, or ethnically ambiguous.[8] Karyn McKinney reflected that just by querying whites about race for her research she set herself up to be read as an outsider despite being white herself.[9] Selecting one or two traits, like race or gender, is a limited way to determine insider–outsider status. There are rather self-evident characteristics a researcher cannot control (e.g., race/phenotype, gender, age, body type), personal characteristics a researcher may elect to reveal or conceal (e.g., affiliations, experiences, identities), and performative aspects a researcher may make conscious decisions around (e.g., dress, demeanor, communication style). I made numerous choices around my self-presentation, not to establish insider status per se, but in the interest of building trust and collecting good data.

Race, gender, class, and age have been noted as the biggest barriers to communication.[10] These factors do not operate in isolation, and this list is not nearly exhaustive, so there is much that impacts their effects. I was race-matched, gender-matched with the women, class-mixed, and the age gap was large. Although I was white like them, by racial perspective I diverged from most of the participants. I had been studying race and racism for several years as a graduate student (and felt confident in my knowledge), and I had come to identify as an antiracist. I chose not to share outright my antiracist identity. *Antiracist* is not a

term many people of that cohort would be familiar with, and I did not
wish to put focus on myself or give the impression that I saw myself as
different from them or opposed to their views. For southerners, regional background takes on heightened importance. It usually came out in
conversation that I was a southerner, through sharing that I am from
Arkansas, or needing to explain that I was getting my degree at Texas
A&M University but living and conducting my research in North Carolina. I was in my mid-20s during the interviews, so to them I was
basically of the "grandchild" cohort. Most participants were comfortable being interviewed and said that they were happy to help out a
student/youngster. Southernness intersected with my race, gender, age,
and student status to provide what seemed a clear expectation for establishing trust—to be deferential. However, with some participants, I was
on edge and felt trapped in "respect your elders" etiquette.

It is quite clear in numerous interview excerpts throughout this book
that many participants were rather forthcoming about their racial views
in ways they were unlikely to have been with a black or multiracial
interviewer. Some people made clear that they read me as white like
them and therefore as aligned with their experience and perspective.
For example, several times Harold referenced our shared whiteness by
using "we/us" language. At one point he said, "*I think* nowadays the
blacks are at the bottom, the Asians are all moving up, the Mexicans are
movin' up. Overall the blacks *aren't* moving up. But *I think* their problem is not you and me holding them down. I think it's them holding
themselves down by chaotic family structure . . . and parents who are
not interested in the kid." Harold not only used "you and me" in
contrast to African Americans, he asserted the two of us as a proxy for
all whites, or mainstream society's structures ("their problem is not you
and me holding them down"). Later in the interview, Harold was more
specific about who *we* represented: "It's much easier, the black race, to
blame you and me—whites or upper class or whatever—on the fact that
the blacks are at the bottom than it is to say, 'We're the one at fault, we
want our kids to go to school, we want 'em to behave . . . and *move*
ourselves *up*.'" By saying "you and me—whites or upper class or whatever," Harold confirmed that we represented upper-income white
Americans/America who bore no responsibility for African Americans'
status. In these statements, I noticed that Harold never looked to me
for affirmation. He expressed his views with ease and gave no indication

that he cared about the extent of my agreement. It is possible that he did not realize his "we" language usage. It seemed—and still seems—to me that if I had intervened, I would have disrupted the flow of his narrative and turned the interview into a forum to debate the realities of racial inequality.

How much did being southern matter? At the point in my life when I was conducting the interviews, I had lost most of my thick southern accent and did not try to conjure it for the interviews for ethical and authenticity reasons. Although it is likely that participants read me as not "from there," regionally or generationally, my being southern did at times seem an important way for building connections. For example, Mack thought that my southernness enabled me to understand segregation like he did:

> Mack: I think in some *strange* way we felt like [segregation] was wrong. We tried in *our* way to make that less painful, maybe, for both of us—our black friends and us. And none of this makes sense 'cause it's convoluted. Inasmuch as you were born and reared in Arkansas, you understand some of it, I'm sure.
> Interviewer: Mm-hm, yeah.

This was one of several moments with Mack—a notably didactic participant—where I question the choices I made. Mack marked me as a white southern insider to whom he did not need to explain everything, and, by simply acquiescing, I let pass the opportunity to solicit an explanation. (In truth, I did not actually "understand some of it.") I may have left the impression that I interpreted race in similar ways to him. Although I cringed when listening to the audio recording and transcribing this exchange, I knew also that I was struggling to interact with a particularly dominant interviewee. Mack displayed much thoughtfulness, critical thinking, and warmth, but drove the interview as if I were the interviewee.

Mack was one of the participants who "jumped the gun" by dominating the interview from the start and not leaving much space for me to ask questions.[11] I found this both perplexing—surely they knew that interviewers are supposed to ask the questions?—and disempowering (thus producing moments like the above). I bristled when people said things with complete confidence that were, to my ears, ill-informed on the facts, patently racist, or condescending to black Americans or to me (as an interviewer, woman, or race scholar). I had to make careful decisions about when and how to challenge or ask for clarification. Ava was one such person who held very strong opinions that were not always rooted in fact. I tired of her diatribes and tried a few times to interrupt her commentary, but she deflected me. Here is an illustrative exchange:

> Ava: If you wanna get prejudice, look at the difference between the salaries of men and women. But we don't have Jesse Jackson or Al Sharpton sayin' women should make a bigger salary . . . all they know how to say is black and white.
> Interviewer: Mm-hm. The—the same, um, there's the same difference between whites and blacks. Whites get paid more than blacks do for jobs.
> Ava: (pause) I don't know.
> Interviewer: It's just something we learn in sociology, that's—
> Ava: Oh. I do know from personal experience, um, uh, that women get paid less than men do.
> Interviewer: Yeah. That's also true.
> Ava: Um, I worked . . . for a company years ago. And they decided to move the office . . . [and my boss] said, "I would rather have you than any five people I've got workin' for me." He said, "But they will *not* transfer you because you're a woman." . . . Uh, if you wanna call it prejudice, the American male has been brought up to believe that he is superior.
> Interviewer: Do you think whites have been brought up that way too? To believe that whites are superior?
> Ava: (pause) *I* don't think so.

I did not forcefully challenge Ava. I first offered a fact about the racial wage gap to see how she would incorporate it into her statements. I then affirmed her argument about the sexism in employment. In the end, she rejected my suggestion that anti-black racism was a reality. This exchange demonstrates the limits of my power as the researcher in the context of this study. It has often been assumed that, because of our high educations, recording equipment, and the fact that we are putting people under the microscope, the researcher is the more powerful party, and our studies will benefit from attempts to level that power dynamic.[12] I did try at times to help participants feel at ease, especially when they were reticent or laconic. However, some individuals engaged in such controlling maneuvers that they did more than enough them-

selves to level power relations. Krista McQueeney and I call these maneuvers *power plays*.

The most difficult power plays occurred late in my data collection,
after I had had overwhelmingly pleasant interactions with most everyone. One man was the only person to request an advance copy of my
interview questions, which I e-mailed to him, but got no reply, so I
entered the interview with trepidation. We met at his workplace; he sat
behind a large desk and I, like a client, sat across from him. When I
turned on the recorder, he reminded me that I was to send him a copy
of the interview transcript as soon as possible (he said he had been
misquoted before), which I assured him would be a high priority.
Throughout the entire interview he sat rigidly upright with his arms
folded across his chest and spoke very carefully, with frequent long
pauses. Despite the personalized nature of my questions, he kept explaining how the racial past had been in general as opposed to what he
had experienced. (For example, if I asked if he had had black domestic
workers in his childhood home, he answered that that was indeed a
common practice at the time.) I grew frustrated that he seemed to be
refusing to provide anything relevant for a project on autobiographical
memories. Why had he even agreed to the interview? In response to my
questions, he said repeatedly that he was "not qualified" to comment, or
told me flatly that what I was asking made no sense. In truth, I was
fumbling over my words as I struggled to concoct phrasings that he
would not reject.

Not surprisingly, that interview was a short one. But once the recorder was turned off, much of his rigidity melted away. His arms came
uncrossed from his chest, and he leaned back comfortably in his chair,
as he asked me with curiosity how he compared to other interviewees.
Although he was visibly more at ease, he did not cede control of our
interaction. He opined at length about the dysfunctions of the black
community, arguing that Ebonics is useless, that blacks are more prejudiced than whites, and that they refuse to assimilate. He even asked me
directly if I agreed with him that black Americans cause their own
problems. I utilized all the strategies I had developed so as to avoid
arguing at the crucial endpoint of the interview. I asked for clarification
("Do I agree with what, exactly?"), but he offered none ("With what I
said"). I employed the "mm-hm" response, encouraging him to continue talking, but that did not always satisfy him. I used my grad student

persona and spoke of how some social science theories might agree somewhat with his views, others not. Perhaps realizing that I was not going to agree with him, he advised me that if I thought carefully about what he had said, I would come to see he was right. I felt condescended to and bullied, and I retreated to my car with haste and exhaustion.

I had begun the research project expecting some resistance; I was interviewing white southerners about the white supremacist past, after all. Power struggles often occur when participants' identities are threatened—common when women interview men and whites are interviewed about race.[13] Given that the research study itself was likely to produce such barriers, I did not emphasize how I differed from participants. I felt it important to accept them on their own terms, so I played down my own critical race perspective in favor of paying full attention to them. I employed active interviewing techniques.[14] I did all I could to make the interview nonthreatening and encouraging so that they could convey rich narratives. Although I am self-critical toward some of the decisions I made, I also feel my approach was functional and, further, not solely within my control.

Sociologist Charles Gallagher has argued that white researchers ought to use interviews as an opportunity to challenge whites' racial views so that they can be exposed to alternative perspectives and forced to respond.[15] He argues for researching whiteness as an antiracist project, because if a researcher allows whites to monologue on faulty assumptions and does not challenge them, she gives them no chance to consider more accurate information and modify their positions: "Do we ask questions which challenge our respondents to think about race as a political category, or do we reproduce, normalize, and continue to make whiteness invisible by uncritically validating the version of whiteness we expect to hear?"[16] The point is well taken. However, I deemed direct challenges of my interview participants to be a risk to the completion of the project itself, for my population was uniquely situated. It is one matter if your subjects are the oft-used college student population of young adults who are well accustomed to having their views challenged by professor-researchers and peers. But I was a young adult myself and interviewing elders on a topic that readily lent itself to mistrust and defensiveness. Because of the demographic restrictions I imposed (lifelong resident of Greensboro and of a certain age), I relied heavily on personal referrals and felt I could not afford to antagonize participants.

I did frequently ask for clarification and elaboration, but the challenges I offered were mild and suggestive rather than contrarian.

I was concerned that, upon hearing about my study, people would be suspicious and decline to participate, limiting my dataset and possibly tarnishing my reputation in the community. There were several moments that verified the need to tread lightly. Some people were "reluctant respondents," either hesitant to give the interview or only opening up off the record.[17] As is clear in the introduction to this book, there was some suspicion of my project among my target population, although the majority of people I contacted readily agreed to give an interview after hearing only a basic description. Among those who turned me down, I could rarely determine their real reasons from what they told me. (The most common excuse was, "I don't have the time.") But I got some indication that some did decline the interview because of the research topic. One woman responded to my standard pitch with "I'd rather not mess with anxious things" and promptly hung up the phone. (Coincidentally, it was late in data collection; I called her just days after Barack Obama won the 2008 presidential election.) Another moment occurred midway through data collection. A female participant told me she had been trying to recruit a male acquaintance of hers for my study and that, despite her assurances as to my reputability, he had adamantly refused and was questioning her own willingness to "get involved with this thing." This conversation gave me a glimpse into the suspicions toward my project and confirmed my need to establish and maintain trust. It also indicated that my being white, southern, young, and female could not eliminate misgivings about my study.

Given all these examples, what really stands out is how generous and open the participants were as a whole. Numerous people expressed that their motivation in the interview was to "help" me. One interesting example was Jolene, who looked uncomfortable throughout the interview and claimed that race was not something she had paid much attention to in her life. The interview was brief—well under an hour—and twice she apologized for not helping me. It seemed clear that she did not want to be sitting for that interview, but she had agreed to it anyway and was disappointed that she was not being of more service. Most people displayed warmth and trust toward me, welcoming me into their homes, sharing their stories, and wishing me well for the completion of my research project and PhD. They clearly read me as a youngster and student—someone who needed their assistance to pursue my education. While there was much truth to this (I *did* need them), this "helping" notion was yet another dynamic that made it feel wrong to challenge their claims.

A couple decades ago Kathleen Blee conducted an interview study on elder women who had, in the 1920s, been members of the Women of the Ku Klux Klan in Indiana. She said that she went into the research expecting to dislike the women but found that her feelings were much more complex as she discovered their diverse views and personalities.[18] I entered my study with milder expectations—I saw my participants as "ordinary" white southerners, not "racists"—but I was nevertheless struck by the range of feelings I had toward them. Some of the most progressive and thoughtful participants, whom I felt great affinity toward, expressed some overtly racist views. Some who had highly problematic views were also quite thoughtful individuals. I love language and delighted in their Carolina accent and colorful turns of phrase.[19] A few people hugged me warmly after the interview, and at different points I was sent home with a bag of local peaches, fresh-cut herbs, and a half pint of homemade jalapeño jelly. Often the difficulties I encountered as a researcher were intensified by the fact that I overwhelmingly liked the participants. They were generous, funny, and unique. Some felt like the grandparents I would like to have had.

Most researchers seek to establish trust and rapport with participants to the extent that they are able, and many of us hope mightily that participants will see us as honest and fair, and not as antagonists. I continue to worry that, through this book and other writings, I will be perceived as having betrayed my participants' trust since I did not explain that I would be critically analyzing their narratives and that I was invested as a scholar in destabilizing the rationalizations and structures of racial inequality. I did, however, often explain what a qualitative sociological analysis was generally—that I would be looking at the interviews as a group rather than individually, and that I did not know in advance what themes would emerge as important. All qualitative researchers have to ask ourselves, Who am I going to be in the field? This is both an ethical and empirical question. Was it enough that I collected data about what people remembered and believed? Or did I miss an opportunity to make them really grapple with contrasting facts and perspectives? Should I have revealed more of myself? And when would have been the right time to do so (before or after the interview)? Had I made a different set of choices, what would have been the effects on the narratives and on my ability to complete the research? I have not reached confident answers to any of these questions. I hope that by sharing some of my experience, however, others can gain some insight into the intricacies of critical qualitative research with dominant group members on sensitive topics.

NOTES

I. "OUR GENERATION HAD NOTHING TO DO WITH DISCRIMINATION"

1. Many of these race-critical white southerners, including Patty Boyle, James Mcbride Dabbs, and Lillian Smith, are profiled in Fred Hobson, *But Now I See: The White Southern Racial Conversion Narrative* (Baton Rouge, LA: Louisiana State University Press, 1999).

2. Wulf Kansteiner, "Finding Meaning in Memory: A Methodological Critique of Collective Memory Studies," *History and Theory* 41 (2002). Examples of the majority of collective memory research that analyzes public "memory projects" like commemorations and memorials includes James W. Loewen, *Lies across America: What Our Historic Sites Get Wrong* (New York: Touchstone, 1999); Renee C. Romano and Leigh Raiford, eds., *The Civil Rights Movement in American Memory* (Athens, GA: University of Georgia Press, 2006); Paul A. Shackel, *Memory in Black and White: Race, Commemoration, and the Post-Bellum Landscape* (Walnut Creek, CA: AltaMira Press, 2003); Barry Schwartz, *Abraham Lincoln and the Forge of National Memory* (Chicago, IL: University of Chicago Press, 2000).

3. Joe R. Feagin, Hernán Vera, and Pinar Batur, *White Racism: The Basics*, 2nd ed. (New York: Routledge, 2001); Karyn D. McKinney, *Being White: Stories of Race and Racism* (New York: Routledge, 2005); Michael Schwalbe et al., "Generic Processes in the Reproduction of Inequality: An Interactionist Analysis," *Social Forces* 79 (2000): 419–52.

4. Kristina DuRocher, *Raising Racists: The Socialization of White Children in the Jim Crow South* (Lexington, KY: University Press of Kentucky, 2011); William H. Chafe, Raymond Gavins, and Robert Korstad, eds., *Remem-*

bering Jim Crow: African Americans Tell about Life in the Segregated South (New York: New Press, 2003); Jennifer Ritterhouse, *Growing Up Jim Crow: How Black and White Southern Children Learned Race* (Chapel Hill, NC: University of North Carolina Press, 2006); Beth Roy, *Bitters in the Honey: Tales of Hope and Disappointment across Divides of Race and Time* (Fayetteville, AR: University of Arkansas Press, 1999); Katherine van Wormer, David W. Jackson III, and Charletta Sudduth, *The Maid Narratives: Black Domestics and White Families in the Jim Crow South* (Baton Rouge, LA: Louisiana State University Press, 2012).

5. Feagin, Vera, and Batur, *White Racism.*

6. For example, Eduardo Bonilla-Silva, "Rethinking Racism: Toward a Structural Interpretation," *American Sociological Review* 62 (1997): 465–80; Philomena Essed, *Everyday Racism: Reports of Women of Two Cultures* (Alameda, CA: Hunter House, 1990).

7. Ritterhouse, *Growing Up Jim Crow.*

8. Stetson Kennedy, *Jim Crow Guide: The Way It Was* (Boca Raton, FL: Florida Atlantic University Press, 1990[1959]).

9. Ibid., 208–9.

10. For a historical analysis of how white southerners responded to the civil rights era, see Jason Sokol, *There Goes My Everything: White Southerners in the Age of Civil Rights, 1945–1975* (New York: Knopf, 2006).

11. Historian William Chafe coined the term "progressive mystique" to describe how Greensboro's progressive reputation has long been contradicted by its race politics. William H. Chafe, *Civilities and Civil Rights: Greensboro, North Carolina, and the Black Struggle for Freedom* (New York: Oxford University Press, 1981).

12. For a good review, see Amanda E. Lewis, "'What Group?' Studying Whites and Whiteness in the Era of Color-Blindness," *Sociological Theory* 22 (2004): 623–46.

13. Lawrence D. Bobo, "Inequalities That Endure? Racial Ideology, American Politics, and the Peculiar Role of the Social Sciences," in *The Changing Terrain of Race and Ethnicity*, ed. Maria Krysan and Amanda E. Lewis (New York: Russell Sage, 2004), 13–42; Eduardo Bonilla-Silva, *Racism without Racists: Color-Blind Racism and the Persistence of Racial Inequality in the United States*, 4th ed. (Lanham, MD: Rowman & Littlefield, 2013).

14. Matthew W. Hughey, *White Bound: Nationalists, Antiracists, and the Shared Meanings of Race* (Stanford, CA: Stanford University Press, 2012), 185.

15. Hughey, *White Bound*; see also Matthew W. Hughey, "The (Dis)similarities of White Racial Identities: The Conceptual Framework of 'Hegemonic Whiteness,'" *Ethnic and Racial Studies* 33 (2010): 1289–1309.

16. For example, David Goldfield, *Still Fighting the Civil War: The American South and Southern History* (Baton Rouge, LA: Louisiana State University Press, 2002); Larry J. Griffin, "'Generations and Collective Memory' Revisited: Race, Region, and Memory of Civil Rights," *American Sociological Review* 69 (2004): 544–57; Maurice Halbwachs, *Collective Memory*, trans. Francis J. Ditter Jr. and Vida Y. Ditter (New York: Harper & Row, 1980 [1950]); Andreas Huyssen, *Twilight Memories: Marking Time in a Culture of Amnesia* (New York: Routledge, 1995); Jeffrey K. Olick, *In the House of the Hangman: The Agonies of German Defeat, 1943–1949* (Chicago: University of Chicago Press, 2005); Schwartz, *Abraham Lincoln*.

17. Barbie Zelizer, *Remembering to Forget: Holocaust Memory through the Camera's Eye* (Chicago: University of Chicago Press, 1998), 3.

18. Catherine K. Riessman, *Narrative Analysis* (Newbury Park, CA: Sage, 1993), 5.

19. See James A. Holstein and Jaber F. Gubrium, *The Active Interview* (Thousand Oaks, CA: Sage, 1995); Alessandro Portelli, *The Death of Luigi Trastulli and Other Stories: Form and Meaning in Oral History* (Albany, NY: State University of New York Press, 1991).

20. I discuss these issues more in depth in the appendix.

21. Joe R. Feagin, *The White Racial Frame: Centuries of Racial Framing and Counter-Framing*, 2nd ed. (New York: Routledge, 2013); Joe R. Feagin, *Systemic Racism: A Theory of Oppression* (New York: Routledge, 2006).

22. This argument is well made in Matthew W. Hughey and Carson Byrd, "The Souls of White Folk beyond Formation and Structure: Bound to Identity," *Ethnic and Racial Studies* 36 (2013): 974–81.

23. The original conceptualization of moral identity was made by Jack Katz, "Essences as Moral Identities: Verifiability and Responsibility in Imputations of Deviance and Charisma," *American Journal of Sociology* 80 (1975): 1369–90. For more recent applications, see Natalia Deeb-Sossa, "Helping the 'Neediest of the Needy': An Intersectional Analysis of Moral-Identity Construction at a Community Health Clinic," *Gender and Society* 21 (2007): 749–72; Sherryl Kleinman, *Opposing Ambitions: Gender and Identity in an Alternative Organization* (Chicago: University of Chicago Press, 1996); Mitchell B. Mackinem and Paul Higgins, "Tell Me about the Test: The Construction of Truth and Lies in Drug Court," *Journal of Contemporary Ethnography* 36 (2007): 223–51; Schwalbe et al., "Generic Processes."

24. Larry J. Griffin and Kenneth A. Bollen, "What Do These Memories Do? Civil Rights Remembrance and Racial Attitudes," *American Sociological Review* 74 (2009): 594–614.

2. "ONLY LOVE UNDER OUR ROOF"

1. Ritterhouse, *Growing Up Jim Crow*.
2. Grace E. Hale, *Making Whiteness: The Culture of Segregation in the South, 1890–1940* (New York: Vintage, 1999); Ritterhouse, *Growing Up Jim Crow*.
3. Chafe, Gavins, and Korstad, *Remembering Jim Crow*; Leon F. Litwack, *Trouble in Mind: Black Southerners in the Age of Jim Crow* (New York: Knopf, 1998).
4. Feagin, *Systemic Racism*; Litwack, *Trouble in Mind*.
5. Ritterhouse, *Growing Up Jim Crow*.
6. Lillian Smith, *Killers of the Dream* (New York: Norton, 1961).
7. Participants' ages are provided in decade ranges: 60s, 70s, and 80s. For confidentiality, the handful of people who were younger than 60 or older than 90 years old have been labeled as 60s and 80s, respectively.
8. Italics within interview excerpts are used to indicate a heightened emphasis in the tone of voice. Pauses in speech three seconds or longer are indicated, while pauses of two seconds or less have been omitted. Most all interview excerpts have been modified slightly for readability, while retaining the speech patterns, tone, and meaning.
9. Smith, *Killers of the Dream*, 83.
10. Notes in parentheses within quotes capture significant nonverbal utterances, such as laughing, sighing, or bodily gestures.
11. Bracketed words in interview excerpts are my own insertions, to either clarify the intended meaning for the reader or remove identifying information about the participant.
12. A classic text on residential segregation is Douglas S. Massey and Nancy A. Denton, *American Apartheid: Segregation and the Making of the Underclass* (Cambridge, MA: Harvard University Press, 1998). A report with national statistics on educational segregation is Erica Frankenberg, Chungmei Lee, and Gary Orfield, "A Multiracial Society with Segregated Schools: Are We Losing the Dream?" The Civil Rights Project Research Report (Cambridge, MA: Harvard University, 2003).
13. Mahnaz Kousha, "Race, Class, and Intimacy in Southern Households: Relationships between Black Domestic Workers and White Employers," in *Neither Separate Nor Equal: Women, Race, and Class in the South*, ed. Barbara E. Smith, 77–90 (Philadelphia, PA: Temple University Press, 1999); Susan Tucker, *Telling Memories among Southern Women: Domestic Workers and Their Employers in the Segregated South* (Baton Rouge, LA: Louisiana State University Press, 1988); Hale, *Making Whiteness*; Litwack, *Trouble in Mind*;

Ritterhouse, *Growing Up Jim Crow*; van Wormer, Jackson, and Sudduth, *Maid Narratives*.

14. Hale, *Making Whiteness*; Litwack, *Trouble in Mind*; van Wormer, Jackson, and Sudduth, *Maid Narratives*.

15. Hale, *Making Whiteness*; Tucker, *Telling Memories*.

16. Hale, *Making Whiteness*, 102–3.

17. Litwack, *Trouble in Mind*, 169.

18. Litwack, *Trouble in Mind*; van Wormer, Jackson, and Sudduth, *Maid Narratives*.

19. Quoted in Litwack, *Trouble in Mind*, 169.

20. Kousha, "Race, Class"; Tucker, *Telling Memories*; van Wormer, Jackson, and Sudduth, *Maid Narratives*.

21. Tucker, *Telling Memories*; see also van Wormer, Jackson, and Sudduth, *Maid Narratives*.

22. Kousha, "Race, Class."

23. Van Wormer, Jackson, and Sudduth, *Maid Narratives*.

24. To protect identities, all names provided within interview excerpts are pseudonyms.

25. Van Wormer, Jackson, and Sudduth, *Maid Narratives*.

26. See also van Wormer, Jackson, and Sudduth, *Maid Narratives*, which also found gift giving to be a theme in interviews of former white employers of black domestic workers.

27. Kennedy, *Jim Crow Guide*; Litwack, *Trouble in Mind*.

28. W. E. B. Du Bois, *Darkwater: Voices from within the Veil* (Amherst, NY: Humanity Books, 2003 [1920]), 131.

29. Kousha, "Race, Class."

30. Chafe, Gavins, and Korstad, *Remembering Jim Crow*; Tucker, *Telling Memories*.

31. Tucker, *Telling Memories*; van Wormer, Jackson, and Sudduth, *Maid Narratives*.

32. Litwack, *Trouble in Mind*, 167.

33. Chafe, Gavins, and Korstad, *Remembering Jim Crow*, 56.

34. Litwack, *Trouble in Mind*; Tucker, *Telling Memories*.

35. Litwack, *Trouble in Mind*.

36. Ruth Thompson-Miller, Joe R. Feagin, and Leslie H. Picca, *Jim Crow's Legacy: The Lasting Impact of Segregation* (Lanham, MD: Rowman & Littlefield, 2015).

37. Tucker, *Telling Memories*; van Wormer, Jackson, and Sudduth, *Maid Narratives*.

38. Ibid.

39. Tucker, *Telling Memories*, 152.

40. Quoted in Tucker, *Telling Memories*, 153–54.

41. Litwack, *Trouble in Mind*; Tucker, *Telling Memories*; van Wormer, Jackson, and Sudduth, *Maid Narratives*.

42. Feagin, *Systemic Racism*, 173.

43. Bonilla-Silva, "Rethinking Racism"; Feagin, *Systemic Racism*.

44. Smith, *Killers of the Dream*, 17–18.

45. Ritterhouse, *Growing Up Jim Crow*.

46. David R. Roediger, *The Wages of Whiteness: Race and the Making of the American Working Class*, rev. ed. (London: Verso, 1999); Tim Wise, *Speaking Treason Fluently: Anti-Racist Reflections from an Angry White Male* (Berkeley, CA: Soft Skull Press, 2008); Hale, *Making Whiteness*.

47. Hale, *Making Whiteness*, 94.

48. This point is also made by van Wormer, Jackson, and Sudduth, *Maid Narratives*.

49. Smith, *Killers of the Dream*, 96.

50. Tucker, *Telling Memories*.

51. Feagin, *Systemic Racism*, 28; see also Feagin, Vera, and Batur, *White Racism*.

52. Ritterhouse, *Growing Up Jim Crow*.

53. C. Vann Woodward, *The Strange Career of Jim Crow: A Commemorative Edition* (New York: Oxford University Press, 2002 [1955]).

54. Ritterhouse, *Growing Up Jim Crow*.

55. Ibid., 9, italics in original.

3. "JUST THE WAY IT WAS"

1. Ritterhouse, *Growing Up Jim Crow*.

2. Litwack, *Trouble in Mind*.

3. Quoted in Sokol, *There Goes My Everything*, 14.

4. Ibid., 15.

5. Van Wormer, Jackson, and Sudduth, *Maid Narratives*.

6. For this decision I am appreciative of one of the anonymous reviewers of this manuscript, who pointed out that "etiquette" implies politeness and decorum and thus draws attention away from white dominant power dynamics.

7. Kennedy, *Jim Crow Guide*.

8. Ibid., 208–9.

9. Ibid., 206.

10. Feagin, *Systemic Racism*, 157.

11. Ritterhouse, *Growing Up Jim Crow*.

12. Ibid.

13. Olivia W. Quinn, "The Transmission of Racial Attitudes among White Southerners," *Social Forces* 33 (1954): 41–47; Ritterhouse, *Growing Up Jim Crow*.

14. Smith, *Killers of the Dream*, 27–28.

15. Sokol, *There Goes My Everything*.

16. Kennedy, *Jim Crow Guide*, 203.

17. Ritterhouse, *Growing Up Jim Crow*.

18. Danielle L. McGuire, *At the Dark End of the Street: Black Women, Rape, and Resistance—A New History of the Civil Rights Movement from Rosa Parks to the Rise of Black Power* (New York: Knopf, 2010); Litwack, *Trouble in Mind*; Thompson-Miller and Feagin, "Reality and Impact."

19. Quoted in Hobson, *But Now I See*, 54.

20. Melton A. McLaurin, *Separate Pasts: Growing Up White in the Segregated South* (Athens, GA: University of Georgia Press, 1998).

21. As described in Hobson, *But Now I See*.

22. A similar argument is made in Michael Maly, Heather Dalmage, and Nancy Michaels, "The End of an Idyllic World: Nostalgia Narratives, Race, and the Construction of White Powerlessness," *Critical Sociology* 39 (2013): 757–79.

23. Sokol, *There Goes My Everything*.

24. Feagin, *Systemic Racism*.

25. Ibid.

26. Ibid, 168.

27. Glenn B. Bracey, "Rescuing Whites: White Privileging Discourse in Race Critical Scholarship," unpublished manuscript.

28. Albion W. Tourgée, *Bricks without Straw*, ed. Carolyn L. Karcher (Durham, NC: Duke University Press, 2009 [1880]); Feagin, *White Racial Frame*; Litwack, *Trouble in Mind*.

29. Woodward, *Strange Career*.

30. W. J. Cash, *The Mind of the South* (New York: Penguin, 1941), 93–94.

31. Smith, *Killers of the Dream*, 57.

32. Feagin, *Systemic Racism*.

33. Feagin, *Systemic Racism* and *White Racial Frame*.

34. Feagin, *White Racial Frame*, 89, emphasis in original.

4. DISTANCING AND REJECTION

1. George M. Frederickson, *The Black Image in the White Mind: The Debate on Afro-American Character and Destiny, 1817–1914* (Middletown, CT: Wesleyan University Press, 1987); Winthrop. D. Jordan, *The White Man's*

Burden: Historical Origins of Racism in the United States (New York: Oxford University Press, 1974); Jan N. Pieterse, *White on Black: Images of Africa and Blacks in Western Popular Culture* (New Haven, CT: Yale University Press, 1992); Ronald Takaki, *Iron Cages: Race and Culture in Nineteenth-Century America* (New York: Oxford University Press, 1990 [1979]; Feagin, *Systemic Racism*; Roediger, *Wages of Whiteness*.

2. Gunnar Myrdal, *An American Dilemma: The Negro Problem and Modern Democracy* (New York: Harper, 1944).

3. DuRocher, *Raising Racists*; Ritterhouse, *Growing Up Jim Crow*.

4. Griffin and Bollen, "What Do These Memories."

5. Griffin, "Generations."

6. Chafe, *Civilities*.

7. Ibid.

8. For reviews of pre-1960 sit-ins, see Beverly W. Jones, "Before Montgomery and Greensboro: The Desegregation Movement in the District of Columbia, 1950–1953," *Phylon* 43 (1982): 144–54; *New York Times*, "Divine's Followers Give Aid to Strikers: With Evangelist's Sanction, They 'Sit Down' in Restaurant," September 23, 1939, 13; *Out of Obscurity*, DVD, directed by Matt Spangler, 2000.

9. Sokol, *There Goes My Everything*.

10. Chafe, *Civilities*.

11. Spoma Jovanovic, *Democracy, Dialogue, and Community Action: Truth and Reconciliation in Greensboro* (Fayetteville, AR: University of Arkansas Press, 2012); Chafe, *Civilities*.

12. Chafe, *Civilities*.

13. Ibid.

14. Ibid., 80.

15. Ibid., 79.

16. Ibid.

17. Ibid., 98.

18. Ibid., 110.

19. Ibid., 112.

20. Ibid.

21. Ibid., 127.

22. Quoted in ibid., 138.

23. Ibid.

24. Myrdal, *American Dilemma*.

25. Howell S. Baum, *Brown in Baltimore: School Desegregation and the Limits of Liberalism* (Ithaca, NY: Cornell University Press, 2010), 3.

26. Derrick Bell, *And We Are Not Saved: The Elusive Quest for Racial Justice* (New York: Basic Books, 1987).

27. Wendy L. Moore, *Reproducing Racism: White Space, Elite Law Schools, and Racial Inequality* (Lanham, MD: Rowman & Littlefield, 2008).

28. Other authors who emphasize the diversity in views among civil rights–era whites include Matthew D. Lassiter and Andrew B. Lewis, *The Moderates' Dilemma: Massive Resistance to School Desegregation in Virginia* (Charlottesville, VA: University of Virginia Press, 1998); Sokol, *There Goes My Everything.*

29. This incident will be discussed at length in chapter 6.

30. Sven-Ake Christianson and Martin A. Safer, "Emotional Events and Emotions in Autobiographical Memories," in *Remembering Our Past: Studies in Autobiographical Memory,* ed. David C. Rubin, 218–43 (New York: Cambridge University Press, 1996).

31. I should make two things clear regarding this section. First, the interview excerpts have been minimally edited in order to show the styles of speech patterns and the numerous missteps. Second, that does not mean that participants made these types of errors all the time. There were clear patterns where people tended to flub certain words or on particular topics.

32. I inserted page numbers as a proxy for time, signifying that this is a string of excerpts that occurred over several minutes of the interview.

33. For extended theorizing on denial and how we can both see and not see inequalities, see Stanley Cohen, *States of Denial: Knowing about Atrocities and Suffering* (Cambridge, UK: Polity, 2001). For theory on how a white-dominant society encourages an "epistemology of ignorance," see Charles W. Mills, *The Racial Contract* (Ithaca, NY: Cornell University Press, 1997).

34. Bracey, "Rescuing Whites."

35. Chafe, *Civilities.*

36. Loewen, *Lies across America.*

37. James W. Loewen, *Lies My Teacher Told Me: Everything Your American History Textbook Got Wrong* (New York: Touchstone, 1995).

38. *Greensboro Record,* "Letters to the Editor," April 9, 1968, A14.

39. James A. Holstein and Gale Miller, "Rethinking Victimization: An Interactional Approach," *Symbolic Interaction* 13 (1990): 106.

40. Ibid., 108–13.

41. Ibid., 105, emphasis in original.

42. Kousha, "Race, Class"; Ritterhouse, *Growing Up Jim Crow*; Tucker, *Telling Memories.*

5. WHITE VICTIMS

1. Meyer Weinberg, *A Chance to Learn: The History of Race and Education in the United States* (New York: Cambridge University Press, 1977).
2. Ibid.
3. Litwack, *Trouble in Mind.*
4. Ibid., 108–9.
5. Weinberg, *A Chance to Learn.*
6. Ibid.
7. Feagin, *White Racial Frame.*
8. Chafe, *Civilities.*
9. Ibid.
10. Ibid., 13.
11. Ibid., 158.
12. Ibid.
13. Ibid.
14. Ibid.
15. Ibid., 158–59.
16. Quoted in ibid., 168.
17. Ibid., 166–69.
18. Ibid., 170.
19. Ibid., 222.
20. Ibid., 222–23.
21. Alexander R. Stoesen, *A Celebration of Guilford County since 1890*, ed. Sydney M. Cone Jr. (Greensboro, NC: The Guilford County Commissioners, 1980), 238.
22. Chafe, *Civilities.*
23. Ibid., 229.
24. *Greensboro Record*, "Boycott Proposal Blasted," August 26, 1971, D1.
25. Chafe, *Civilities*, 230–31.
26. W. K. Lee Jr., "Group Talks Boycott," *Greensboro Daily News*, August 24, 1971, B1, B14.
27. Barbara Ross, "County School Rolls Swell," *Greensboro Record*, August 24, 1971, B1; Stoesen, *A Celebration of Guilford County since 1890.*
28. *Greensboro Daily News*, "Enrollment in Private Schools Soars," August 27, 1971, B11.
29. Ibid.
30. See from the *Greensboro Daily News*, "Public Pulse: Mr. Nixon and the Busing Question" and "Tyranny," August 21, 1971, A6; "Public Pulse: Time to Act," September 3, 1971, A6; "Public Pulse: 'Busing' and the Welfare of the

Children," September 4, 1971, A4; "Public Pulse: ACT Chairman Reaffirms His Position," September 7, 1971, A6.

31. *Greensboro Daily News*, "Public Pulse: 'Busing.'"

32. *Greensboro Daily News*, "Public Pulse: School Busing Is a Red Herring," August 29, 1971, E5.

33. Lassiter and Lewis, *Moderates' Dilemma*.

34. Ronald P. Formisano, *Boston against Busing: Race, Class, and Ethnicity in the 1960s and 1970s* (Chapel Hill, NC: University of North Carolina Press, 2004).

35. David L. Chappell, *Inside Agitators: White Southerners in the Civil Rights Movement* (Baltimore, MD: Johns Hopkins University Press, 1996).

36. Charles C. Bolton, *The Hardest Deal of All: The Battle over School Integration in Mississippi, 1870–1980* (Jackson, MS: University Press of Mississippi, 2005); Lassiter and Lewis, *Moderates' Dilemma*.

37. Davison M. Douglas, *Reading, Writing, and Race: The Desegregation of the Charlotte Schools* (Chapel Hill, NC: University of North Carolina Press, 1995); Lassiter and Lewis, *Moderates' Dilemma*.

38. Chafe, *Civilities*, 230.

39. Feagin, *White Racial Frame*, 87–88.

40. Chafe, *Civilities*.

41. Holstein and Miller, "Rethinking Victimization."

6. REFLECTING ON A LIFETIME

1. For example, Shackel, *Memory in Black*.

2. This survey was conducted in 2000. See Bobo, "Inequalities." An example of a qualitative study showing similar views among whites is Nancy DiTomaso, Rochelle Parks-Yancy, and Corinne Post, "White Attitudes toward Equal Opportunity and Affirmative Action," *Critical Sociology* 37 (2011): 615–29.

3. Bonilla-Silva, *Racism without Racists*.

4. Ibid.

5. Ibid.

6. Feagin, *White Racial Frame*.

7. This survey was conducted in 2001. See Bobo, "Inequalities." The statistics for black respondents were much lower, at 13 percent (lazy), 21 percent (aggressive), and 10 percent (prefer welfare).

8. Ibid. The numbers for black respondents were much higher, at 60 percent (law abiding), 66 percent (good neighbors), and 78 percent (hardworking).

9. Bonilla-Silva, *Racism without Racists*.

10. See Jay Livingston, "Blaming the Media I," *Montclair SocioBlog*, June 2, 2012, accessed May 3, 2014, http://montclairsoci.blogspot.com/2012_06_01_archive.html.

11. 2001 survey, cited in Bobo, "Inequalities." Among black respondents, 24 percent expressed agreement with this characterization.

12. I acknowledge Krista McQueeney for her analytical insight here on politics of representation.

13. Jovanovic, *Democracy*.

14. *Greensboro Truth and Reconciliation Final Report* (Greensboro, NC: Greensboro Truth and Reconciliation Commission, 2006), accessed May 5, 2014, http://www.greensborotrc.org/.

15. The documentary film *Greensboro's Child*, 2002, includes the original footage.

16. *Greensboro Truth*.

17. *Greensboro Truth*; Jovanovic, *Democracy*.

18. David Cunningham, Colleen Nugent, and Caitlin Slodden, "The Durability of Collective Memory: Reconciling the 'Greensboro Massacre,'" *Social Forces* 88 (2010): 1517–42.

19. Jovanovic, *Democracy*.

20. *Greensboro Truth*.

21. Jordan Green, "City Council Splits along Racial Lines over Truth Process," *Yes! Weekly*, April 27–May 3, 2005, 7–8.

22. Ibid.

23. *Greensboro Truth*.

7. MEMORY AND WHITE MORAL IDENTITY

1. Roy F. Baumeister and Stephen Hastings, "Distortions of Collective Memory: How Groups Flatter and Deceive Themselves," in *Collective Memory of Political Events: Social Psychological Perspectives*, ed. James W. Pennebaker, Dario Páez, and Bernard Rimé (New York: Psychology Press, 1997), 292.

2. See Jan Assmann, "Collective Memory and Cultural Identity," *New German Critique* 65 (1995): 125–33; David W. Blight, *Race and Reunion: The Civil War in American Memory* (Cambridge, MA: Harvard University Press, 2001); W. Fitzhugh Brundage, "No Deed But Memory," in *Where These Memories Grow: History, Memory, and Southern Identity*, ed. W. F. Brundage, 1–28 (Chapel Hill, NC: University of North Carolina Press, 2000); Jeffrey K. Olick and Joyce Robbins, "Social Memory Studies: From 'Collective Memory' to the Historical Sociology of Mnemonic Practices," *Annual Review of Sociolo-*

gy 24 (1998): 105–40; Baumeister and Hastings, "Distortions"; Olick, *In the House*; Schwartz, *Abraham Lincoln*.

3. Baumeister and Hastings, "Distortions."

4. Ibid., 277.

5. Ibid.

6. Feagin, *White Racial Frame*, 17.

7. Sokol, *There Goes My Everything*.

8. Leslie Carr, *"Color-Blind" Racism* (Thousand Oaks, CA: Sage, 1997); Michael Omi and Howard Winant, *Racial Formations in the United States: From the 1960s to the 1990s*, 2nd ed. (New York: Routledge, 1994); Bobo, "Inequalities"; Bonilla-Silva, *Racism without Racists*.

9. For example, Ruth Frankenberg, "The Mirage of an Unmarked Whiteness," in *The Making and Unmaking of Whiteness*, ed. Birgit B. Rasmussen et al., 72–96 (Durham, NC: Duke University Press, 2001); Bobo, "Inequalities"; Bonilla-Silva, *Racism without Racists*.

10. Michael G. Lacy, "White Innocence Myths in Citizen Discourse: The Progressive Era (1974–1988)," *Howard Journal of Communications* 21 (2010): 20–39; Feagin, *White Racial Frame*.

11. Eduardo Bonilla-Silva and Tyrone A. Forman, "'I Am Not a Racist But . . .': Mapping White College Students' Racial Ideology in the USA," *Discourse and Society* 11 (2000): 50–85; Charles A. Gallagher, "White Reconstruction in the University," in *Privilege: A Reader*, ed. Michael S. Kimmel and Abby L. Ferber, 300–18 (Boulder, CO: Westview, 2003); Jennifer C. Mueller, "Tracing Family, Teaching Race: Critical Race Pedagogy in the Millennial Sociology Classroom," *Teaching Sociology* 41 (2013): 172-–87.

12. See Hughey, "(Dis)similarities," and Lewis, "What Group?" for conceptualization of "hegemonic whiteness" as the set of characteristics that, in a given context, become seen as the ideal, normal qualities of being white. This concept allows for the ways in which whites sometimes contrast themselves against other types of "deviant" whites—such as "white trash" or "white hippies"—in order to elevate themselves and define ideal whiteness.

13. Although I never indicated that I believed this, I was a kind of representative of post–civil rights generations.

14. Daniel J. Goldhagen, *Hitler's Willing Executioners: Ordinary Germans and the Holocaust* (New York: Vintage, 1997); Eric A. Johnson, *Nazi Terror: The Gestapo, Jews, and Ordinary Germans* (New York: Basic Books, 1999).

15. Olick, *In the House*.

16. Kathleen M. Blee, *Women of the Klan: Racism and Gender in the 1920s* (Berkeley, CA: University of California Press, 1991).

17. Smith, *Killers of the Dream*.

18. Cohen, *States of Denial*, 5.

19. Ibid., 249.
20. Gallup, "Black-White Relations in the United States: 2001 Update" (Washington, DC: The Gallup Organization, 2001); Tim Wise, *Colorblind: The Rise of Post-Racial Politics and the Retreat from Racial Equity* (San Francisco: City Lights Publishers, 2010), 65.
21. Feagin, *White Racial Frame* and *Systemic Racism.*
22. Wise, *Speaking Treason*, 38.
23. C. Vann Woodward, *Origins of the New South: 1877–1913* (Baton Rouge, LA: Louisiana State University Press, 1971); Blight, *Race and Reunion*; Goldfield, *Still Fighting.*
24. Blight, *Race and Reunion.*
25. Ibid.
26. Feagin, *Systemic Racism*, 44.
27. Cohen, *States of Denial*, 5.
28. Mills, *Racial Contract*, 17–19.
29. Peter Burke, "History as Social Memory," in *Memory: History, Culture, and the Mind*, ed. Thomas Butler, 97–113 (Oxford, UK: Blackwell, 1989), 110.
30. Du Bois, *Darkwater*, 59.

APPENDIX

1. This concern is discussed throughout France Winndance Twine and Jonathan W. Warren, eds., *Racing Research, Researching Race: Methodological Dilemmas in Critical Race Studies* (New York: New York University Press, 2000).
2. For example, see Kathleen M. Blee, "White on White: Interviewing Women in U.S. White Supremacist Groups," in *Racing Research*, 99–100.
3. McKinney, *Being White*, xviii.
4. Charles Gallagher makes this argument in "White Like Me? Methods, Meaning, and Manipulation in the Field of Whiteness Studies," in *Racing Research*, 67–92; and "'The End of Racism' as the New Doxa: New Strategies for Researching Race," in *White Logic, White Methods: Racism and Methodology*, eds. Tukufu Zuberi and Eduardo Bonilla-Silva, 163–78 (Lanham, MD: Rowman & Littlefield, 2008).
5. For example, see Howard S. Becker, "Afterword: Racism and the Research Process," in *Racing Research*, 252.
6. Krista B. McQueeney and I tackle this question in an unpublished manuscript, "Emotional Labor in Critical Ethnographic Work: In the Field and Behind the Desk." See also Elizabeth A. Hoffman, "Open-Ended Interviews, Power, and Emotional Labor," *Journal of Contemporary Ethnography* 36

(2007): 318–46; Sherryl Kleinman and Martha A. Copp, *Emotions and Fieldwork* (Newbury Park, CA: Sage, 1993).

7. France W. Twine has an excellent critical discussion of this in "Racial Ideologies and Racial Methodologies," in *Racing Research*, 7–16.

8. Gallagher, "End of Racism, 172–73.

9. McKinney, *Being White*, xviii.

10. Becker, "Afterword," 251.

11. For strategies that interviewees use to wrest control over the research process, including "jumping the gun," see Terry Arendell, "Reflections on the Researcher-Researched Relationship: A Woman Interviewing Men," *Qualitative Sociology* 20 (1997): 341–68.

12. See, for example, Studs Terkel, "Interviewing an Interviewer," in *The Oral History Reader*, eds. Robert Perks and Alistair Thomson, 123–28 (New York: Routledge, 2006); Holstein and Gubrium, *Active Interview.*

13. Michael L. Schwalbe and Michelle Wolkomir, "Interviewing Men," in *Handbook of Interview Research: Context and Method*, eds. Jaber F. Gubrium and James A. Holstein, 203–19 (Thousand Oaks, CA: Sage, 2002).

14. Holstein and Gubrium, *Active Interview.*

15. See Gallagher, "White Like Me?" and "End of Racism."

16. Gallagher, "White Like Me?," 86.

17. Patricia A. Adler and Peter Adler, "The Reluctant Respondent," in *Handbook of Interview Research*, 515–35.

18. Blee, *Women of the Klan* and "White on White."

19. This is why I chose, in the transcript and editing, to retain much of their speech patterns (for example, clipped words like *thinkin'* instead of *thinking*), so that the reader would get a clearer sense of how they expressed themselves.

BIBLIOGRAPHY

Adler, Patricia A., and Peter Adler. "The Reluctant Respondent." In *Handbook of Interview Research: Context and Method*, edited by Jaber F. Gubrium and James A. Holstein, 515–35. Thousand Oaks, CA: Sage, 2002.

Arendell, Terry. "Reflections on the Researcher-Researched Relationship: A Woman Interviewing Men." *Qualitative Sociology* 20 (1997): 341–68.

Assmann, Jan. "Collective Memory and Cultural Identity." *New German Critique* 65 (1995): 125–33.

Baum, Howell S. *Brown in Baltimore: School Desegregation and the Limits of Liberalism.* Ithaca, NY: Cornell University Press, 2010.

Baumeister, Roy F., and Stephen Hastings. "Distortions of Collective Memory: How Groups Flatter and Deceive Themselves." In *Collective Memory of Political Events: Social Psychological Perspectives*, edited by James W. Pennebaker, Dario Páez, and Bernard Rimé, 277–93. New York: Psychology Press, 1997.

Becker, Howard S. "Afterword: Racism and the Research Process." In *Racing Research, Researching Race*, edited by France W. Twine and Jonathan W. Warren, 247–53. New York: New York University Press, 2000.

Bell, Derrick. *And We Are Not Saved: The Elusive Quest for Racial Justice.* New York: Basic Books, 1987.

Blee, Kathleen M. "White on White: Interviewing Women in U.S. White Supremacist Groups." In *Racing Research, Researching Race: Methodological Dilemmas in Critical Race Studies*, edited by France Winddance Twine and Jonathan W. Warren, 93–109. New York: New York University Press, 2000.

——. *Women of the Klan: Racism and Gender in the 1920s.* Berkeley, CA: University of California Press, 1991.

Blight, David W. *Race and Reunion: The Civil War in American Memory.* Cambridge, MA: Harvard University Press, 2001.

Bobo, Lawrence D. 2004. "Inequalities That Endure? Racial Ideology, American Politics, and the Peculiar Role of the Social Sciences." In *The Changing Terrain of Race and Ethnicity*, edited by Maria Krysan and Amanda E. Lewis, 13–42. New York: Russell Sage, 2004.

Bolton, Charles C. *The Hardest Deal of All: The Battle over School Integration in Mississippi, 1870–1980.* Jackson, MS: University Press of Mississippi, 2005.

Bonilla-Silva, Eduardo. *Racism without Racists: Color-Blind Racism and the Persistence of Racial Inequality in the United States*, 4th ed. Lanham, MD: Rowman & Littlefield, 2013.

——. "Rethinking Racism: Toward a Structural Interpretation." *American Sociological Review* 62 (1997): 465–80.

Bonilla-Silva, Eduardo, and Tyrone A. Forman. "'I Am Not a Racist But . . .': Mapping White College Students' Racial Ideology in the USA." *Discourse and Society* 11 (2000): 50–85.
Bracey, Glenn B. "Rescuing Whites: White Privileging Discourse in Race Critical Scholarship." Unpublished manuscript.
Brundage, W. Fitzhugh. "No Deed But Memory." In *Where These Memories Grow: History, Memory, and Southern Identity*, edited by W. F. Brundage, 1–28. Chapel Hill, NC: University of North Carolina Press, 2000.
Burke, Peter. "History as Social Memory." In *Memory: History, Culture, and the Mind*, edited by Thomas Butler, 97–113. Oxford, UK: Blackwell, 1989.
Carr, Leslie. *"Color-Blind" Racism*. Thousand Oaks, CA: Sage, 1997.
Cash, W. J. *The Mind of the South*. New York: Penguin, 1941.
Chafe, William H. *Civilities and Civil Rights: Greensboro, North Carolina, and the Black Struggle for Freedom*. New York: Oxford University Press, 1981.
Chafe, William H., Raymond Gavins, and Robert Korstad, eds. *Remembering Jim Crow: African Americans Tell about Life in the Segregated South*. New York: New Press, 2003.
Chappell, David L. *Inside Agitators: White Southerners in the Civil Rights Movement*. Baltimore, MD: Johns Hopkins University Press, 1996.
Christianson, Sven-Ake, and Martin A. Safer. "Emotional Events and Emotions in Autobiographical Memories." In *Remembering Our Past: Studies in Autobiographical Memory*, edited by David C. Rubin, 218–43. New York: Cambridge University Press, 1996.
Cohen, Stanley. *States of Denial: Knowing about Atrocities and Suffering*. Cambridge, UK: Polity, 2001.
Cunningham, David, Colleen Nugent, and Caitlin Slodden. "The Durability of Collective Memory: Reconciling the 'Greensboro Massacre.'" *Social Forces* 88 (2010): 1517–42.
Deeb-Sossa, Natalia. "Helping the 'Neediest of the Needy': An Intersectional Analysis of Moral-Identity Construction at a Community Health Clinic." *Gender and Society* 21 (2007): 749–72.
DiTomaso, Nancy, Rochelle Parks-Yancy, and Corinne Post. "White Attitudes toward Equal Opportunity and Affirmative Action." *Critical Sociology* 37 (2011): 615–29.
Douglas, Davison M. *Reading, Writing, and Race: The Desegregation of the Charlotte Schools*. Chapel Hill, NC: University of North Carolina Press, 1995.
Du Bois, W. E. B. *Darkwater: Voices from within the Veil*. Amherst, NY: Humanity Books, 2003 [1920].
DuRocher, Kristina. *Raising Racists: The Socialization of White Children in the Jim Crow South*. Lexington, KY: University Press of Kentucky, 2011.
Essed, Philomena. *Everyday Racism: Reports of Women of Two Cultures*. Alameda, CA: Hunter House, 1990.
Feagin, Joe R. *Systemic Racism: A Theory of Oppression*. New York: Routledge, 2006.
———. *The White Racial Frame: Centuries of Racial Framing and Counter-Framing*, 2nd ed. New York: Routledge, 2013.
Feagin, Joe R., Hernán Vera, and Pinar Batur. *White Racism: The Basics*, 2nd ed. New York: Routledge, 2001.
Formisano, Ronald P. *Boston against Busing: Race, Class, and Ethnicity in the 1960s and 1970s*. Chapel Hill, NC: University of North Carolina Press, 2004.
Frankenberg, Erica, Chungmei Lee, and Gary Orfield. "A Multiracial Society with Segregated Schools: Are We Losing the Dream?" The Civil Rights Project Research Report. Cambridge, MA: Harvard University, 2003.
Frankenberg, Ruth. "The Mirage of an Unmarked Whiteness." In *The Making and Unmaking of Whiteness*, edited by Birgit B. Rasmussen, Eric Klinenberg, Irene J. Nexica, and Matt Wray, 72–96. Durham, NC: Duke University Press, 2001.
Frederickson, George M. *The Black Image in the White Mind: The Debate on Afro-American Character and Destiny, 1817–1914*. Middletown, CT: Wesleyan University Press, 1987.
Gallagher, Charles A. "'The End of Racism' as the New Doxa: New Strategies for Researching Race." In *White Logic, White Methods: Racism and Methodology*, edited by Tukufu Zuberi and Eduardo Bonilla-Silva, 163–78. Lanham, MD: Rowman & Littlefield, 2008.

———. "White Like Me? Methods, Meaning, and Manipulation in the Field of Whiteness Studies." In *Racing Research, Researching Race: Methodological Dilemmas in Critical Race Studies*, edited by France W. Twine and Jonathan W. Warren, 67–92. New York: New York University Press, 2000.

———."White Reconstruction in the University." In *Privilege: A Reader*, edited by Michael S. Kimmel and Abby L. Ferber, 300–18. Boulder, CO: Westview, 2003.

Gallup. "Black-White Relations in the United States: 2001 Update." Washington, DC: The Gallup Organization, 2001.

Goldfield, David. *Still Fighting the Civil War: The American South and Southern History*. Baton Rouge, LA: Louisiana State University Press, 2002.

Goldhagen, Daniel J. *Hitler's Willing Executioners: Ordinary Germans and the Holocaust*. New York: Vintage, 1997.

Green, Jordan. "City Council Splits along Racial Lines over Truth Process." *Yes! Weekly*, April 27–May 3, 2005, 7–8.

Greensboro Daily News. "Enrollment in Private Schools Soars." August 27, 1971, B11.

———. "Public Pulse: ACT Chairman Reaffirms His Position." September 7, 1971, A6.

———. "Public Pulse: 'Busing' and the Welfare of the Children." September 4, 1971, A4.

———. "Public Pulse: Mr. Nixon and the Busing Question" and "Tyranny." August 21, 1971, A6.

———. "Public Pulse: School Busing Is a Red Herring." August 29, 1971, E5.

———. "Public Pulse: Time to Act." September 3, 1971, A6.

Greensboro Record. "Boycott Proposal Blasted." August 26, 1971, D1.

———. "Letters to the Editor." April 9, 1968, A14.

Greensboro Truth and Reconciliation Final Report. Greensboro, NC: Greensboro Truth and Reconciliation Commission, 2006. Accessed May 5, 2014, http://www.greensborotrc.org.

Griffin, Larry J. "'Generations and Collective Memory' Revisited: Race, Region, and Memory of Civil Rights." *American Sociological Review* 69 (2004): 544–57.

Griffin, Larry J., and Kenneth A. Bollen. "What Do These Memories Do? Civil Rights Remembrance and Racial Attitudes." *American Sociological Review* 74 (2009): 594–614.

Halbwachs, Maurice. *Collective Memory*. Translated by Francis J. Ditter Jr. and Vida Y. Ditter. New York: Harper & Row, 1980 [1950].

Hale, Grace E. *Making Whiteness: The Culture of Segregation in the South, 1890–1940*. New York: Vintage, 1999.

Hobson, Fred. *But Now I See: The White Southern Racial Conversion Narrative*. Baton Rouge, LA: Louisiana State University Press, 1999.

Hoffman, Elizabeth A. "Open-Ended Interviews, Power, and Emotional Labor." *Journal of Contemporary Ethnography* 36 (2007): 318–46.

Holstein, James A., and Jaber F. Gubrium. *The Active Interview*. Thousand Oaks, CA: Sage, 1995.

Holstein, James A., and Gale Miller. "Rethinking Victimization: An Interactional Approach." *Symbolic Interaction* 13 (1990): 103–22.

Hughey, Matthew W. "The (Dis)similarities of White Racial Identities: The Conceptual Framework of 'Hegemonic Whiteness.'" *Ethnic and Racial Studies* 33 (2010): 1289–1309.

———. *White Bound: Nationalists, Antiracists, and the Shared Meanings of Race*. Stanford, CA: Stanford University Press, 2012.

Hughey, Matthew W., and W. Carson Byrd. "The Souls of White Folk beyond Formation and Structure: Bound to Identity." *Ethnic and Racial Studies* 36 (2013): 974–81.

Huyssen, Andreas. *Twilight Memories: Marking Time in a Culture of Amnesia*. New York: Routledge, 1995.

Johnson, Eric A. *Nazi Terror: The Gestapo, Jews, and Ordinary Germans*. New York: Basic Books, 1999.

Jones, Beverly W. "Before Montgomery and Greensboro: The Desegregation Movement in the District of Columbia, 1950–1953." *Phylon* 43 (1982): 144–54.

Jordan, Winthrop. D. *The White Man's Burden: Historical Origins of Racism in the United States*. New York: Oxford University Press, 1974.

Jovanovic, Spoma. *Democracy, Dialogue, and Community Action: Truth and Reconciliation in Greensboro.* Fayetteville, AR: University of Arkansas Press, 2012.

Kansteiner, Wulf. "Finding Meaning in Memory: A Methodological Critique of Collective Memory Studies." *History and Theory* 41 (2002): 179–97.

Kennedy, Stetson. *Jim Crow Guide: The Way It Was.* Boca Raton, FL: Florida Atlantic University Press, 1990 [1959].

Kleinman, Sherryl. *Opposing Ambitions: Gender and Identity in an Alternative Organization.* Chicago: University of Chicago Press, 1996.

Kleinman, Sherryl, and Martha A. Copp. *Emotions and Fieldwork.* Newbury Park, CA: Sage, 1993.

Kousha, Mahnaz. "Race, Class, and Intimacy in Southern Households: Relationships between Black Domestic Workers and White Employers." In *Neither Separate Nor Equal: Women, Race, and Class in the South*, edited by Barbara. E. Smith, 77–90. Philadelphia, PA: Temple University Press, 1999.

Lacy, Michael G. "White Innocence Myths in Citizen Discourse: The Progressive Era (1974–1988)." *Howard Journal of Communications* 21 (2010): 20–39.

Lassiter, Matthew D., and Andrew B. Lewis. *The Moderates' Dilemma: Massive Resistance to School Desegregation in Virginia.* Charlottesville, VA: University of Virginia Press, 1998.

Lee, W. K., Jr. "Group Talks Boycott." *Greensboro Daily News*, August 24, 1971, B1, B14.

Lewis, Amanda E. "'What Group?' Studying Whites and Whiteness in the Era of Color-Blindness." *Sociological Theory* 22 (2004): 623–46.

Litwack, Leon. F. *Trouble in Mind: Black Southerners in the Age of Jim Crow.* New York: Knopf, 1998.

Loewen, James W. *Lies across America: What Our Historic Sites Get Wrong.* New York: Touchstone, 1999.

———. *Lies My Teacher Told Me: Everything Your American History Textbook Got Wrong.* New York: Touchstone, 1995.

Mackinem, Mitchell B., and Paul Higgins. "Tell Me about the Test: The Construction of Truth and Lies in Drug Court." *Journal of Contemporary Ethnography* 36 (2007): 223–51.

Maly, Michael, Heather Dalmage, and Nancy Michaels. "The End of an Idyllic World: Nostalgia Narratives, Race, and the Construction of White Powerlessness." *Critical Sociology* 39 (2013): 757–79.

McGuire, Danielle L. *At the Dark End of the Street: Black Women, Rape, and Resistance—A New History of the Civil Rights Movement from Rosa Parks to the Rise of Black Power.* New York: Knopf, 2010.

McKinney, Karyn D. *Being White: Stories of Race and Racism.* New York: Routledge, 2005.

McLaurin, Melton A. *Separate Pasts: Growing Up White in the Segregated South.* Athens, GA: University of Georgia Press, 1998.

McQueeney, Krista B., and Kristen Lavelle. "Emotional Labor in Critical Ethnographic Work: In the Field and Behind the Desk." Unpublished manuscript.

Mills, Charles W. *The Racial Contract.* Ithaca, NY: Cornell University Press, 1997.

Moore, Wendy L. *Reproducing Racism: White Space, Elite Law Schools, and Racial Inequality.* Lanham, MD: Rowman & Littlefield, 2008.

Mueller, Jennifer C. "Tracing Family, Teaching Race: Critical Race Pedagogy in the Millennial Sociology Classroom." *Teaching Sociology* 41 (2013): 172–87.

Myrdal, Gunnar. *An American Dilemma: The Negro Problem and Modern Democracy.* New York: Harper, 1944.

New York Times. "Divine's Followers Give Aid to Strikers: With Evangelist's Sanction, They 'Sit Down' in Restaurant." September 23, 1939, 13.

Olick, Jeffrey K. *In the House of the Hangman: The Agonies of German Defeat, 1943–1949.* Chicago: University of Chicago Press, 2005.

Olick, Jeffrey K., and Joyce Robbins. "Social Memory Studies: From 'Collective Memory' to the Historical Sociology of Mnemonic Practices." *Annual Review of Sociology* 24 (1998): 105–40.

Omi, Michael, and Howard Winant. *Racial Formations in the United States: From the 1960s to the 1990s*, 2nd ed. New York: Routledge, 1994.

Out of Obscurity. DVD. Directed by Matt Spangler, 2000.

Pieterse, Jan N. *White on Black: Images of Africa and Blacks in Western Popular Culture*. New Haven, CT: Yale University Press, 1992.

Portelli, Alessandro. *The Death of Luigi Trastulli and Other Stories: Form and Meaning in Oral History*. Albany, NY: State University of New York Press, 1991.

Quinn, Olivia W. "The Transmission of Racial Attitudes among White Southerners." *Social Forces* 33 (1954): 41–47.

Riessman, Catherine K. *Narrative Analysis*. Newbury Park, CA: Sage, 1993.

Ritterhouse, Jennifer. *Growing Up Jim Crow: How Black and White Southern Children Learned Race*. Chapel Hill, NC: University of North Carolina Press, 2006.

Roediger, David. R. *The Wages of Whiteness: Race and the Making of the American Working Class*, rev. ed. London: Verso, 1999.

Romano, Renee C., and Leigh Raiford, eds. *The Civil Rights Movement in American Memory*. Athens, GA: University of Georgia Press, 2006.

Ross, Barbara. "County School Rolls Swell." *Greensboro Record*, August 24, 1971, B1.

Roy, Beth. *Bitters in the Honey: Tales of Hope and Disappointment across Divides of Race and Time*. Fayetteville, AR: University of Arkansas Press, 1999.

Schwalbe, Michael, Sandra Godwin, Daphne Holden, Douglas Schrock, and Michele Wolkomir Thompson. "Generic Processes in the Reproduction of Inequality: An Interactionist Analysis." *Social Forces* 79 (2000): 419–52.

Schwalbe, Michael L., and Michelle Wolkomir. "Interviewing Men." In *Handbook of Interview Research: Context and Method*, edited by Jaber F. Gubrium and James A. Holstein, 203–19. Thousand Oaks, CA: Sage, 2002.

Schwartz, Barry. *Abraham Lincoln and the Forge of National Memory*. Chicago, IL: University of Chicago Press, 2000.

Shackel, Paul A. *Memory in Black and White: Race, Commemoration, and the Post-Bellum Landscape*. Walnut Creek, CA: AltaMira Press, 2003.

Smith, Lillian. *Killers of the Dream*. New York: Norton, 1961.

Sokol, Jason. *There Goes My Everything: White Southerners in the Age of Civil Rights, 1945–1975*. New York: Knopf, 2006.

Stoesen, Alexander R. *A Celebration of Guilford County since 1890*, edited by Sydney M. Cone Jr. Greensboro, NC: The Guilford County Commissioners, 1980.

Takaki, Ronald. *Iron Cages: Race and Culture in Nineteenth-Century America*. New York: Oxford University Press, 1990 [1979].

Terkel, Studs. "Interviewing an Interviewer." In *The Oral History Reader*, edited by Robert Perks and Alistair Thomson, 123–28. New York: Routledge, 2006.

Thompson-Miller, Ruth, Joe R. Feagin, and Leslie H. Picca. *Jim Crow's Legacy: The Lasting Impact of Segregation* Lanham, MD: Rowman & Littlefield, 2015.

Tourgée, Albion W. *Bricks without Straw*, edited by Carolyn L. Karcher. Durham, NC: Duke University Press, 2009 [1880].

Tucker, Susan. *Telling Memories among Southern Women: Domestic Workers and Their Employers in the Segregated South*. Baton Rouge, LA: Louisiana State University Press, 1988.

Twine, France Winddance. "Racial Ideologies and Racial Methodologies." In *Racing Research, Researching Race: Methodological Dilemmas in Critical Race Studies*, edited by France W. Twine and Jonathan W. Warren, 1–34. New York: New York University Press, 2000.

Twine, France Winddance, and Jonathan W. Warren, eds., *Racing Research, Researching Race: Methodological Dilemmas in Critical Race Studies*. New York: New York University Press, 2000.

Van Wormer, Katherine, David W. Jackson III, and Charletta Sudduth. *The Maid Narratives: Black Domestics and White Families in the Jim Crow South*. Baton Rouge, LA: Louisiana State University Press, 2012.

Weinberg, Meyer. *A Chance to Learn: The History of Race and Education in the United States*. New York: Cambridge University Press, 1977.

Wise, Tim. *Colorblind: The Rise of Post-Racial Politics and the Retreat from Racial Equity*. San Francisco: City Lights Publishers, 2010.

———. *Speaking Treason Fluently: Anti-Racist Reflections from an Angry White Male*. Berkeley, CA: Soft Skull Press, 2008.

Woodward, C. Vann. *Origins of the New South: 1877–1913*. Baton Rouge, LA: Louisiana State University Press, 1971.

———. *The Strange Career of Jim Crow: A Commemorative Edition*. New York: Oxford University Press, 2002 [1955].

Zelizer, Barbie. *Remembering to Forget: Holocaust Memory through the Camera's Eye*. Chicago: University of Chicago Press, 1998.

INDEX

Baldwin, James, 1
black community leaders/activists,
  165–166, 170–172. *See also* civil rights
  movement activists; Jackson, Jesse;
  King, Martin Luther, Jr.; Sharpton, Al
Blee, Kathleen, 201
Blight, David, 190
Bonilla-Silva, Eduardo, 160, 162
Boyle, Patti, 58
Bracey, Glenn, 73–74
Brown v. Board of Education, 49, 91,
  125–127, 131, 150

Cash, W. J., 82
Chafe, William, 90–92, 109, 127
civil rights movement, 88, 90; activists,
  103–105, 109–114, 116, 120–123;
  faulty recall, 88, 97–99; fear of,
  115–119; misuse of terms, 100–102;
  survey data, 189; violence, perceptions
  of, 89, 114–119, 121–122. *See also*
  Greensboro civil rights activism;
  integration; school integration; white
  victimhood
class. *See* social class
Cohen, Stanley, 189, 190–191. *See also*
  memory denial
collective memory. *See* memory
color-blind discourse, 3, 7, 159–160,
  176–177, 185–186; abstract liberalism,
  160–161, 165–166, 169; minimization

of racism, 169; naturalistic reasoning,
  23–24, 75–77, 160; rhetorical
  incoherence, 162–163. *See also* racial
  perspectives, contemporary
cultural racism. *See* criticism of black
  Americans; racial perspectives,
  contemporary

Dabbs, James McBride, 57
desegregation. *See* integration; school
  integration
domestic labor, 27; black views of white
  employers, 27, 38–39; exploitation of
  blacks, 27, 31, 33, 35, 37–39; family-
  like relations, assertions of, 29–33
Du Bois, W. E. B., 33, 191

emotion, 1–3, 9–10, 100, 164, 168,
  187–188
empathy, 44–48, 100, 149, 189
equal opportunity. *See* racial perspectives,
  contemporary

family: childhood teachings, 17–19,
  39–40, 44–46; goodwill toward blacks
  stories, 19–20, 31–32, 41–43. *See also*
  white protectionism
Feagin, Joe, 11, 39, 67, 182, 190
Formisano, Ronald, 133

Gallagher, Charles, 194, 199

portrayals of, 9–10, 56–57, 89, 118;
white supremacist ideology
undergirding, 7, 15, 51–54, 73, 84,
185. *See also* civil rights movement
misuse of terms; domestic labor;
family
segregation stress syndrome, 37
Sharpton, Al, 170–172. *See also* Jackson,
Jesse
sit-in movement. *See* Greensboro civil
rights activism
slavery, 19, 125, 171–172
Smith, Lillian, 16, 18, 39–40, 44, 46,
54–55, 83
social class, 7, 28, 68–69, 82–83; classism,
42–43; wealthier whites, 32, 65–66,
107; working-class and poor whites,
34–35, 70. *See also* school integration
social class divisions; segregation
paternalism
Sokol, Jason, 52, 60

Thompson-Miller, Ruth, 37
truth and reconciliation, 191; assessments
of, 175–178; "Greensboro massacre,"

173–174; Greensboro Truth and
Reconciliation Commission (GTRC),
172–174
Tucker, Susan, 27–28, 38

Walker, Alice, 27
white flight. *See* segregation
neighborhoods
white moral identity, 11–12, 85, 183–185,
190; white innocence constructions,
93, 96, 154, 184–185
white protectionism, 16–17, 21–26, 183
white racial frame, 11, 186–187, 189
white southerners, 4–9, 164, 181–182,
183, 189, 201; racial awareness during
segregation, 43–48, 57–58, 62–66, 94,
102
white victimhood, 114–115; civil rights
protests, 115–123, 184; contemporary,
171; school integration, 126, 150,
153–154. *See also* school integration;
white moral identity
Woodward, C. Vann, 49, 77

ABOUT THE AUTHOR

Kristen M. Lavelle is assistant professor at the University of Wisconsin–Whitewater. Kristen earned her PhD in sociology from Texas A&M University, her master's from the University of Florida, and her bachelor's from the University of Arkansas. Her research focuses on race, memory, and identity. Prior to her current job, Kristen taught at Montana State University and Salem College, a small women's institution in North Carolina. She teaches courses in race and ethnicity, inequality, research methods, and general sociology and enjoys introducing students to a sociological perspective, training them in good research practice, and encouraging them to put knowledge into practice in their daily lives.

Born and raised with four siblings in rural Arkansas by two of the hardest working people on the planet for parents, Kristen learned early on that hard work is tempered by factors beyond our control: geographic location and its economic patterns, access to quality education, gender, and social norms, to name a few. Her childhood experiences were vital to Kristen's path toward studying sociology and structures of inequality and how individuals and groups negotiate the world around them.